Mary Hollis Johnston
Philip S. Holzman

Assessing Schizophrenic Thinking

A Clinical and Research Instrument
for Measuring Thought Disorder

Jossey-Bass Publishers
San Francisco • Washington • London • 1979

ASSESSING SCHIZOPHRENIC THINKING
A Clinical and Research Instrument
for Measuring Thought Disorder
by Mary Hollis Johnston and Philip S. Holzman

Copyright © 1979 by: Jossey-Bass Inc., Publishers
433 California Street
San Francisco, California 94104
&
Jossey-Bass Limited
28 Banner Street
London EC1Y 8QE

Library of Congress Cataloging in Publication Data

Johnston, Mary Hollis, 1946–
    Assessing schizophrenic thinking.

    (The Jossey-Bass social and behavioral science series)
    Bibliography: p.
    Includes index.
    1. Schizophrenics—Language. 2. Schizophrenia—Diagnosis. I. Holzman, Philip S., 1922– joint author. II. Title.
    RC514.J58   616.8'982   79-88771
    ISBN 0-87589-434-8

Manufactured in the United States of America

JACKET DESIGN BY WILLI BAUM

FIRST EDITION

Code 7936

The Jossey-Bass
Social and Behavioral Science Series

Special Advisor,
Methodology of Social and
Behavioral Research
DONALD W. FISKE
University of Chicago

Preface

One person in 100 can expect to be hospitalized for a schizophrenic condition at some time during his or her life. Forty percent of all hospital beds are occupied by mental patients, and of these, over half are persons with schizophrenic conditions. The prevalence of the illness is without doubt a major public health problem.

Questions about the origin and treatment of schizophrenia have been a major focus of research since the middle of the nineteenth century, but few satisfactory answers have emerged. Investigators have looked at biogenetic, epidemiological, biochemical, psychological, social, and familial interaction factors, and for the most part, each investigator has promulgated his or her own theory of schizophrenia. Single-factor theories, however, do not adequately explain the diversity of schizophrenic symptoms or the complexity of the disorder, which manifests itself differently not only among individuals but also within a single person.

A meaningful approach to understanding schizophrenia would include a description of both the behavioral manifestations of the disorder and the internal processes that underlie or produce the behavior observed. We are simply unable as yet to make such specifications, although many attempts have been made within different frames of reference. This volume does not attempt to explain schizophrenia but rather to help clarify one of its important characteristics—thought disorder.

Examination of theories about schizophrenic thinking reveals that the term *schizophrenia,* as currently understood, is itself a *disjunctive* category. [Bannister (1971) stated that although schizophrenia is defined by five major characteristics—thought disorder, primary delusions, loss of volition, incongruous or flattened affect, and disturbance of motility—any patient who is called schizophrenic will manifest some but not necessarily all of these characteristics.] Individuals within a group of schizophrenics may not even share the same characteristics. Consequently, Bannister suggested that researchers should not study schizophrenia as a single, general category but should focus instead on a specified subset of characteristics that define the illness. This book takes such an approach by focusing on thought disorder as one of the characteristics most consistently included in a comprehensive definition of schizophrenia.

Obviously, in order to study thought disorder, it is first necessary to describe and measure it. The major purpose of this book, therefore, is to present a valid, reliable instrument that assays thought disorder in an objective, quantifiable, and replicable manner; we call this instrument the Thought Disorder Index or TDI. Such an instrument should provide the researcher with two important resources: (1) a means of assessing a population with regard to thought disorder and (2) a measure with the potential for yielding results that can be meaningfully interrelated with other aspects of schizophrenic pathology.

Within the field of research on schizophrenic thinking, several approaches exist: broad, general theories concerning the na-

ture of schizophrenic thinking and its central importance in
schizophrenia; attempts to describe subjectively the multitudinous
facets of schizophrenic thinking; and empirical studies of single
aspects of, and fine distinctions within, schizophrenic thinking.
The broad theories are probably the ones most familiar to clinicians
and investigators. These theories include those formulated by
Kraepelin, Bleuler, Goldstein, and Cameron, who focused on special aspects of schizophrenic thinking that appeared to them to
describe most completely the fundamental underlying disturbance.
All subsequent research was influenced by their ideas. The
Thought Disorder Index (TDI) presented in this book focuses on
many aspects of schizophrenic thinking first noted by these writers,
although it is not limited to these aspects.

       We believe that a metric that assesses thought disorder can
bypass the issue of whether a patient should be called "schizophrenic" or not. Such a measure classifies subjects instead on the
basis of various quantities and qualities of thought disorder. From
this perspective, those concerned with research methods in
psychopathology can derive a workable tool for studying some of
the cognitive aspects of the major functional psychoses. Clinicians
seeking ways to chart change in patients may also find value in this
approach.

       In Chapters One, Two, and Three, by reviewing early
theories of thought disorder as well as later attempts to test them,
we shall set the stage for presenting the TDI and how we used it.
Chapter One includes a brief review of the classical theories concerning the role of thought disorder in schizophrenia, remarks
about the relationship between normal and disturbed thinking, and
a discussion of the difficulty of defining thought disorder. Chapter
Two describes the procedures that have been used to define and
measure thought disorder, with particular focus on methodological
problems that have arisen in the past and must now be taken into
account. Chapter Two also discusses quantifiable aspects of
thought disorder supported as valid by empirical research and
used as basic dimensions in the construction of our instrument.
Chapter Three describes some studies of thought disorder in subject groups that are not clinically schizophrenic, such as the relatives of schizophrenic patients.

Chapter Four describes the empirical origins of the TDI and presents the scoring manual for the instrument and details of administration and scoring. Chapter Five presents the design of our validation study—how and why the particular groups of subjects were chosen and the choice of instruments used to discriminate among the subject groups. Chapter Six describes the results of the validation study using the TDI as well as brief discussions of the meaning of the separate results.

Chapter Seven is an attempt to pull together the substantive findings and to discuss them as a whole. The final "Case Illustrations" section contains complete protocols of representative subjects—schizophrenic, manic, nonpsychotic—at different stages of their disorder. The records of some parents of subjects are also included. Thought disorder is scored for these records using the TDI and brief case notes with historical and interpretative sections included.

It is a paradox that a set of disorders called schizophrenia, which is recognized by deviant behavior and pathological thinking, has defied recent advances into its *psychological* process while yielding, or promising to yield, answers to *somatic* interrogatories. The pharmacologic, biochemical, and genetic advances are, of course, aided by the availability of viable research methods and tools. Progress on the psychological dimension seems slowed by the relative absence of such techniques. Because of the prominence of thought disorder in psychosis, the measurement of thought disorder should be a prerequisite for deeper studies into the psychology of schizophrenia. The TDI can help fill that requirement.

The authors gratefully acknowledge the help of many people at various stages of this project. Sally Haimo, James Otteson, Ira Rosofsky, David Clark, and Steven Hurt administered some of the psychological tests. The Psychosomatic and Psychiatric Institute of Michael Reese Hospital, the Illinois State Psychiatric Institute, and the Manteno State Hospital in Illinois provided facilities and access to patients. Roy R. Grinker, Sr., and Herbert Y. Meltzer made it possible to test many of the patients in the Chicago area. Sally Haimo and Randall Rowlett helped to score protocols both for thought disorder and for communication deviance. Donald W. Fiske of the University of Chicago generously gave methodological advice. LaJune Whitney and Mary Ann Perkins ably typed the manuscript. Joyce Nevis-Olesen helped to make some difficult and turgid passages more readable.

This study is based on a dissertation written for the Ph.D. degree by Mary Hollis Johnston. The research was supported by grants from the U.S. Public Health Service (MH-19477 and MH-31340), the State of Illinois (131-13-RD), and from the Benevolent Foundation of the Scottish Rite to Philip Holzman, who was a recipient of Public Health Service Research Scientist Award (MH-70900). This work was also supported in part by Public Health Service funds (MH-31154) awarded to Seymour S. Kety.

September 1979   MARY HOLLIS JOHNSTON
Chicago, Illinois

PHILIP S. HOLZMAN
Cambridge, Massachusetts

Contents

Preface   vii

The Authors   xiii

I.   Theories of Schizophrenic Thinking   1

II.   Definitions and Measurements of Thought Disorder   18

III.   Thought Dysfunction in Nonschizophrenic Subjects   38

IV. Development and Scoring Manual of the
     Thought Disorder Index   56

V.   Testing the Thought Disorder Index   102

VI. Test Results and Substantive Findings   129

VII. Implications for Using the Thought
     Disorder Index in Research and
     Clinical Practice   168

     Case Illustrations and Interpretations   178

     References   288

     Index   303

The Authors

MARY HOLLIS JOHNSTON is assistant professor of psychology and psychiatry at the University of Illinois Medical Center, Chicago, in the Early Childhood Assessment Program of the Child Psychiatry Clinic. In addition, she is a faculty member of the Erikson Institute for Early Education, psychological consultant to the Virginia Frank Child Development Center, and in private practice.

As an undergraduate at Carleton College, Johnston was nominated to Phi Beta Kappa and Sigma Xi, and she presented the outstanding undergraduate psychology research paper (1968) to the Minnesota Psychological Association on a study of language development in children. She was graduated summa cum laude with the B.A. degree in psychology (1968). The recipient of a NDEA fellowship for graduate study in clinical psychology at the

University of Chicago, she was awarded the M.A. and Ph.D. degrees from the Committee on Human Development (1970, 1975). Her research interests have been in the study of language and thinking disturbances in psychopathology. Another current interest is the study of early developmental distortions in object relations and ego development.

PHILIP S. HOLZMAN is professor of psychology in the Department of Psychology and Social Relations, Faculty of Arts and Sciences, and in the Department of Psychiatry, Faculty of Medicine, at Harvard University. He is also a training and supervising psychoanalyst in the Boston Psychoanalytic Society and Institute.

Holzman was awarded the B.A. degree from the College of the City of New York (1943) and the Ph.D. degree in psychology from the University of Kansas (1952). He was a clinical psychologist for twenty-two years on the staff of the Menninger Foundation, Topeka, Kansas, where he studied with David Rapaport and Karl Menninger. He became director of research training at the Menninger Foundation and a training and supervising analyst in the Topeka Institute for Psychoanalysis. He was professor of psychology and psychiatry at the University of Chicago (1968–1977) and then accepted a professorship at Harvard University. In addition to his teaching positions, he is chief of the Psychology Laboratory at the Mailman Research Center, McLean Hospital, and works in close collaboration with scientists representing neuroanatomy, genetics, pharmacology, and clinical sciences.

Holzman has written extensively on cognitive consistencies, psychoanalytic topics, and schizophrenia. He has published over eighty papers. Among the books he has authored or co-authored are: *Cognitive Controls* (with R. W. Gardner, G. S. Klein, H. Linton, and D. Spence, 1959), *Psychoanalysis and Psychopathology* (1970), *The Theory of Psychoanalytic Technique* (with K. Menninger, 2nd ed., 1973), *Psychology Versus Metapsychology* (with M. M. Gill, 1976). He is currently working on issues of thought disorder in psychosis and on psychophysiological dysfunctions in schizophrenia.

Assessing Schizophrenic Thinking

A Clinical and Research Instrument
for Measuring Thought Disorder

I

Theories of
Schizophrenic Thinking

Consider the following scene, which took place in a state hospital meeting room. It involved Marian, a 23-year-old schizophrenic woman; her father and mother; Joan, a 20-year-old schizophrenic woman; her father; a psychiatrist; and a psychiatric nurse. The group had begun to discuss the discomfort Marian experienced just prior to her hospitalization.

Marian: I'm responsible for my own motives. I keep my mouth closed and my nose open.

Nurse: Can you say things a bit more clearly to let us know what's going on?

Marian: Just ask my autograph book who was signing it all the time. It's not my fault it's ripped up.

Psychiatrist: Did you think we'd know what you meant when you said that?

Marian: I *know* you all know what I meant.

Psychiatrist: I didn't.

Marian: That's not your fault.

Nurse:	I suspect no one else in this room knew what you were talking about.
Marian:	I said I could remember when my mother's hair was down her back and she kept cutting it off.
Psychiatrist:	I don't know what that means.
Marian:	That's what I mean. There's been a pass over me. I've been passed over.
Psychiatrist:	I still don't know.
Marian:	Well, look at the dark shadows. What do you see? Same old monkeys.
Marian's mother:	(abruptly and with irritation) Get on the subject.
Marian:	Why in the hell should I get on the subject?
Psychiatrist:	Do you know the subject?
Marian:	No.
Marian's father:	I think she'd 'a made more progress if she'd had her glasses sooner. She'd 'a been more quiet.
Marian:	I have 'em now.
Marian's mother:	She was going to school and working at the same time. There was a lot of pressure on her. She'd stay up late at night and her Dad would holler.
Joan's father:	Would the hollering bother you, Marian?
Marian:	No.
Marian's mother:	She always told me it did.
Nurse:	Do you agree with what your mother is saying?
Marian:	Yes, that's it. I got in the middle of everything and that's where I'm gonna stay, in the middle.
Psychiatrist:	What do you mean?
Marian:	They used to argue all the time, and that would make me sick.
Marian's mother:	We did argue too much. If I said something, he thought he was right, and . . .
Marian's father:	(interrupting) That's not the way . . .
Marian:	(shrilly) You're interrupting the woman! See? That's why I'm here!

Marian's father:	You're interrupting both of us.
Marian:	That's what I mean, that's why I'm sitting up here in your face.
Marian's mother:	He would get angry with all the children.
Marian's father:	I need rest. Can't you see that?
Psychiatrist:	(to Marian) Being sick permits you to say anything to your father.
Marian:	Sure. You all don't want me to laugh, you're telling me I'm supposed to sit up here and cry?
Joan's father:	I'm pretty argumentative. I'm short-fused with the family. Most families do this. The family is a place where there's no contest, no battle. When a difference of opinion comes up I get angry.
Joan:	Who is married to whom?
Joan's father:	No, Joan, you're not so far gone that you can't understand.
Joan:	(abruptly stands up and begins to leave the room) Damn it! (turns and speaks angrily) I was upset with my father because I lost my dreaming ability. I had a good nap. Maybe I sound like I'm crazy, but I'm not angry in my mind.
Joan's father:	I'm annoyed with you because you haven't participated in the conversation.
Joan:	Conversation or conversations?
Marian:	Let the man finish.
Joan:	It's all a tangle.
Joan's father:	But there are common threads.
Joan:	The stupid English lesson.
Joan's father:	We're not talking about that.
Joan:	Well, if I can explain myself outwardly maybe you can explain yourself inwardly and you'll feel better and help your pupils.
Joan's father:	That's not what I'm concerned about here. This group . . .
Joan:	Little closed circuit—closed group—like Marian said.
Marian:	My name's not Marian, it's Markey.
Joan:	(rhythmically) You say your name is Marian.

	You say your name is Valerie.
	You say your name is Markey.
	You say your name is Joan.
	You say your name is Happy.
	You say your name is Sad. This. That. I get
	mixed up. I don't understand the chemistry in-
	volved in smoking.
Joan's father:	Joan gets upset when there's a change.
Joan:	I feel terrible, and it has to do with what hap-
	pened before I came into the hospital. And I
	don't want to talk about it. I just want good
	grooming.

The cacophony of meanings jars the observer. Wild swings of direction intrude upon lines of discourse barely begun. Ideas that apparently have deep personal significance ("I said I can remember when my mother's hair was down her back . . .") are offered as explanations for another obscure reference ("Just ask my autograph book . . ."). Rhythmic, compulsively repetitive phrases appear ("You say your name is . . ."). Sudden bursts of anger exaggerate the dissonance. And it is not only the patients whose communications are difficult to follow. Marian's father, perhaps fueled by anxiety, shame, anger, or remorse, contributes his own labyrinthine thoughts to the discussion ("I think she'd 'a made more progress if she'd 'a had her glasses sooner").

Classical Theories of
Thought Disorder

Confronted by the range of disordered communicating such as that evinced in this excerpt, early observers of schizophrenia tried to describe the nature of disordered thinking that evoked such communicating and then to determine the essential process that could explain it. Kraepelin ([1896]1919), for example, united several clinical psychiatric syndromes conceptually under the name *dementia praecox*, which identified those psychoses that begin relatively early in life and progress to intellectual and social deterioration. He gave as evidence of this deterioration the incoherence and "derailments" of thought sequences that characterize the speech of patients manifesting these syndromes.

Influenced by the associationist psychology popular in the latter decades of the nineteenth century, classical theorists, for the most part, proposed that schizophrenic thinking was an outcome of impaired associations among ideas. In this respect Bleuler ([1911] 1950) placed special emphasis on the appearance of a "splitting of the psychic function" (p. 9), by which he meant that in the course of speaking or thinking, a patient's ideas and feelings appear fragmented and separated from each other, and different levels of functioning compete or coexist, some showing deterioration, some preservation. He attributed this "splitting" to a "loosening of associations" that occurs in the thinking of schizophrenic patients and argued that this loosening of associations is a primary symptom of schizophrenia that produces secondary symptoms such as delusions. Disturbances of association, he wrote, reflect blocking or pressure of alien thoughts, a lack of unifying goal direction, condensation of several ideas into one, and perseverations. When associative connections and relationships between thoughts and ideas are lost, confusion and illogic result, and thinking appears bizarre and unpredictable: "Often thinking stops in the middle of a thought; or in the attempt to pass to another idea, it may suddenly cease altogether, at least as far as it is a conscious process (blocking). Instead of continuing the thought, new ideas crop up which neither the patient nor the observer can bring into any connection with the previous stream of thought" (Bleuler, [1911] 1950, p. 9).

While Kraepelin and Bleuler explained schizophrenic thinking as the result of a breakdown in associative connections, other early theorists called attention to the primitive language usage which they believed characterized schizophrenia. Storch (1924), for example, following the comparative orientation of Werner (1948), who sought links among thought processes of adults, children, and "primitives," noted the "syncretic" quality of thinking—the merging of motor and affective elements in perception and the blurring of boundaries between concepts—that appear to be characteristic of both schizophrenic patients and members of primitive cultures.

Within this mode of thought, innocuous objects may become invested with portentous meanings or inanimate things may be regarded as alive.

The efforts of Goldstein (1944), like those of Storch and Werner, represented a decisive break with the associationist theories. Rather than emphasizing the connections between ideas, Goldstein focused on the manner in which one approaches a cognitive problem and described two levels of capacity to relate oneself to the external world—concrete and abstract. The concrete attitude or mode, on the one hand, reflects a loss of or a deficiency in the ability to categorize; it represents a basic disturbance in the total functioning of the organism. The abstract attitude, on the other hand, permits a person to choose from among mental sets and to shift a particular set to include different aspects of a situation, to keep in mind several aspects simultaneously, to look at the whole as well as at separate parts, and then to generalize, plan, and think symbolically. Goldstein believed that schizophrenia brings with it a loss of this abstract attitude.

Arieti (1974) described a process of "active concretization," by which abstract ideas are transformed into concrete representations, and suggested that this transformation occurs because the abstract idea is too anxiety provoking. Thus, rather than losing the capacity to abstract, the schizophrenic patient regresses to developmentally earlier types of thinking as a protective, purposeful, defensive maneuver.

While Goldstein and others characterized schizophrenic speech and thinking as *concrete,* some investigators labeled similar samples of speech as excessively *abstract.* For example, Barison (1948, 1949) observed that the schizophrenic patient prefers the use of abstract terms to concrete terms and that this substitution represents a defensive attempt to heal a rupture in smooth thinking. However, while some patients constrict the connotative realm of words, others push words beyond their usual connotative boundaries. In the former group, words no longer represent classes of things but only the specific object being considered at the moment; this decrease in connotative power is an expression of the concrete attitude. In the latter group, concrete referents are totally absent;

the resulting impression may therefore be that their thinking is overly abstract.

The idea that schizophrenic thinking is literal and restricted was rejected by Cameron (1944), who proposed the term *overinclusiveness* to describe what he believed to be the fundamental disturbance in schizophrenic thinking. For Cameron, overinclusion describes the inability to maintain conceptual boundaries, with the result that irrelevant and tangential ideas are included in the stream of thought. This in turn leads to vagueness, incomprehensibility, and confusion. Cameron characterized schizophrenic language as having the following characteristics: (1) asyndetic thinking, in which logical connections are missing and the ability to restrict attention and to focus on a task is thereby lost; (2) the use of metonyms and a personal idiom containing imprecise approximations as substitutes for more exact terms; (3) an interpenetration of themes, in which an individual's fantasies mingle with more realistic concerns in a fragmented, disorganized manner; (4) a distortion of the reality situation; and (5) an incongruity between words and actions.

Although Goldstein and Cameron appear to disagree about whether schizophrenic conceptualizing is excessively narrow, limited, and concrete or excessively broad, generalized, and overinclusive, they do agree that schizophrenics have difficulty in appropriately categorizing and in focusing on the most relevant aspects of a situation.

The apparent inability to reason logically about the relationships between objects and events is still another quality of schizophrenic thought; von Domarus (1944) specifically addressed this dimension of cognition, which he called *paralogical thinking*. Such thinking follows a "law of predicate logic," in which two things are identified on the basis of a common predicate rather than on the basis of a common subject. Arieti (1974) held that predicative thinking, which he termed *paleological,* is an essential part of the schizophrenic's tendency to "retreat from reason."

Arieti disagreed with Bleuler's idea that associations break down in schizophrenia. He noted in people who suffer from only a mild form of schizophrenia that most of their thoughts are indeed connected by associations, although some ideas may be without logical direction or purpose. (It is also true, however, that in normal individuals in very relaxed states, thoughts tend to arise spontaneously without apparent purposive selection or direction.) Arieti used the term *associative link* to describe the connection between two ideas that originally were merely temporally contiguous or shared some common quality. Predicative thinking involves a process of ascribing identity to ideas that share such associative links, as in the statement of the patient who believed she was the Virgin Mary because "the Virgin Mary was a virgin and I am a virgin."

In more advanced stages of schizophrenia, ideas are associated and connected through the sharing of sound properties (for example, clang associations) or phonetic symbols of words, so that the meaning of the word is ignored. In the most severe cases, there is a tendency to perceive similarly sounding words and ideas as identical. Arieti proposed that these thinking processes represent a more primitive stage of thinking in which differentiation is rudimentary, logic is ignored, and a part cannot be separated or dissociated from the whole context.

Psychoanalytic Theories

Some psychoanalytic writers have viewed schizophrenic thinking and language usage as manifestations of the "primary process," representing a regression to an earlier, infantile state of psychic development. In *The Interpretation of Dreams*, Freud ([1900] 1953) explicated an ontogenetic theory of thinking, which holds that in the wake of mounting appetitive tension and excitation (referred to as *needs* or *drives*), the young infant perceives a vivid sensory image of the need-satisfying object. This image represents a memory of previous experiences of gratification that arises when the need-satisfying experience is absent. The first ideas about objects are both substitutes for the missing real object (hallucinatory wish fulfillment) and attempts to master the real object magically. This process of thinking, which is responsive to the need for tension discharge and which, in its extreme form, constitutes hallucinatory wish fulfillment, is referred to as the *primary process*. A characteristic of this mode of thinking is that the gratifying image may reflect both the need *and* the need-satisfying object. Thus, primary process thinking appears to be illogical because parts and whole, means and end, can be equated.

During the course of maturation, the theory continues, as a result of adaptive necessities and of the requirements for delaying gratification, a more logical, reality-oriented thinking develops, called the *secondary process*. A principal characteristic of the secondary process is seen in an individual's conceptual organization of ideas and memories. This ability makes possible the delay of drive-motivated actions and the preparation of appropriate, reality-oriented actions. It also permits making plans when need tensions have not yet arisen.

Because of the hallucinatory qualities and the alienation from reality of both dreaming and schizophrenic thinking, classical psychoanalytic theory has regarded these phenomena as regressive and as reinstating primary process thinking. Schizophrenic thinking, according to Fenichel (1945, p. 421), is "identical with primitive, magical thinking, that is, with a form of thinking that also is found in the unconscious of neurotics, in small children, in normal persons under conditions of fatigue, as antecedents of thought, and in primitive man."

Gill (1967), however, has pointed out that primary process thinking is not necessarily an indicator of disordered thinking. Its mechanisms of condensation, displacement, the simultaneous existence of mutually contradictory ideas, and linkage among ideas by loose associations, assonance, and rhymes are operationally manifested not only in hallucinations and symptom formation but in normal thinking as well—in dreaming and humor, for example. Freud ([1900] 1953) claimed that the primary process is one of the singular characteristics of unconscious functioning. Gill's proposal, in contrast, is to regard primary and secondary processes not as dichotomous constructs but as a continuum along which the major mechanisms of condensation and displacement function. Thus, the mere presence of these mechanisms in thought does not brand the thought as primary process or as necessarily pathological.

The idea that primary process thinking is in itself pathological, archaic, and maladaptive was also rejected by Rycroft (1975, p. 27): "If one starts from another assumption, that the primary and secondary processes coexist from the beginning of life and that under favorable conditions they may continue to function in harmony with each other, one providing the imaginative, the other the rational basis of living, then creative people may be conceived to be those who retain into adult life something of that imaginative freedom which healthy children display openly but too many grownups in our present rationalist, bourgeois culture lose when they enter the adult world." Arieti (1974) also stressed that primary process thinking is present in the psychological life of everyone. He described three distinctive features of the primary process as manifested in schizophrenic patients:

1. It involves a larger segment of mental life than in the nonschizophrenic.

2. At least in its pathological manifestation, it is not corrected, neutralized, or rejected by the secondary process; rather, it resists or overpowers the influence of the secondary process.

3. Except in rare cases, it is not harmoniously integrated with the secondary process to form a creative product.

Thus, it appears that the clinical phenomenon of thought disorder, as well as "normal thinking" and imaginative thinking, cannot be explained by a dichotomy of primary process versus secondary process thinking. There is a need for a conceptual continuum that takes account of motivational as well as nonmotivational factors in the production of thinking disorders.

In his consideration of the nature of thought pathology, Rapaport (1951) attempted to encompass both the motivational variables introduced by psychoanalysis and the empirical data from nonpsychoanalytic studies. We summarize his conclusions:

1. Thought disorder may present the preparatory phases as well as the end-product of a process of thinking.

2. It varies according to individual personality characteristics.

3. Thought disorder may rigidify what is usually flexible in normal thought and deautomatize what is usually fixed.

4. Thinking may become less goal directed and purposive as more primitive and less controlled motivations become apparent.

5. Different states of consciousness are associated with particular qualities of thought organization. Thus, thought disorder is a reflection of the interruption of thought organization within a particular state of consciousness rather than a shift in state of consciousness that carries its associated thought organization with it.

6. Thought disorder, as Freud suggested, may take the form either of overvaluing abstractions or of lacking the capacities necessary for abstraction. Thus, both abstract and concrete thinking may be aspects of thought disorder.

7. Thought disorder probably involves all aspects of thinking—attention, concentration, reasoning, and so forth.

8. Motivational considerations alone cannot explain thought organization or its pathology.

The classical theories concerning the nature of schizophrenic thinking and the psychoanalytic theories about primary process thinking and regression were suggested by clinical observations of schizophrenic patients illustrated by the excerpt that began this chapter. However, different theorists have interpreted their own observations in particular ways and have not agreed on which aspects of schizophrenic thinking were of principal or subsidiary importance. No theory has successfully encompassed the range of dysfunction in schizophrenic thinking. It may be necessary at this juncture to clarify the relationship of "disordered" to "ordered" thinking: What is nonpathological thinking, and can disordered thinking be clearly separated from it?

Language and Thought

Language is the structure through which thought is communicated and reflects the way people organize their experiences. Cameron (1944, pp. 51–52) described the interaction between language and thought in the development of the child and how the deterioration of communication means the deterioration of organized, conceptual thinking:

> As the child gradually acquires speech, the organization of the thinking slowly changes because of it; and since

the organization of his language is determined by his social
environment, his thinking tends to become progressively
more socialized. . . . [In schizophrenic disorganization] social communication is gradually crowded out by fantasy;
and the fantasy itself, because of its nonparticipation in and
relation to action, becomes in turn less and less influenced
by social patterns. The result is a progressive loss of organized thinking, and ultimately an incapacity for taking
the role of others when this is necessary to enable one to
share adequately in their attitudes and perspectives.

Lidz (1973) suggested that it is through language that individuals
learn from others and also transmit their own experiences to
others. In order to perceive, understand, reflect on, and talk about
experience, one must categorize one's own experiences. The use of
words reflects that organization of the inner world of thought.

The use of the term *disordered thinking* implies that the nature of ordered thinking is understood. Within the present discussion, nonpathological or ordered thinking refers to the process by
which a person selects and organizes perceptions for presentation
in the course of ongoing adaptive functioning and problem solving.
Cognitive processes are internal events that mediate between external stimuli and the subject's response to those stimuli. Adaptive
functioning requires selective attention to the outside world with
the deletion of irrelevant material, ongoing assessment of the ap-
propriateness of a thought or a percept, and the discrimination
of internal perceptions from external ones. Language provides
the framework through which these cognitive activities can be
represented.

Purposeful, organized thinking should be distinguished
from the alogical, primitive, drifting reveries, associations, and images that occur continually "in the back of our mind," as it were.
Sullivan (1944) attempted to differentiate "language operations as
thought" from "language operations as communication" in the following manner: Language as thought can be autistic and idiosyncratic, perhaps the direct expression of reveries and images, much
like the language of dreams; language as communication, however,
is an organization of the revery process and is attuned to other
people as potential listeners. "The more completely one becomes
self-centered, the more utterly he becomes cut off from integra-

tions with other more or less real people, and the more utterly novel, perfectly magical, and wholly individual become the symbols which he uses as if they were language" (Sullivan, 1944, p. 9). The schizophrenic patient has the greatest difficulty in the more formal, disciplined organization of revery which requires critical observation of one's own thought and the inhibition of irrelevant associations. In Sullivan's terms, disordered thinking represents a disturbance in "the final refinement of the reverie process," a breakdown in the capacity to organize so that the logical, abstract, intentional thinking expected of adult members of our society no longer predominates.

Referring to some aspects of language operations as a disturbance of communication may trouble some readers. Sapir (1921) distinguished several levels of language, each of which can serve a different purpose, ranging from image representation and concrete particularities to presentation of abstract concepts and their relations. This latter level of language he called *reasoning*. "Thus the outward form only of language is constant; its inner meaning, its psychic value or intensity varies freely with attention or the selective interest of the mind, also, needless to say, with the mind's general development" (Sapir, 1921, p. 14). We say that individuals manifest a disturbance of thinking when they cannot move flexibly from one level of language to another in appropriate response to the situation at hand. Though this disorder is reflected in the level of language used, it is not simply a problem in communicating. It reflects, we believe, a disturbance in the *thought process* which the language is portraying.

Lorenz (1961) believed that there may not necessarily be a fixed relationship between language and thought. Language may equal thought or it may reflect thought. In its use of metaphor, simile, and analogy, language may express private meanings that can be shared only if the listener recognizes and understands the symbolism. Language can *represent* private experience and thoughts in a public, understandable communication or it can *present* thoughts without transformation, so that what is spoken is private and noncommunicative. Language can disguise and distort thought. And, finally, language can order, categorize, and organize experience.

Like Sapir, Lorenz believed that there are levels of language and individual dispositions to choose particular levels. An instance of apparent concrete thinking, she wrote, may represent a disposition to organize experience in a particular way rather than an inability to think abstractly. It may reflect a disposition for viewing the world in terms of its variety and multiplicity of instances rather than in terms of its common denominators. Schizophrenic pathology, in this framework, could be viewed as an inflexible overemphasis on modes of thought that exclude logical thinking.

This viewpoint has much in common with the previously discussed psychoanalytic description of primary and secondary process thinking. Language that is more expressive and that presents thoughts and images without transformation is closer to primary process thinking, while language that organizes and transforms thoughts in order to communicate is closer to secondary process thinking. However, neither mode is in itself pathological; it is the way in which the modes are employed that brand the thinking as disordered.

Dichotomy or Continuum?

The ideas of Lorenz (1961) and Sapir (1921) appear to be congruent with Gill's (1967) belief that the levels of language use —as revealed in primary process and secondary process thinking modes—occur on a continuum and are not necessarily mutually exclusive. However, in the classifications of several of the theorists discussed (Bleuler, [1911] 1950; Goldstein, 1944; Cameron, 1944) the assumption is implicit that there are indeed two types of thinking: the one comprising normal, everyday rationality and even extending to scientific and pure logic; and the other comprising disordered thinking, extending from the mildly peculiar to the bizarre. The classical theorists have employed their own ordering schemes—abstract-concrete, paralogical-logical, primary process–secondary process—and all of the schemes seem to apply to some patients. That is, one can discern in the language and thought products of schizophrenic patients examples of disordered thinking that fit one's preferred classifications. Yet not all schizophrenic patients manifest one particular kind of thought disorder, nor are all the kinds of disorders demonstrably present in any particular patient. It therefore becomes difficult to maintain that the thought disorder in schizophrenia reflects this or that particular, specific process.

Philosophically, the search for the single, specific characteristic of schizophrenic thinking itself reveals a preference for class-theoretical modes of thinking rather than field-theoretical modes, as discussed by Lewin (1935). In a class-theoretical orientation, the ideal thought process is rational and scientific: logic and syntax are predictable and follow rules that are, at least superficially, fairly easy to specify. The *ideal* process contrasts with the *pathological* thought processes, which either replace or transform the former into allusive images, symbols, distant associations, or connotative or concrete ideas.

class-theor. models

Lewin recounted the characteristics of such class-theortical concepts: their valuative character; their abstract classifatory constraints (the class defines the characteristics of an ject); their exclusion of the conceptually unintelligible (thus, the individual case, the complex, and the irregular are banned from consideration). In contrast, the field-theoretical approach, which Lewin called the Galilean mode of thought, replaces dichotomies with continua, class laws with homogenization (the same laws govern the stars and the stones), and abstract classifications with concreteness (a full description of the concrete actually is required for understanding).

Consistent with the Galilean mode, formulation of laws of thinking—rather than laws of schizophrenic thinking—seem to us a reasonable and profitable goal for the research pursuits of experimental psychopathologists. Concrete and abstract thinking, paralogical and logical thought, primary and secondary process, syncretistic and narrowed conceptualization, and other formulations occur across the continuum on which normal to pathological thinking ranges. In fact, many different kinds of thought processes are commonplace in nonpathological as well as pathological persons, in highly civilized as well as so-called primitive cultures, and in children as well as in adults. The pure form of any extreme of thinking—primary or secondary process, for example—is, as Freud noted, a fiction. The view we adopt is that thought processes represent constructions that cannot be considered apart from the

context in which they occur. This context includes reality constraints, the social-interpersonal setting, and the personal purposes, wishes, and state of the organism. The reciprocal interplay
among these factors will determine the quality of thinking.

Holt (1977) reminded us that Freud coupled the primary
process to the pleasure principle and the secondary process to the
reality principle. This parameter can be applied to the issue of
pathological thinking: The more a thought can be characterized as
an unrealistic search for immediate gratification divorced from
reality-adaptive constraints, the more it can be considered deviant
or disordered; the more intention, purpose, and context guide the
thinking, the more it can be considered appropriate and realistic.
The more peremptory is the thought product, with relative absence
of modulating controls, the more pathological is the thought
(Klein, 1967). Holt (1977, p. 377) commented in this respect that "In
much of what Freud wrote about [the primary and secondary proc-
esses] it is fairly clear that he did not think of them dichoto-
mously, but as defining the extremes of a logical continuum. Any
actual thought process, even that of a baby or a deteriorated
schizophrenic, has to be located somewhere in between the two
poles."

Similar transformations of thinking can occur both in
psychosis and in artistic creation. This is illustrated by the following
anecdote: James Joyce consulted C. G. Jung about the former's
daughter, whose behavior had so concerned Joyce that he sought
psychiatric help for her. Jung conducted a lengthy examination
and then concluded that she was suffering from *dementia praecox*.
"How do you know, Dr. Jung?" Joyce asked. Jung replied that her
thinking and speech were so deviant and distorted that he could
conclude that she was suffering from this particular form of mad-
ness. Joyce protested that in his own writing, he purposefully
stretched the English language, distorted words, fused thoughts
and images. "What is the difference?" he asked. Jung replied that
Joyce and his daughter were like two people going to the bottom of
a river, but whereas Joyce dove into the deep water, his daughter
fell into it. Jung later wrote, "The ordinary patient cannot help
himself talking and thinking in such a way, while Joyce willed it and
moreover developed it with all his creative forces" (Ellman, 1959,
p. 692).

A crucial parameter in the differentiation of creative production from psychotic ravings is that of control voluntarism and purposefulness. The schizophrenic patient appears to be driven by his thoughts; the artist orders them. The patient's thoughts are peremptory and insistent; the artist's are formed and modulated. The patient with a religious delusion may, on the face of it, behave no differently from the faithful, scrupulous, and devoted churchgoer. Religion in both may even serve defensive purposes. The peremptory quality of the religious behavior will, however, betray the deluded person.

Holt (in Rapaport, Gill, and Schafer, 1968, p. 425) phrased the relationship between controlled and uncontrolled thinking this way: "By paying close attention to the effectiveness (or ineffectiveness) with which the subject uses his controls and defenses in coping with the emergence of his own primary processes, I have found it possible and fruitful to distinguish between uncontrolled, pathological breakthroughs of primary process material (maladaptive regression) and more ego-syntonic, socialized, acceptable expressions (adaptive regression)."

The mere expression of odd, difficult-to-comprehend material does not by itself signal the breakdown of logical thinking and hence of psychotic incursions on cognitive functioning. One must evaluate the speaker's purpose, his efforts to control the material, the pervasiveness of the breakthrough, the effects on the speaker and on his audience, and the speaker's capacity to shift to more socialized discourse. In short, incomprehensibility is not a definition of thought disorder, although products of disordered thinking may be incomprehensible. The process by which such incomprehensibility emerges helps to determine whether or not it is a result of thought disorder. Assessment of the manifestations and meanings of such thought processes presents a major challenge to research efforts.

II

Definitions and
Measurements
of Thought Disorder

The first theorists to describe schizophrenic thinking were clinicians who observed schizophrenic patients on hospital wards or in the physician's office. Their astute descriptions of overinclusive, primitive, or associatively loose thinking were valid for those patients they observed, and such patients can usually be found on psychiatric wards today. However, an individual patient may display overinclusive thinking during one observation and concrete thinking at the next; or the patient may be both primitive and loose at the same time. Research attempts to assess thought disorder have focused either on the measurement of single aspects of disordered thinking, such as overinclusion or concreteness, or on a more global assessment of disordered thinking, assuming a continuum of severity of disturbance.

A variety of procedures for systematically eliciting disordered thinking and for describing the results has been employed.

Chapman and Chapman (1973) have observed that these procedures differ in the degree of specification and restriction of the stimulus situation, the alternatives for responding, and the categories for scoring responses. For example, clinical theorists describe anecdotally the unstructured, free speech of their patients. Some investigators have classified this deviant speech into predetermined categories by rating scales or checklists (Gottschalk and Gleser, 1969; Reilly and others, 1975; Andreasen, in press). Rorschach ([1922] 1942); Klopfer (1942); Beck (1944); Rapaport, Gill, and Schafer (1968), and others have standardized the stimulus situation through the use of projective tests and then have evaluated the responses to these tests. Others (Chapman and Chapman, 1973) have employed standardized tests with multiple choice questions and restricted response choice.

Single Aspects of Thought Disorders

The majority of recent empirical studies of thought disorder have continued to look for a fundamental, underlying deficit and have thus examined specific aspects of thinking disturbance. Chapman and Chapman (1973) listed a number of characteristics of schizophrenic thinking that have been investigated empirically: excessive yielding to normal biases, such as responding to the stimulus that is strongest, most recent, most novel, or most familiar; loss of abstract thinking ability; errors in syllogistic reasoning; overinclusion; regressive thinking; and impairment of attention. We will briefly review the empirical studies that relate to five areas of thinking: (1) concept formation; (2) cognitive focusing; (3) reasoning; (4) modulation of affect; and (5) reality testing (as summarized by Weiner, 1966).

Concept Formation

Theories about schizophrenic thinking typically have focused on disturbances in conceptualizing, with special emphasis on the presence of concreteness and overinclusion. Concrete thinking, defined as the loss of the ability to abstract, has been labeled a pathognomonic indicator of schizophrenia by Vygotsky (1962), Benjamin (1944), and Goldstein (1944). Cameron's concept of overinclusion (1944) has been subjected to more empirical studies than any other characteristic of schizophrenic thinking, and has been generally accepted as one of the "distinctive and diagnostically useful features of schizophrenic concept formation" (Weiner, 1966, p. 94). Concreteness and overinclusion are most often measured by tests that were designed to assess concept formation: the Object Sorting Test (Vygotsky, 1934, 1962; Hanfmann and Kasanin, 1942; and Goldstein, 1939) and the Proverbs Test (Benjamin, 1944; Gorham, 1956).

Concreteness. Concreteness refers to the tendency of a subject to stay within the bounds either of the immediate specific stimulus situation or of his or her own personal experiences. Such thinking is manifest on the Object Sorting Test, for example, when the subject adheres very narrowly to the starting object that is presented; on the Proverbs Test, it appears when a subject uses words directly from the proverb without translating them into a more general meaning.

Early descriptions of concrete attitude were derived from observations of chronic schizophrenic patients. However, this quality has not characterized the thinking of less chronic schizophrenic patients. Shimkunas, Gynther, and Smith (1966, 1967), for example, gave the Gorham Proverbs Test to schizophrenics at hospital admission and again after the patients had been receiving phenothiazines for five weeks. The proverb responses were scored as concrete or as "autistic," which the authors defined as "bizarre, idiosyncratic, inappropriate, tangential to the meaning of the proverb." They found that autism was a more significant characteristic of the schizophrenic patients' responses than was concreteness and that autistic reponses fluctuated in synchrony with clinically rated pathology.

Harrow, Adler, and Hanf (1974) found that, during the acute phase of psychiatric disturbance, some limited impairment in abstract thinking occurred in both schizophrenic and nonschizophrenic patients, with the more chronic, insidiously developing schizophrenics (so-called *process schizophrenics*) tending to be more concrete than other patients, including the more acute and episodic conditions (so-called *reactive schizophrenics*). They reported, however, that intelligence level was a powerful influence on the abstract-concrete dimension. Improvement in abstracting ability, found in the recovery phase, was related to improvement in intellectual efficiency. Thus, abstracting ability reflects the intactness of general cognitive functioning, and both are disrupted by acute disturbance.

A report by Tutko and Spence (1962) suggested that the concrete thinking observed in some schizophrenics represents not an inability to conceptualize but a difficulty in maintaining a set from which to abstract. They found, for example, that, although process schizophrenics and patients with organic brain damage were similarly unable to perform an object-sorting task successfully, the manner in which they made errors differed. Process schizophrenics, in contrast to the brain-damaged patients, were sometimes able to produce appropriate abstract responses but were inconsistent in their ability to reach an adequate solution. Reactive schizophrenics, however, actively searched for solutions, to the point of making inappropriate, overinclusive ones. The finding that all schizophrenic patients did not share the same kind of conceptualizing disturbance suggests that schizophrenics may be grouped into subtypes—at least process and reactive types—on the basis of thought organization.

Overinclusion. The group of schizophrenics studied by Payne and Hewlett (1960) was strikingly heterogeneous with respect to thought organization. These psychotic patients could be classified by the different kinds of thought disorder they presented: those with moderate retardation; those with severe retardation and flattened affect; and those with overinclusive thinking. Only one third to one half of the acute psychotic patients they tested showed overinclusive thinking.

In their review of the concept of overinclusive thinking, Hawks and Payne (1972) noted the discrepancy between Cameron's definition of such thinking and later attempts to measure it. Cameron's original description of overinclusiveness was based on studies of chronic schizophrenics, but Payne (1962) found overinclusive thinking only in acute schizophrenics. It appears that measurements of overinclusiveness have confounded verbal overproductivity with overinclusion. The level of overinclusiveness was measured principally by verbal productivity, and the higher scores of acute schizophrenics probably reflected their greater verbal responsivity.

Harrow and others (1972a) explained some of the confusion in research on overinclusion by the fact that at least three different phenomena had been studied as overinclusion without distinguishing among them: (1) behavioral overinclusion, which, as studied by Payne and his associates, is based on the quantitative aspects of the subject's overt behavior; (2) conceptual overinclusion, which involves an assessment of the level of abstraction of concepts used; and (3) stimulus overinclusion, which consists of difficulty in attending to relevant stimului. Bromet and Harrow (1973) held that *behavioral overinclusion* does not reveal overinclusive thinking; rather, it reveals excessive behavioral output or overproductivity. They investigated the occurrence of behavioral overinclusion during the acute stage of psychiatric disturbance and at a post-hospital stage, and found that schizophrenics did not differ from nonschizophrenics at either stage. A high correlation occurred between behavioral overinclusion at the acute and at the post-hospital stage, suggesting that behavioral overinclusion is a stylistic or trait variable that remains consistent within individual patients over time and cuts across diagnostic groups (cf. Otteson and Holzman, 1976; Gardner, 1953).

Harrow and others (1972a) found that *conceptual overinclusion* was significantly more prevalent in acute schizophrenic patients than in nonschizophrenic patients and that it correlated significantly with the presence of delusions. Harrow and others (1973) also found that schizophrenic patients showed a significant reduction in conceptual overinclusion during the post-hospital phase (eight months after hospital discharge), when they no longer showed greater overinclusion than nonschizophrenic patients. It appeared that conceptual overinclusion was greatly influenced by disorganization.

Chapman (1960) investigated overinclusion and overexclusion in a conceptual sorting task that used cards naming fruits, vegetables, and sports equipment and systematically varied the breadth of the concept the subjects were asked to sort for. When the task called for a narrow concept, the schizophrenics overincluded; when it called for a broader concept, they overexcluded.

Chapman and Chapman (1973) found that incorrect but conceptually similar objects were overincluded more often than incorrect but dissimilar objects. They interpreted these findings to indicate that conceptually similar objects are sorted according to common, popularly shared, and even stereotypic meanings of the objects.

Richness of association. Using the Object Sorting Test, Harrow and others (1972a) scored the subject's *richness of association,* that is, responses indicating originality and awareness of a variety of possible categorizing principles. They found no difference between a group of acute schizophrenic patients and nonschizophrenic patients. However, in a second study (Harrow and others, 1972b) chronic schizophrenics showed significantly fewer rich associations than did acute schizophrenics or nonschizophrenics.

In summary, the quality of concept formation differs in acute and chronic schizophrenics. The cognitive impairment characterizing chronic schizophrenics is discernible in impaired abstracting ability; chronic schizophrenics show greater concreteness and fewer rich associations than do acute patients. However, acute schizophrenic patients, who are generally psychologically disorganized, show greater conceptual overinclusion.

Cognitive Focusing

There is clear-cut experimental evidence that schizophrenic patients have difficulty focusing on relevant stimuli, appropriately changing a mental set, and inhibiting extraneous associations (Weiner, 1966). Investigators have noticed these difficulties in a variety of tasks, but most specifically on items of the Wechsler Adult Intelligence Scale (WAIS) and the Rorschach Test. Examples of such problems include: clang associations; peculiar and queer verbalizations (Rapaport, Gill, and Schafer, 1968); blocking or pressure of thought; perseveration (Friedman, 1953; Becker, 1956); and loose or tangential associations.

Stimulus overinclusion. This concept was defined by Shield, Harrow, and Tucker (1974, p. 2) as "perceptual experiences characterized by the individual's difficulty in attending selectively to relevant stimuli, or by the person's tendency to be distracted by or to focus unnecessarily on a wide range of irrelevant stimuli." They found that while such experiences are frequently described by schizophrenics, they are not exclusive to schizophrenics and appear to be associated with acute emotional disturbances, especially anxiety and depression.

Idiosyncratic thinking. Deviant or idiosyncratic thinking refers to content that deviates from usual social norms or expectations, is inappropriate to the task at hand, and thus appears confused, contradictory, or illogical. Such responses include the peculiar and queer verbalizations described by Rapaport, Gill, and Schafer (1968). Weiner and Exner (1978) scored "deviant verbalizations" on the Rorschach Test and reported that nonpatient adolescents and adults produced fewer such verbalizations than their patient counterparts. Harrow and others (1972a) and Harrow, Tucker, and Adler (1972), in evaluating reponses to proverbs and to the Comprehension subtest of the WAIS, found a significantly greater amount of idiosyncratic thinking in acute schizophrenics than in other patients. They therefore suggested that strange, idiosyncratic ways of thinking and behaving are as characteristic of schizophrenic thinking as are other qualities of thought disorganization, such as overinclusion. Chronic schizophrenics also scored high on both idiosyncratic thinking and conceptual overinclusion (Harrow, and others, 1972b). Quinlan and others (1978), comparing different aspects of disordered thinking, found that idiosyncratic responses scored from the WAIS comprehension items were a stronger index of disturbed thinking than were measures from the Object Sorting Test.

A decrease in idosyncratic thinking was found in all patients during a phase of partial recovery from acute disturbance (Adler and Harrow, 1974), although it remained higher in schizophrenics than in nonschizophrenics. In a longitudinal study, Harrow and others (1973) found that in a subgroup of the schizophrenic patients following discharge from the hospital, overinclusion significantly diminished but idiosyncratic thinking remained high. It would appear, then, that overinclusive thinking is a characteristic of acute schizophrenic disturbance and decreases following recovery from the acute illness. Idiosyncratic thinking, however, abates but remains conspicuous even after the acute illness in some patients.

Excessive yielding to normal biases. Chapman and Chapman

(1973) proposed that schizophrenic thought shows accentuation of normal response biases. Thus, in schizophrenic patients a strong association appears in place of a correct response. This is similar to normal subjects' tendency to give their strongest association when they do not know the correct answer to a vocabulary or information item. Chapman and Chapman argue that many aspects of schizophrenic thinking—such as concreteness, loss of set, overinclusion, and predicative reasoning—can be explained by the patient's tendency to give the most accessible response. They admit, however, that the process underlying the tendency to yield excessively to normal biases is not understood and that the theory does not account for the bizarre and autistic quality of many schizophrenic responses.

   Looseness of associations. Cameron (1944) described what he termed "asyndetic thinking" in schizophrenic subjects—a paucity of causal links in a train of associations so that the speaker tends to lose the focus of thought and expresses lines of irrelevant and loosely connected associations. In mild instances, there may be only a subtle discontinuity between the appropriate focus and the subject's verbalization; in severe schizophrenic disorganization, irrelevant associations may pervade and interfere with communication.

   Looseness of associations in the free-verbalization interviews of acutely disturbed psychiatric patients was studied by Reilly and others (1975), who found that loose associations were more frequent and more severe in the schizophrenic group. Looseness was found in combination with vagueness of ideas and gaps in communication. The use of *private meaning,* that is, words or phrases that are unique to and only understood by the speaker, occurs to a moderate degree and only in the schizophrenic patients. The authors hypothesized that during the acute schizophrenic episode, as a result of the thought disturbance, there is a temporary incapacity to maintain consistent, coherent, and effective verbal and interpersonal contact.

   Overspecific responses on the Rorschach Test are defined by Quinlan and others (1972) as irrelevant, personalized, and tangential associations, with elaboration beyond what is justified by the qualities of the inkblot. In their study, schizophrenic patients showed significantly more overspecific responses than neurotic depressive patients did, and overspecificity correlated both with ratings of bizarre behavior and with thought quality scores.

In summary, schizophrenic patients have difficulty in maintaining cognitive focus, as manifested by the appearance or intrusion of irrelevant and inappropriate associations and bizarre thinking. Idosyncratic thinking appears to be an enduring characteristic of cognition in some schizophrenics, even after remission of their acute disturbance.

Reasoning

A major aspect of schizophrenic thinking, according to many investigators, is the inability to reason logically about the relationships between objects and events, along with a tendency to draw conclusions about events in an unconventional way. Weiner (1966) discussed the disturbed reasoning of schizophrenics according to (1) overgeneralized thinking, (2) combinative thinking, and (3) circumstantial thinking.

Overgeneralized thinking. Overgeneralization, according to Weiner (1966), involves drawing conclusions on the basis of minimal evidence and investing experiences with elaborate meanings. Extended fabulizations, confabulations, and absurd responses, which occur on the Rorschach, are examples and represent significant indicators of thought disorder.

Combinative thinking. Also called *fluidity of conceptual boundaries,* combinative thinking occurs when there is a condensation of perceptions and ideas in a way that appears to disregard usual conceptual boundaries between ideas and objects. This is most often seen on the Rorschach in incongruous combinations, fabulized combinations, and contaminations. Quinlan and Harrow (1974) and Blatt and Wild (1975) defined a continuum of what they called "disturbance of boundary articulation," ranging from fabulized combinations through contaminations. The latter is indicative of the most severe boundary disturbance and is limited to the most psychotic patients. These researchers assumed that disturbances of boundaries in Rorschach Test responses reflect loss of self-other distinctions, intrusions of unconscious material into consciousness, loss of intrapsychic boundaries, and loss of interobject boundaries.

Harrow and Quinlan (1977) found that acute schizophrenics had significantly more contaminations and fabulized combinations on the Rorschach than did borderline or other nonschizophrenic patients. Quinlan and Harrow (1974) reported, moreover, that contaminations and fabulized combinations were not necessarily limited to the schizophrenic group: 41 percent of the schizophrenics had one or more contaminations; 11 percent of the nonschizophrenics had one or more such scores. Contaminations were strongly associated with the occurrence of fabulized combinations, bizarre verbalization, affective elaboration, and overspecificity on the Rorschach, as well as with ratings of disturbed behavior.

In a recent study, Weiner and Exner (1978) found that while adolescent nonpatients had more incongruous and fabulized combinations than did adult nonpatients on the Rorschach, they still had fewer such combinative responses than did disturbed adolescents. Adult patients had more combinative and contaminated responses than did nonpatients, with 12 percent of the adult schizophrenic inpatients producing contaminations (no nonpatient adults gave contaminated responses).

Circumstantial thinking. Arieti's (1974) description of paleologic or predicative thinking is an example of circumstantial thinking, in which incidental aspects of a situation are used as a basis for fallacious conclusions. Although circumstantial thinking is implicit in overgeneralization and combinative thinking, when it occurs explicitly as a statement of purposeful, faulty logic cast in syllogistic form, it is called *autistic logic.*

In their normative study of disordered thinking on the Rorschach, Weiner and Exner (1978) found that adolescent nonpatients had fewer autistic logic responses than did adolescent patients; however, as these authors had found with respect to combinative thinking, the adolescent nonpatients had more such responses than nonpatient adults. Nonpatient adults also had fewer such responses than did adult outpatients and adult inpatient schizophrenics.

A "thought quality index," which assesses thought disorganization on a four-point scale, was devised by Quinlan and others (1970). Levels 1 and 2 include bizarre, idiosyncratic responses—

what Rapaport called peculiar or queer verbalizations. Levels 3 and 4 score autistic logic. Thought quality scores significantly discriminated acute schizophrenics from other patient groups and correlated highly with overspecificity, boundary disturbance, and very poor form level on the Rorschach. Thought quality also correlated with ratings of bizarre behavior (Quinlan and others, 1972; Quinlan and Harrow, 1974). In a later study, Harrow and Quinlan (1977) found that schizophrenic and nonschizophrenic patients were not distinguishable on level 1. At the more severe levels, schizophrenics were indeed differentiated from nonschizophrenics, although level 2 responses were frequent among nonschizophrenics. Level 3 and 4 scores occurred infrequently in nonschizophrenic groups.

In summary, disturbances in reasoning—as reflected in overgeneralization, combinative thinking, and circumstantial reasoning (autistic logic) on the Rorschach—are found to a much greater degree in schizophrenics than in other patient groups. However, as was found for conceptualizing difficulties and for cognitive focusing, these disturbances are also found in other acutely disturbed patients. The *degree* to which these disturbances are manifest appears to differentiate schizophrenics from other psychiatric patients, with schizophrenics producing them more often.

Modulation of Affect

Intrusion of affect into cognitive activities, sometimes referred to as "failure of repression" and "inconsistent affective modulation," implies that the adaptive integration of affective experiences has broken down. Several investigators have hypothesized that affect-laden stimuli result in increased thought disorder in schizophrenic patients. Chapman and Chapman (1973) reviewed empirical studies that tested this theory, including their own studies of response to emotional and neutral vocabulary items. They concluded that "the great majority of published findings of greater schizophrenic deficit with affective materials than with neutral materials are artifactual" (p. 239).

Quinlan and others (1972) and Quinlan and Harrow (1974), investigating affective elaboration on the Rorschach (defined partially as the subject's verbalizations of his or her own affective reactions to the card), reported that schizophrenics tended to elaborate neutral stimuli affectively more than did nonschizophrenic patients. Harrow, Tucker, and Adler (1972) defined personally overinvolved responses as those that used a first-person pronoun or that were elaborated in a highly personal manner. Although these responses occurred more frequently in schizophrenics, they are common in most psychiatric patients. Adler and Harrow (1974) found no significant differences between schizophrenic and nonschizophrenic patients in personally overinvolved thinking at either the acute phase or a phase of partial recovery. Nonschizophrenic patients who were acutely disturbed gave personalized responses that were not idiosyncratic; in contrast, acute schizophrenics gave both personalized and idiosyncratic responses.

The "Rorschach Indices of Drive-Dominated Ideation," which score primary process content on the Rorschach, were devised by Holt and Havel (1960) and further developed by Holt (1977, 1978) for various research purposes. The investigators scored both libidinal (oral, anal, sexual) and aggressive drive content at two levels: level 1 for the more direct, intense, and blatant expressions of drives and level 2 for the muted, more socialized or sublimated expressions of drives. This scoring system was used to assess Rorschach responses of acute psychiatric patients by Harrow and others (1976). They found that both schizophrenics and nonschizophrenics rated high on primitive drive content, and patients with high ratings on sociopathic or rule-breaking behavior showed more primitive drive-dominated thinking.

Thus, although schizophrenics experience difficulty in modulating affect, this aspect of their disorder does not appear to be specific. Further, thought disorder apparently occurs in contexts that may or may not involve strong affective stimulation.

Reality Testing

Reality testing is a term used by Freud ([1911] 1958) to refer to the process by which a person distinguishes stimuli originating in the outside world from those emanating from internal bodily sources. Successful discrimination determines whether an experience is "real" or a hallucination. If it is real, motor action can influence it. Another role for reality testing is to distinguish between a percept and an idea. In psychotic impairment there is confusion between stimuli that arise internally and externally, one's own wishes and another's demands, and mental representations and perceptions.

Disturbances in perception that occur in schizophrenics reflect autism—detachment from adaptive reality contact. One measure of veridical interpretation of reality is the extent to which Rorschach responses are more or less congruent with their reality denotation, that is, the extent to which the form quality of a response is "good." Responses on the Rorschach that correspond to a more or less consensual interpretation of the inkblots are scored F+; those that distort the form are scored F− (see Weiner, 1966; Rapaport, Gill, and Schafer, 1968). After reviewing some of the different criteria for scoring F+ as well as research studies examining F+ percentages in schizophrenics, Weiner concluded that an F+ of 60 percent is a good cut-off point "below which a schizophrenic impairment of reality testing is indicated" (1969, p. 110).

Multiple Aspects of Thought Disorder

In addition to studies of single aspects of thought disorder, there have been studies focusing on the problem of describing and defining thought disorder in a more comprehensive, all-inclusive manner. Such measures include (1) scales for rating all aspects of thought disorder as they occur in interviews or structured tests and (2) systems for scoring the Rorschach in order to obtain an overall score of all instances of thought disorder.

Rating Scales

Rating scales assume a conception of thought disorder as occurring on a continuum of severity. Bellak (1969), in his research on patterns of ego functioning in schizophrenia, devised a rating scale to assess thought processes. Components of thinking to be rated included (1) adaptive adequacy of processes that guide thoughts, such as attention, concentration, anticipation, concept formation, memory, language, and (2) degree of organization and reality orientation of thinking. In Bellak's study, patients were rated on a seven-point scale on their responses to a structured interview situation. Anchor points on the scale were as follows:

1. Extreme disruption of control processes and/or extreme breakdown of reality orientation and organization: loss of abstracting ability, difficulty in communicating, extreme distraction, bizarre or delusional thought content, loose and fluid associations, autistic logic, fragmentation, symbolization, condensation, and contradictions.

3. Episodic failure of control processes and reality orientation: frequent but circumscribed disruptions of attention, difficulty in sustaining thought, rigidity, circumscribed delusions or temporary disorganization, with some thinking free of distortion.

5. Minor failures of control processes and reality orientation under stress: some distractibility, vagueness, tangentiality, occasional peculiarities.

7. Optimal functioning of control processes and reality orientation: unimpaired concentration, no disruption from associations, flexible conceptualizing, integrated and logical thinking, and no peculiarities.

Cancro (1969) developed a scale for rating thought disorder and found a relationship between severity of thought disorder and duration of hospital stay. His four-point scale was as follows: (0) no formal signs; (1) circumstantiality, literalness, concreteness; (2) autistic intrusion, predicative reasoning, loosening of association; and (3) perseveration, echolalia, blocking, neologisms, and incoherence.

A scale for rating "language problems" was included in the Schizophrenia State Inventory of Grinker and Holzman (1973). The seven points on the scale represent degrees of severity of thought disorder:

0. Well-modulated, no impairment discernible.
1. Mild paucity of thought and reduced richness in language.
2. Language well modulated in reference to impersonal things, but occasional impairment with reference to the self or a threat to the self.
3. Circumstantiality, literalness, concreteness.

4. Antithetical meanings manifested.

5. Autistic intrusions, predicative thinking, loosening of associations, blocking.

6. Perseverations, echolalia, neologisms, incoherence.

A comparison of these rating scales shows considerable agreement among different investigators as to what is more or less severe thought disorder. The Thought Disorder Index, described in Chapter Four, also scores "levels" of thought disorder and shares with other rating scales the conception of thought disorder as ranging from mild "slippage" to bizarre incoherence.

The reliability of global judgments of thought disorder is critical in determining their usefulness. Hunt and Arnhoff (1965), Hunt and Jones (1958), and Jones (1959) assessed reliability of clinical judgments of thought disorder made for single test responses (on the WAIS) and for complete test protocols. Interrater reliability was high, and a repeat reliability assessment showed that the raters' initial ratings correlated highly with ratings fifteen months later, thus lending support to the assumption that these scales possess usable reliabilities.

Rorschach Scoring Systems

The search for single signs of schizophrenic thinking on such tests as the Object Sorting Test, the Proverbs Test, and the subscales of the WAIS has gradually become a search for interrelated signs or symptoms that identify schizophrenic thinking. Research using the Rorschach has followed a similar progression. The single most influential early research effort using projective and nonprojective tests was the study of Rapaport, Gill, and Schafer (1968), which consisted of intensive clinical perusal of Rorschach, Wechsler-Bellevue (the predecessor of the WAIS), word association, sorting test, and TAT records of schizophrenic patients and comparisons between these records and those of several classes of nonschizophrenic subjects. The authors published a meticulously compiled listing of scoring categories that appeared to distinguish the groups. Although some methodological criticism has been leveled at the statistical treatment of the data and at the comparability of the samples, Rapaport and his colleagues provided a conceptual basis for viewing and predicting differences among groups of neurotic and psychotic patients.

Beyond an analysis of location, determinants, form level, and content of the responses on the Rorschach, the Rapaport study referred to "the fifth category"—the associative process—and elaborated on its verbalization and interrelationship with the perceptual process. Disturbance in verbal association conveys a disturbance in the subject's reality testing. The contribution of Rapaport, Gill, and Schafer can be summarized by their own statement: "Verbalizations . . . have been used by many investigators for interpretation of test results. But what has been lacking thus far was a psychological rationale to systematize the conspicuous verbalizations and to attempt to explain the psychological processes leading to deviant ones" (1968, p. 425). Rapaport, Gill, and Schafer defined deviant thinking as that which does not adhere to the reality of the test situation, "as defined by attitudes, responses, and verbalizations of the general normal population" (p. 427).

Delta Index. Watkins and Stauffacher (1952) attempted to quantify Rapaport's clinical categories by developing what they called the Delta Index of deviant verbalization. The Delta Index is a system of weights applied to instances of thought disorder on the Rorschach Test, with minor deviations receiving the lowest weight (.25), moderate instances receiving intermediate weights (.5 and .75), and major cases of pathological verbalization receiving the highest weight (1.0). The delta index score is computed as the sum of all the weighted scores divided by the number of Rorschach responses, expressed as a percentage. The various types of responses that contribute to the delta scoring are presented in Table 1. A more detailed understanding of the meaning of most of the categories can be obtained by referring to our revision of the Delta Index—the Thought Disorder Index Manual for Scoring—which appears in Chapter Four.

Watkins and Stauffacher scored the records of twenty-five normal college students, twenty-five neurotic outpatients, and twenty-five psychotic schizophrenics. Interscorer reliability for the normals was .04, for the neurotics .47, and for the psychotics .91. The overall reliability for the combined groups was .78. The low reliability in the normal sample appeared to be a function of the

Table 1. Weights for the Delta Index

Type of Response	Delta Value
1. Fabulized responses	.25
2. Fabulized combinations	
a. Spontaneously corrected or recognized	.25
b. Not corrected or recognized	.5
3. Confabulations	
a. Extreme affect loading or specificity	.5
b. Far-fetched elaboration	1.0
c. DW (inappropriate generalization from one detail to the entire inkblot)	1.0
4. Contamination	1.0
5. Autistic logic	1.0
6. Peculiar verbalization	.25
7. Queer verbalization	
a. Usual	.5
b. Extreme	1.0
8. Vagueness	.25
9. Confusion	.5
10. Incoherence	1.0
11. Overelaborate symbolism	
a. Moderate	.25
b. Extreme	.5
12. Relationship verbalization	
a. Between two percepts (same or different cards)	.25
b. Within a series of cards	
1. Corrected or recognized	.25
2. Not corrected or recognized	.5
13. Absurd responses	1.0
14. Deterioration color	
a. Pure color	1.0
b. With form	.5
15. Mangled or distorted concepts	.25

Source: Watkins and Stauffacher, 1952.

low occurrence of scorable responses in normals and the limited within-group variability. The delta score significantly differentiated among the groups. All normals fell below a delta index of 5; therefore the authors suggested the score of 5 as the cut-off point in nonpsychiatic cases. When they used a delta index of 10 as the cut-off for a positive indication of schizophrenia, 8 percent of the neurotics were falsely identified and 48 percent of the psychotics were correctly identified.

Powers and Hamlin (1955) found a reliability of .88 for the overall Delta Index, with 60 percent agreement on the index level but little agreement on the specific category within a particular level. They obtained delta index scores on five groups of subjects (ten subjects per group)—socially adjusted, anxiety neurotics, latent schizophrenics, paranoid schizophrenics, and catatonic schizophrenics—and obtained significant differences among the five groups. A cut-off point of 10 identified twenty-six out of thirty schizophrenics and misidentified five of the nonschizophrenics. As the criterion score for schizophrenics, they suggested a score of 20, which correctly labeled fourteen of the schizophrenics and included none of the nonschizophrenics.

Pope and Jensen (1957) modified the Delta Index by scoring each response on a five-point pathology scale. They obtained an overall scoring reliability of .85, using a partial rank-order correlation. They also observed a low percentage of scorer agreement on individual categories and suggested that the index should be modified to omit infrequently used categories.

Kataguchi (1959) also modified the Delta Index by eliminating the categories Confusion, Relationship Verbalization, Absurd Responses, and Vagueness, and adding a category of Perseveration. He also eliminated the weighted distinctions within categories (such as the three degrees of Confabulation). He found marked differences between schizophrenics and neurotics in a Japanese sample.

Developmental Level. Other Rorschach scoring systems that focus on differential signs of schizophrenia have been employed, but less frequently than the Delta Index. The majority of attempts to find schizophrenic indicators within content and determinants of Rorschach responses have not been fruitful. The one exception has been the determinant of poor form level, which consistently indicates severe pathology. Friedman's Developmental Level Scoring System (1953) takes into account the structural and organizational aspects of the percept. Developmentally low scores indicate less structuring of the world and include the syncretic mode of functioning, in which affective, sensory, and motor modes are blended together. Confabulation, fabulized combinations, and contaminations are at the lowest developmental level. Becker (1956) devised a single developmental level (DL) score that assigned weights to the categories and represented the average weighting for the entire protocol.

In an evaluation of Friedman's scoring system, Goldfried, Stricker, and Weiner (1971) concluded that it is a good measure of the developmental level of functioning and that it adequately differentiates normal adults from neurotics and schizophrenics at different levels of disturbance. Unfortunately, however, there is lack of information about the overlap of DL scores among types of pathological and nonpathological groups, the applicability of the scoring to females (since the normative data concentrated on males), and whether or not norms should take account of Rorschach response productivity.

Summary

Empirical studies have shown that disturbances in concept formation, cognitive focusing, reasoning, and reality testing are important components of thought disorder. The particular aspects of thinking that best exemplify these disturbances are overinclusiveness, idiosyncratic verbal responses, circumstantial and combinative thinking with disruption of logical thought, and overelaboration, particularly of affective material. All of these aspects of thought disorder can occur at different levels of severity. Although the diagnosis of schizophrenia appears to be the single most important factor in locating a subject with thought disorder, Harrow and his associates suggest that any acute psychiatric disturbance increases the probability of the appearance of thought disorder in the patient. This group of investigators has examined a range of thought disorders rather than confining themselves to a single category.

There is impressive evidence suggesting that responses on both the WAIS verbal subtests and the Rorschach Test provide opportunity for observing many of the thought disorders implicated in psychotic conditions. The Harrow group also demonstrated the necessity in cross-sectional studies for collecting data at uniform stages of the psychiatric disorder, whether at the most acute phase, at partial recovery, at remission, or at post-hospitalization. Only such controls make the data comparable among subjects and permit one to decide which features of thought disorder are characteristic of different phases of the illness and which thought disorder variables distinguish schizophrenic patients from other acutely disturbed psychiatric patients and from nonpatients.

Our review of empirical research of thought disorder has led us to accept the concept of a continuum ranging from mild slippage to bizarre verbalization. It is thus possible to place individuals at different points on this continuum and to compare severity of thought disorder both within a single individual over time and also across individuals. This formulation corresponds to a similar conceptualization concerning the disorder of schizophrenia itself. This "schizophrenic spectrum" (Kety and others, 1975) has been described as a continuum of schizophrenic disturbance that embraces some nonpsychotic conditions (see Holzman, 1978) as well as classical schizophrenic disorders (Rosenthal, 1971).

III

Thought Dysfunction in Nonschizophrenic Subjects

Many of the biological relatives of schizophrenic patients have been described as showing mild pecularities of thought without ever being psychiatrically ill, and many schizophrenic patients frequently show similar peculiarities even before their illness began (Mayer-Gross, Slater, and Roth, 1969). Bleuler ([1911] 1950) called such people "latent schizophrenics," while Kretschmer (1936) spoke of a "schizophrenic constitution." More recently such individuals have been referred to as "schizoid" (cf. Heston, 1970).

According to Planansky (1966), the term *schizoid* connotes a structural relationship to or psychopathological derivation from schizophrenia. Those individuals designated as schizoid show life-long constriction of both intellectual functioning and social interaction. Social adaptation is characterized by aloofness, avoidance of social contacts, and an inclination to introversion and private fantasy. Although schizoid individuals share personality features with schizophrenic patients, the specifically schizophrenic components seem to be integrated into a stable character structure without psychotic disruption or deterioration. How or why this autistic mode can continue as a stabilized pattern of life in schizoid individuals while becoming part of a psychotic process in schizophrenic patients is not known, although issues of competence and capacity for coping with adversity must play a role (Garmezy, 1973).

Atkinson and others (1966) noted a significantly higher prevalence of psychiatric disorder within families of schizophrenic patients than within families of neurotic or surgical patients. These findings are consistent with other studies that have reported concordance not only in occurrence of schizophrenia but also in other abnormal schizoid characteristics in first-degree relatives—that is, parents, children, and siblings of schizophrenics. Heston (1966), for example, found that children born to schizophrenic mothers and reared in foster homes displayed a wide range of psychopathology: 16.6 percent became schizophrenic; others were observed to be retarded, sociopathic, or severely neurotic; and 21 percent appeared to be unusually creative and interesting people without significant psychopathology. Heston reported that the psychopathology as well as the creativity was significantly more pronounced in the offspring of schizophrenic mothers than in normal mothers' offspring who also had been reared in foster homes. Such studies suggest a genetic basis for at least the predisposition to schizophrenic pathology.

In this connection, Rosenthal (1968) wrote that it is not schizophrenia itself that is inherited but some outcome whose essential character we have not yet discovered. Wynne (1968) suggested that investigators look for specific traits or aspects of temperament that may constitute the genetic contribution to schizophrenia. It is possible that thought disorder is one of these dimensions, with a significant genetic component that underlies schizophrenia. To test this hypothesis, it is, of course, necessary to assess thought disorder quantitatively. The TDI proposed in Chapter Four of this volume can serve that purpose.

Investigators who have studied the families of schizophrenic patients in both psychotherapeutic and research contexts claim that frequency of psychological disturbance has been underestimated in the immediate families of patients (Wynne, 1968; Lidz, 1973). They propose examining the family as a social system in which individual symptomatology is an essential ingredient of overall family functioning. The entire nuclear family of a schizophrenic patient becomes the locus of disturbance, and the patterns of relating and communicating within these families are believed to be etiologically linked to the basic pathology of the schizophrenic patient, who may be the point of least resistance in this pathological system.

A recent review of the current status of "the family's contribution to the etiology of schizophrenia" summarizes the assumptions investigated in this direction during the past ten years:

> Assumption 1: Families of schizophrenics are discriminably different from those containing other offspring with other types of disturbances, particularly in role relationships, affect, and communication style.
> Assumption 2: These differences occur early enough in the life experiences of the potential schizophrenic to have a significant impact on his development.
> Assumption 3: These disordered family relationships are a necessary but not sufficient condition for the development of schizophrenia [Goldstein and Rodnick, 1975, pp. 48-49].

The majority of early investigators of the family focused on the first assumption. Most of these researchers attempted to explain the observations concerning shared family characteristics in terms of etiological, developmental theories. But studies of families after one member has already become schizophrenic are retrospective and thus cannot give direct evidence concerning familial factors that earlier may have influenced the development of schizophrenia (Garmezy, 1974; Holzman, 1977).

Research into the characteristic thinking of relatives of schizophrenic patients has generally fallen into one of two broad types of studies: (1) studies that examine transactions within the family and look either for congruent thinking styles in parents and their children or for complementary patterns in which the child's behavior can be regarded as a reaction to parental behavior and (2) studies of individual relatives' response dispositions, symptoms, and styles of thinking and communicating that can be regarded as similar to that found in the patients. Hirsch and Leff (1975) extensively and cogently reviewed many of these investigations. Their review covers reports based on case studies and interviews, questionnaires, and analyses of small group interactions. Rather than repeat the research descriptions in their review, with which we are in general agreement, in this chapter we will describe only those studies of abnormalities in communication and thinking that have used psychological tests as the principal instruments.

Transmission of Deviance by the Family

Lidz (1973) proposed that the families of schizophrenic patients "transmit irrationality," and that within these families the parents of schizophrenic patients respond principally to their own needs rather than to those of their offspring. Such structuring of the family environment results in distortions, inconsistencies, and contradictions in interpreting events. Thus, in Lidz's view, the schizophrenic's problems in testing reality grow out of biased intrafamilial communication patterns that distort reality but meet some of the egocentric needs of the parents. Lidz summarized, in interrogative form, what may happen to language development when there is some disturbance in the parents: "Do some children, because of their parents' difficulties in communicating, or because of the peculiarities of the meanings and reasoning used within the family, develop confused meanings that distort perceptions of experiences and perhaps impede efforts at problem solving? . . . Do they grow up learning that meanings of words can be changed to defend against emotional turmoil? . . . Can the ensuing impairment in adaptive capacities and in ego functioning make them prone to schizophrenic disorganization?" (Lidz, 1973, p. 63).

Singer and Wynne (1965a and 1965b) have studied the formal, structural features of communication disorders, emphasizing the ways in which experience and behavior are organized and the development of individual response dispositions that focus attention in particular ways. These authors view parental styles of communicating as codeterminants, along with other experiential and genetic factors, of the thinking and communications defects in the schizophrenic offspring. As they state: "[We] have focused upon those enduring aspects of family styles which might impair and undermine the development of the basic cognitive and closely related capacities which are especially impaired in schizophrenic disorders: capacities to attend selectively, to maintain major sets, and to sustain goal-directed thinking; the ability to differentiate body image and self-concept from non-self; the capacity to trust the validity of one's immediate perceptions; the ability to organize object relations adaptively . . ." (Singer and Wynne, 1965a, p. 191).

Wynne and Singer (1963) used Werner's organismic conception of development to characterize two classes of schizophrenic thinking, *amorphous* and *fragmented.* Amorphous thinking is global and undifferentiated; it is characterized by vagueness, indefiniteness, and impoverishment and leads to major impairments of perceptual and cognitive capacities. *Fragmented* thinking represents some degree of differentiation and thus is further along the development continuum. But here too, failures of hierarchic integration occur. Fragmented thinking is related to the loosening of associations described by Bleuler ([1911] 1950) and the overinclusiveness described by Cameron (1944). Wynne and Singer (1963) described a third kind of cognitive organization among parents. This mode of thinking is one of *constriction,* which seals off or protects the person from potential cognitive disorganization.

According to Singer (1967), communication in families of schizophrenics is disturbed because the parents fail to establish and maintain shared foci of attention. A transaction in which something is shared must proceed sequentially through four phases; it begins with (1) "one person's effort to select some event, feeling, perception, or idea; proceeds with (2) his efforts to orient the other person to the same "set"; continues with (3) a sustained transaction in which the same set and focus of attention is shared if all goes well; and optimally concludes with (4) closure around meaning or 'point' which is understood by both" (Singer, 1967, p. 148).

The process of sharing foci of attention is manifested in patterns of communication within the family. Because cognitive development occurs through a continuing series of transactions with the environment, at each point there must be a "fit" between a person's innate and previously acquired capacities and the stimuli and responsiveness of the environment. For any person to develop appropriate cognitive focusing, his or her family environment must have provided healthy transactional models. Thus, constitutional and experiential influences interact at each developmental phase to create new potentialities, which in turn determine the next phase.

Personality development is affected not only by growing children's capacity to engage and interact with their parents, from whom they can then learn, but also by parents' ability to engage their children's attention and to direct them in the learning of speech, reasoning, and behavior, which will be important to successful adaptation. If either parent or child has difficulty at these early stages of engagement and shared attention, then the child's core ego functions, especially cognitive focusing and reasoning, may be impaired.

Measurement of Communication Deviance

The communication deviance scoring system of Singer and Wynne (1966a), an outgrowth of their series of transactional studies, approaches most closely the research method of assessing thought disorder in the comprehensive, quantitative way proposed in this book with the use of the TDI. Singer and Wynne, however, emphasize that they were not evaluating thought disorder in the parents; rather, they concentrated on aspects of the communication styles of parents that are hypothesized to contribute to thought disorder in their offspring.

The rationale of the communication deviance scoring system maintains that the learning of language requires the learning of cognitive categories and is thus the means by which an individual shapes experience. The family mediates this learning and so influences both the development of meanings and the organization of experience. Wynne and Singer have attempted in their studies to discover how members of the family establish and maintain task sets among themselves and with the examiner. Typically, subjects are tested individually, but the results are interpreted within the framework of the family as a social system. The Rorschach Test, the Thematic Apperception Test (TAT), and verbatim transcriptions of family interviews were used as samples of communication.

Using only the test protocols of the parents, Singer was able to infer the diagnosis, form of thinking, and severity of disorganization of the patient based upon "(1) familial patterns of dealing with attention and meaning; (2) erratic and inappropriate kinds of interpersonal distance and closeness; (3) underlying feelings of pervasive meaninglessness, pointlessness, and emptiness; and (4) a psychologically encompassing overall family structure which is confusingly organized around the denial or reinterpretation of the reality' of major anxiety-provoking feelings and events" (Singer and Wynne, 1965a, pp. 199–200).

For the offspring of thirty-five families, Singer predicted the following at a high level of significance: a diagnosis of schizophrenia, borderline schizophrenia, or neurosis; form of thinking as amorphous, mixed, fragmented, or constricted; and severity of ego disorganization on a five-point scale. She also blindly matched offspring with their parents correctly for forty-one out of forty-six matchings (Singer and Wynne, 1965b).

Singer and Wynne (1966a) use the Rorschach in the form of a structured interview. Inquiry into the responses is made after all ten cards have been viewed; this is carried out in an open-ended manner, exploring the point of view and reasoning about the percept without pushing subjects beyond their usual style of responding. Everything the subjects say, as well as their nonverbal behavior, is recorded. They are asked to share the focus offered by the tester, must attend to images and ideas that occur to them in response to the card, and then must select and express those that seem appropriate. What they say about the task presumably reflects the attentional process involved, and it is assumed that the language elicited is representative of how subjects deploy and guide attentional processes in other interpersonal situations. The extent to which the listener can share meaning with the subject is dependent on whether the listener can follow and visualize what is being described.

Singer and Wynne (1966a) developed manuals for analyzing attention, reasoning, and language deviations in response to the Rorschach and the TAT. Using these manuals for scoring Communication Deviance, the rater scores the protocols for each family member separately and rates items in each response. On the

Rorschach, only the first response and the inquiry into that response are scored for each card.

The categories of scored communication defects are clustered into three classes: (1) *closure problems,* in which the communication is not completed, because of either (a) closure that is premature—that occurs before understanding has been reached or (b) closure that is delayed—because the percept is not visualizable or because an originally clear idea has been disqualified; (2) *disruptive behavior,* in which the speaker distracts attention from the task at hand; and (3) *peculiar language and logic, in* which idiosyncratic language interferes with the listener's ability to understand the ideas or percepts which the speaker has in mind. (Singer, 1977, reclassified the categories into five clusters: commitment problems, referent problems, language anomalies, disruptions, and contradictory, arbitrary sequences.) Table 2 lists the forty-one scoring categories used. The communication deviance (CD) score is obtained by dividing the number of scored categories by the number of transactions; the number of transactions equals the number of first responses plus the inquiry to those responses, and thus the maximum and usual number of transactions is 20.

In a study of fifty-nine parent pairs—parents of schizophrenics, neurotics, and normals—the first responses to each of the ten Rorschach cards were scored for both Becker's genetic level score and communication deviance (Singer, 1967). Groups did not differ on the former. The important finding was that the communication deviance scores of the parents of schizophrenics were significantly higher than the scores of the other parent groups, with none of the schizophrenics' parents having scores below the total group median (Wynne, 1967). An ancillary finding was that mothers of the schizophrenics used more words to convey their responses than did the mothers in the other two groups.

In another study—based on data from 116 families of normals, neurotics, borderline schizophrenics, and process and reactive schizophrenics (Wynne, 1970; Wynne and others, 1977)—the frequency of communication deviances of parents on the Rorschach test was significantly related to the severity of psychiatric illness in the offspring. All of the parental pairs of schizophrenics were above the common median, while only two of forty-six pairs

Table 2. Rorschach Scoring Codes for Communication Deviance

Code	
I. Closure Problems	III. Peculiar Language and Logic

Code

I. Closure Problems

a. *Ambiguous Remarks*

110 Uncorrected speech fragments

120 Unintelligible remarks

130 Unstable percepts

140 Gross indefiniteness and tentativeness

150 Responses in negative form

160 Subjunctive "if" responses

170 "Question" responses

181 Contradictory information

182 Inconsistent and ambiguous references

183 Incompatible alternatives

b. *Disqualifications*

191 Derogatory, disparaging, critical remarks

192 Nihilistic remarks

193 Failures to verify own responses

194 Retractions and denials

195 Forgetting responses

196 Partial disqualifications

II. Disruptive Behavior

211 Interruptions of examiner's speeches

212 Extraneous questions and remarks

213 Odd, tangential, inappropriate remarks

220 Nonverbal, disruptive behavior

230 Humor

240 Swearing

250 Hopping around among responses

260 Negativistic, temporary card rejection followed by a response

270 Concrete-set responses

280 References to "they" and to the intent of others

Code

III. Peculiar Language and Logic

a. *Peculiar Word Usages, Constructions and Pronunciations*

310 Ordinary words or phrases used oddly or out of context

311 Odd sentence construction

312 Quaint, private terms or phrases

313 Euphemisms

314 Slips of tongue

315 Mispronounced words

316 Foreign terms used for no particular reasons

317 Cryptic remarks

318 Clang associations, rhymed phrases and word play

319 Abstract, global terms

b. *Reiteration*

320 Repetition of words or phrases

c. *Peculiar Logic*

330 Illogical combinations of percepts and categories

331 Non sequitur reasoning

332 Assigning meaning illogically on basis of nonessential attributes of cards

333 Contaminations

Source: Singer and Wynne, 1965a, 1965b.

of parents of nonschizophrenic offspring were above the median. The parental pairs of borderlines were almost equally divided above and below the median. The communication patterns of the parents of the neurotics were similar to those of the normals.

Even when neither parent of a schizophrenic offspring had a history of serious psychopathology, the parental pair still had high communication deviance scores, indicating that these scores do not necessarily reflect previous or manifest psychotic symptoms. The communication patterns of the parents of schizophrenics differed from the patterns of their schizophrenic offspring in that the parents scored in categories not usually regarded as manifestations of thought disorder: responses in negative form; subjunctive "if" responses; inconsistent and ambiguous references; question responses; derogatory remarks; uncorrected speech fragments; failures to verify own responses; and contradictory information. The schizophrenic offspring frequently scored in areas usually associated with symptoms, such as clang associations and nonverbal disruptive behavior.

Hirsch and Leff (1975), using a British sample population, attempted to replicate Wynne and Singer's finding that parents of schizophrenics had a higher level of communication deviance (CD) than did parents of other patients. Although they did not find the clear separation between parents of schizophrenics and parents of neurotics and controls that Wynne and Singer had found, they did find that parents of schizophrenics scored significantly higher on communication deviance scores than did the parents of nonschizophrenic psychiatric patients. They found a mean communication deviance score of 1.33 for the parents of schizophrenics and .88 for the parents of neurotics. The fathers of the schizophrenics had significantly higher CD scores than either parent of the neurotics, but the mothers of the schizophrenics did not show a significant elevation of CD score. Hirsch and Leff interpreted their results as not supporting Wynne and Singer's earlier findings and believed that the differences between their groups were related to the higher word count of the parents of schizophrenics. Although there were some differences in methodology between the Hirsch and Leff study and the Wynne and Singer studies, the most important differences appeared to be in the sample of schizophrenic patients in both studies: The Hirsch and Leff British sample of schizophrenics was composed of recently admitted acute schizophrenic patients. The Wynne and Singer American sample was divided into three groups of schizophrenics: (1) seriously disturbed, nonremitting, process schizophrenics; (2) remitting, reactive schizophrenics; and (3) borderline schizophrenics, including patients who showed classic schizophrenic symptoms for only a short time, with no relapse of symptoms. Although there was no overlap between the CD scores of parents of schizophrenics and parents of neurotics and controls, the CD scores of parents of borderlines did overlap with the CD scores of all of the other groups. This classification difference could account for the discrepancies in the two studies: CD scores of the parents of schizophrenics in the British sample were lower than those of the parents of schizophrenics in the American sample. However, the presence of CD in the parents of nonschizophrenic patients does suggest that communication deviance in parents may be neither necessary nor sufficient for the development of schizophrenia in offspring.

A study in which TAT stories of the parents of disturbed adolescents were scored for communication deviance was reported by Jones and others (1977). By means of factor score patterns, the authors established three categories of risk for schizophrenia in the offspring based on communication patterns in the parents. Families with a high risk for schizophrenia were those having (1) active family conflict, (2) withdrawn teenagers, or (3) a significant tendency for deviant patterns both of speech and of focal attention to emerge during family interactions. These deviant patterns were related to higher scores for communication deviance on the TAT.

The generalizability of the findings of Wynne and Singer was widened by examining communication deviance as affected by several demographic variables. By using the Object Sorting Test rather than the Rorschach, Wild and others (1965) tested parents of schizophrenic and normal subjects who were matched for age and education—after discovering low but significant correlations between transactional thinking (communication deviance) scores and these variables. They found a significant difference between the two groups, with 75 percent of the parents of schizophrenics scoring above the median compared with 31 percent of the parents of normals.

Communication processes in lower-class (Hollingshead-Redlich classes IV and V) black and white families of schizophrenic patients and normal controls were studied by Behrens, Rosenthal, and Chodoff (1968), using a Rorschach procedure. They scored communication on the basis of clarity of expression, the subject's understanding of the task and what was said, and the degree of cooperation (ranging from collaboration to disruption). The black families of schizophrenics were significantly less adequate in communication and more disturbed in attention than were the black families of normal subjects. Black schizophrenics and white schizophrenics showed similar score distributions.

Communication Deviance and Thought Disorder

Wynne and Singer did not specifically study thought disorder; rather, they centered their interest on communication or transactional difficulties within the family. Thus, it is important to ask how and whether these transactional problems differ from thought disorder. The transactional approach assumes that the communication patterns in parents produce thought disorder and schizophrenic symptoms in offspring. Wynne and Singer were not trying to define thought disorder, and communication deviance in parents may not be the same as thought disorder in parents. But if communication deviance does not reflect thought disorder, it is unclear what it does reflect.

A study of both thought disorder and communication deviance would make use of the same samples of verbal material, but the former would draw inferences about intrapsychic thought processes, the latter about transactional processes. However, although the inferences proceed in different directions, we still have not shown that the two measures tap different phenomena. Communication deviance, in fact, could be the transactional manifestation of thought disorder, and thus, what we regard as two different phenomena may actually be the same.

There are, however, some suggestions that such an identity may not be the case. Although thought disorder is a symptom of schizophrenia, and its severity allegedly correlates with the severity of illness, communication deviance in parents does not correlate highly with ratings of severity of illness in those parents, even though it does correlate highly with severity of illness in their offspring. In fact, in one study (Wynne and others, 1977) the communication deviance scores of the parents predicted the severity of illness of the psychotic offspring even better than did the deviance scores of the offspring themselves. As we shall see, many of the categories scored as communication deviance are not indications of thought disorder, and it is these categories that may be elevated in the deviance scores of the parents of schizophrenics.

Processes of attention and focusing are fundamental in effective communicating, and we have seen that thought disorder affects cognitive focusing, reasoning, and concept formation. Thus, we would expect thought disorder and communication deviance to overlap when attention and focusing are disturbed or when normally shared frames of reference are disrupted and produce a communication that is difficult to understand. As we have noted, communication deviance is comprised of three classes: closure problems, disruptive behavior, and peculiar language and logic (see Table 2, p. 46). We shall discuss each of these from the vantage point of thought disorder.

Several of the categories of communication deviance scored as *closure* problems (Class I) reflect deviations from the task set offered by the examiner. Speech fragments (110), use of the negative (150), subjunctive (160) or question responses (170), inconsistent and ambiguous references (182), and all of the categories scored as "disqualifications" do not necessarily reflect thought disorder, although they may sometimes indicate difficulties in thought organization. Such categories reflect the actions of a subject who imposes his or her own set on the task, a set which may be negativistic, vacillating, or anxious. Thought disorder appears most clearly when the closure problems seem to result from the subject's inability to organize his or her thinking: confusion may result in contradictions (181); idiosyncratic word usage results in unintelligible remarks (120); a perception of self and the external world as fluid, with unstable boundaries, results in unstable percepts (130); and circumstantial and combinative thinking result in combining incompatible aspects of a percept into one response (183b).

Behavior that interrupts the task set is scored as *disruptive behavior* (Class II). Interruptions and extraneous comments (211,

212, 213), behavior inappropriate to the test-taking situation (220, 230, 240), and temporary rejections of cards (260) are not usually considered examples of thought disorder. Aspects of thought disorder such as loss of distance, inability to adopt an appropriate set, personalizing, overabstracting, and looseness can result in odd or tangential remarks (213) or concrete-set responses (270). Although categories 213 and 270 may reflect some aspects of thought disorder, they do not necessarily imply thought disorder.

Class III, *peculiar language and logic,* includes the greatest overlap between communication deviance and thought disorder. These categories score the idiosyncratic associations, autistic logic, loose associations, combinatory and contaminated thinking which characterize thought disorder. Only the repetition of words or phrases (320) and euphemisms (313) are not necessarily indicative of thought disorder.

Quinlan and others (1978) investigated the relationship between transactional thinking (communication deviance) on the Object Sorting Test and other measures of disordered thinking. There were significant correlations between transactional thinking on the one hand and conceptual overinclusion, bizarreness, and idiosyncratic thinking on the other. They hypothesized that the communication deviance scoring system was broadly based enough to pick up diverse signs of thought disorder. Thus, although some communication deviance categories score aspects of response styles that do not reflect thought disorder, the communication deviance scoring system appears to be highly correlated with thought disorder measures. The relationship between communication deviance and thought disorder requires further exploration and clarification.

Thought Disorder in First-Degree Relatives

Apart from the studies of Singer and Wynne and that of Hirsch and Leff, most of the research on thought disorder in families has done little to clarify the nature of the thought disorder that occurs in the first-degree relatives of schizophrenics. Although studies agree that these relatives show some disturbance of thinking, there is little agreement on the kind of disturbance and whether one parent is to be singled out as being more disturbed than the other parent. Several studies have found the thinking of parents of psychiatric patients to be disturbed in the following ways: parents of psychotic patients had more idiosyncratic and less common word associations than parents of controls (Ciarlo, Lidz, and Ricci, 1967); biological parents of schizophrenics had more deviant associations than adoptive parents of schizophrenics (Zahn, 1968); families of schizophrenics more frequently misidentified objects, had a greater degree of inappropriate conceptualization, and had more impaired focal attention than families of nonschizophrenics (Feinsilver, 1970); and schizophrenic patients and their parents were scored higher on conceptual overinclusion and idiosyncratic thinking than nonschizophrenic patients and their parents (Schultz and others, 1975). The assessment of thought disorder in parents is affected by many variables, such as the type of schizophrenia of the patient offspring; intelligence, education, and socioeconomic class of the parents; and the particular test used to measure thought disorder and system used to score the test.

Romney's (1969) study of thought disorder, using the Object Sorting Test and Bannister's Grid Test, reported no differences between relatives of schizophrenics and relatives of normal controls. However, Muntz and Power (1970), using a vocabulary test and the Bannister Grid Test, differentiated thought-disordered schizophrenic patients from patients without thought disorder. They then found that the parents of the thought-disordered patients had significantly more thought disorder than did the parents of patients without thought disorder.

Education, Intelligence, and Socioeconomic Class

The presence or absence of thought disorder in relatives of schizophrenic patients is apparently affected by the sex, education, intelligence, and socioeconomic class of the parents being studied. Rosman and others (1964), using the Object Sorting Test, found significantly greater thought disorder among parents of adult schizophrenics than in the normal control group. There were low correlations between thought disorder and vocabulary-information scores, education, and occupation in the control group. Among the subjects characterized simultaneously by low intelligence, less than high school education, and low occupational level, it was not possi-

ble to discriminate parents of schizophrenics from parents of normal controls. Wild and others (1965) found that scores on the Object Sorting Test for transactional thinking were higher in individuals with lower levels of education. They interpreted this as due
to the nature of the Object Sorting Test, which is a test of concept
formation that challenges intellectual ability.

Effects of Stress

Schopler and Loftin (1969) questioned whether thought disorder, as measured by the Object Sorting Test, was primarily a
function of situational stress rather than an internal disposition
toward disordered thinking. They found that parents of psychotic
children, tested when the parents were told that the testing was
part of a study of psychiatric disturbance, showed significantly
more impairment than did parents of normal children. These findings were comparable to other reports of thought impairment in
parents of adult schizophrenics. The authors, however, invited a
second group of parents of psychotic children to participate in a
research project with a different task set—one that focused on how
parents with a disturbed child were able to be successful in the
rearing of their other children. After these parents were encouraged to discuss their normal children, they were then given the
Object Sorting Test. This second group of parents did not differ
significantly from either the group of normal parents in conceptual
thinking or from the first group of parents of psychotic children:
rather, their scores were arrayed between the two groups. Schopler
and Loftin suggested that the Object Sorting Test is sensitive to
anxiety reactions rather than to formal thought disorder in the
subjects. They do admit, however, that because there was a trend
for the second group of parents to have higher conceptual impairment than normals, there may be a predisposition toward impaired
conceptual thinking in the parents of schizophrenics.

It is hard to refute Schopler and Loftin's major point that
performance on the Object Sorting Test is sensitive to variations in
the testing circumstances and therefore may not be a suitable measure of a predisposition toward thought disorder. This, however,
would be a criticism of the instruments employed and not of the
hypothesis that thought disorder occurs frequently in the

nonpsychotic family members of schizophrenic patients. The fact that degree of thought disorder is influenced by situational variables does not mean that thought disorder is merely a manifestation of anxiety, just as the exacerbation of tremor by anxiety in a person with Parkinson's disease does not implicate anxiety as the etiological factor in the tremor. Schizophrenic patients do become more disturbed and speak in more bizarre and idiosyncratic ways when they are under increased stress, but it is questionable whether situational stress by itself is a sufficient condition for the appearance of thought disorder.

The disordered thinking of schizophrenics fluctuates; at times it is worse than at others. But is thought disorder unique to schizophrenics, or is everyone susceptible to it if subjected to enough stress? Or does such susceptibility vary among individuals—some requiring little stress for thinking to become disordered, others requiring greater amounts, and still others remaining quite immune to such disorganization no matter what the stress? Perhaps thought disorder reflects a predisposition in some vulnerable people to react to stress by becoming less able to conceptualize, focus attention, and reason logically. It is also possible that persons with manifest thought disorder require less stress than do normal people for their thinking to be affected.

Consideration of stress and anxiety effects dictates that any investigation of thought disorder not only take account of the factors that affect thought disorder but also specify the nature of the testing situation and, if possible, control the amount of stress. It is thus important in any such study to include a group of family members of acutely disturbed nonschizophrenic psychiatric patients as well as a group of family members of schizophrenic patients. Since both of these groups share the experience of having a psychiatrically ill family member, they could be presumed to have similar degrees of anxiety about being tested.

Allusive Thinking

In addition to finding thought disorder in relatives of schizophrenic patients, there have also been indications that some aspects of thought disorder may occur in normal subjects as well. In a study of what they called *allusive thinking*, McConaghy and Clancy

(1968) found a significant degree of "loosening of concept span" on the Object Sorting Test in normals. They characterized allusive thinking as overgeneralized, vague, and sometimes irrelevant. Not only did they find such loosening in normal college students, but they also found that students with high scores tended to have at least one parent with a high score. However, allusive thinking in the students did not correlate with academic success or the MMPI-F scale scores, and these investigators decided that such thinking was not related to schizophrenic pathology. Of special interest for the present study is their finding of a normal mode of thinking that is influenced by family factors—genetic or transactional—and that is also related to what has been defined as thought disorder but occurs without other schizophrenic symptomatology. This suggests that thought disorder can be a disposition toward a particular kind of thinking and may not always be a "disorder."

Attempts to define the precise nature of thought disorder may have foundered on efforts to fit disordered thinking into a single conceptual scheme. Although the term *thought disorder* is often used as if it refers to a single phenomenon, we have seen that it occurs in heterogeneous ways as well as in a wide variety of individuals, some of whom are not seriously disturbed. Clinicians continue to regard flagrant disturbances of thinking as pathognomonic of schizophrenia, but they lack a systematic means of describing and assessing thought disorders within clinical and research populations. We now require techniques that permit the natural variability and special qualities of schizophrenic thinking to be sampled. We need methods that allow us to observe, describe, and validate the quality of disordered thinking, without excluding any type of slippage that may occur and without undue restriction of the opportunity for the patient to respond.

IV

Development and Scoring Manual of the Thought Disorder Index

Our review of prior research has shown that no single unitary measure can adequately reflect the complexity and variation of thought disorder. The kind of measure most successful in differentiating groups of subjects by degree of psychopathology has been one that involves an aggregate of measures—a global system that takes account of different indications of thought disorder. The Thought Disorder Index (TDI) is such a global measure, in that its focus is not limited to one aspect of thought disorder; it recognizes that a variety and range of thought disturbances exist and that some categories (such as contaminations and neologisms) are more serious indicators of psychosis than others (such as peculiar word usage).

Empirical Precursors

The TDI is based upon the early study by Rapaport, Gill, and Schafer (1968, first published in 1946), which qualitatively specified the variety of thought deviations in schizophrenia. In their 1946 study of a mixed clinical population, Rapaport and his colleagues collected and categorized a large set of verbalizations they designated as deviant and then studied the degree to which people in the different diagnostic groups produced each type. The authors did not claim that their list of deviant verbalizations was complete, nor did they assume that the distinctions they fashioned between some of the categories of verbalizations were wholly consistent or even easy for other investigators or clinicians to make. They did assert, however, that their set was a good starting point for constructing a taxonomy of deviant verbalizations and thus for making some conceptual order out of the congeries of pathological responses that emerge in the testing situation. The Rapaport group divided pathological verbalizations into two major categories: (1) those that pertained to the nature of the Rorschach or WAIS response itself—its rooting in reality, for example—and (2) those that described the type of verbalization by which a response, whether good or poor, was conveyed.

An example of the first type of pathological verbalization would be the response "Niagara Falls" to a card on the Rorschach Test that contains no perceptual justification for such a response. Such responses permit the scorer to infer slippage in reality-rooted cognitive activity. Thought disorder may also be inferred when two responses, both justified by some structural resemblance to the blot, are given but combined in an arbitrary way. An example would be the response "a clown" to a large area of Card II and "a fountain pen" to a small projection in the lower part of the same card, combined in the following: "a clown dancing on a fountain pen." In such a response, Rapaport, Gill, and Schafer note that the subject may be taking the spatial arrangement of the blot too literally and thereby giving it too much reality. The reality of the testing situation itself is admittedly difficult to specify, however:

> By and large, normal subjects will understand the testing situation and the test instructions to mean that they

are to give responses for which sufficient justification may be found in the perceptual qualities of the inkblot; that their responses must be completely acceptable to everyday conventional logic; and that, just as they should not give responses they cannot confirm by reference to the inkblot, so their responses should not be so dominated by the perceptual configurations of the inkblot that they are no longer subject to critical control, and thus become absurdly combined or absurdly integrated [Rapaport, Gill, and Schafer, 1968, p. 429].

This justification is not as subjective as it may first appear. The testing situation is a standardized one. When responses from large numbers of subjects are recorded verbatim and then subjected to close examination, some responses appear to depart from logic and comprehensibility and from the "usual" responses given by most nonpathological subjects.

The second major category—that of deviance in the way responses are communicated, without reference to the percept itself—reflects the verbal end-products of pathological thought processes rather than those processes themselves. Thus peculiar, queer, vague, fluid, or confused verbalizations are alleged to express degrees of antecedent thought slippage. "Male red hair" may seem a benign enough response, but the overspecificity of "male" is strange. Many of these deviant verbalizations—especially those classified as "peculiar"—can be overlooked as unremarkable in ordinary conversation or even in psychiatric interviews. And some peculiar verbalizations occur in normal records (but rarely in abundance), at least in the normal comparison groups studied by Rapaport, Gill, and Schafer.

The analysis of verbalization was without doubt the most original and generative feature of the Rapaport study. But it was left as a set of descriptive clinical statements with no quantification. As described in Chapter Two, Watkins and Stauffacher (1952) introduced a system of quantifying the Rorschach categories of pathological thinking as defined by the Rapaport group. They called this system the Delta Index, and it is this system that we have used as the basis of our Thought Disorder Index. Watkins and

Stauffacher assigned weighted scores of .25, .5, .75, and 1.0 to Rorschach verbalizations, with higher weightings indicating greater pathology. The summary delta score consisted of the sum of all the weights, multiplied by 100 and divided by the number of responses in the record. Oddly, the Delta Index has not been widely employed in studies of psychosis, for several possible reasons: only small numbers of subjects were studied; the measure was used only with the Rorschach, while its application to other tests, like the WAIS, was clearly appropriate; some of the categories seem not to have much clinical meaning; and the papers reporting the use of the Delta Index were not detailed enough to enable readers to learn and apply the scoring system.

There is a need for a measure of thought disorder that permits a wide sample of types of thought slippage to be recorded and assessed. The Rapaport categories and Watkins and Stauffacher's logical and simple method of quantification seem to us superior to other attempts reviewed in earlier chapters. Therefore, for our measure of thought disorder we selected the Delta Index of Watkins and Stauffacher (1952), which we revised (see Johnston, 1975) and renamed the Thought Disorder Index (TDI). This revision eliminated categories that did not provide evidence of thought disorder and those that occurred rarely or were too difficult to identify. We added other categories that were specific for the WAIS. In renaming the instrument, we preferred the label Thought Disorder Index because it is more informative than Delta Index. The idea of quantifying Rapaport's deviant verbalization categories was a significant advance. But Watkins and Stauffacher employed the Delta Index only as a diagnostic tool—one that would distinguish schizophrenics from nonschizophrenics on the basis of the quantity of thought disorder. The investigators apparently did not see the value of their index for purposes other than diagnostic. In fact, with such a measure patients can be ranked, compared, and monitored with respect both to each other and to themselves, and the index can be valuable beyond its validity as a diagnostic discriminator.

The TDI, then, is a system of weighting verbal responses according to their pathological quality. Less pathological expressions receive lower weightings than expressions that are more pathological. The TDI has retained the four level weightings (.25, .5, .75, and 1.0) introduced by Watkins and Stauffacher (1952).

Assessment Instruments

The TDI uses the WAIS and the Rorschach tests to elicit verbal samples from which thought disorder is measured. Admittedly, the administration of the WAIS and the Rorschach is time consuming, requiring between two and three hours. Both require some capacity for attention and perseverance in subjects. Thus the complete battery probably cannot be used effectively to study thinking processes in the most disturbed patients, whose attention spans are severely limited. It is apparent, however, that essentially reliable assessments of thought disorder can be estimated from abbreviated forms of the Rorschach (see Hurt and others, 1978).

The Wechsler Adult Intelligence Scale

The WAIS consists of six verbal and five nonverbal or performance tests (Wechsler, 1955). The verbal tests are relevant for assessing thought disorder because they require verbalizations that permit elucidation of the process by which the subject arrives at the answer.

The WAIS is a measure of the efficiency of intellectual functioning at the moment the test is given and is particularly suited to an investigation of forms of psychopathology that fluctuate and selectively encroach upon certain intellectual functions. The WAIS requires the subject to perform tasks for which there is wide social agreement about appropriate and inappropriate responses. It is therefore partially a test of a person's knowledge of social expectations, reactions to those expectations, and compliance with them. In responses of thought-disordered subjects, there may be evidence of conflicting response dispositions; although the subject may have the skills and the social knowledge to give a correct response, he or she may, at the same time, experience pressure to reinterpret the task in a personal way. Thought-disordered subjects may reveal distortion of information, faulty reasoning, overgeneralization, bizarre personalizing, failure to maintain an appropriate cognitive focus, peculiar idiosyncratic expressions, associative looseless, and intrusions of irrelevant information during the course of the test. An extended discussion of the WAIS and other nonprojective tests as instruments for assessing psychopathology may be found in Rapaport, Gill, and Schafer (1968) and Rapaport (1946).

The Rorschach

The testing situation is standardized for both the WAIS and the Rorschach, which permits evaluation of responses for departure from usual reactions of subjects or for personalized interpretation of the testing situation. Whereas the WAIS calls for habitual reactions and the social frame of reference is implicitly dictated, the social expectations in the Rorschach are less obvious; in the latter the subject is asked to choose a frame of reference by which to organize his or her perceptions. In 1946, Rapaport, Gill, and Schafer (1968) described the process by which a Rorschach response is produced: "In the first phase, the salient perceptual features of the blot initiate the associative process; in the second, this process pushes beyond these partial perceptual impressions and effects a more or less intensive organization and elaboration of the inkblot; in the third, the perceptual potentialities and limitations of the inkblot act as a regulating reality for the associative process itself" (p. 276). Failures in this normal process of organization and regulation will result in faulty reasoning, failure to focus or to attend in appropriate ways, and unusual concept formation.

At this juncture we present a description of the TDI, including a manual for identifying and scoring degrees of thought disorder.

The Thought Disorder Index
Scoring Manual

The TDI is a global or composite system for scoring instances of deviant verbalizations on the Wechsler Adult Intelligence Scale (WAIS) and the Rorschach Test. A zero score indicates an absence of any scorable example of thought disorder. There is no theoretical limit to the upper end of the range. Mild instances of thought disorder receive low weights (.25), moderate ones receive intermediate weights (.5 or .75), and the most serious or bizarre examples receive the maximum weight (1.0). High scores can be obtained by an accumulation of many low-weighted instances or by a smaller number of high-weighted instances. The manual will first describe some basic principles of test administration and the procedure for computing the TDI. A detailed description of the scoring categories follows.

Administration ~

Verbal responses on the WAIS and the Rorschach Test are used by the TDI to assess thought disorder. In general, the examiner should be nonintrusive. The purpose of these tests is to evaluate the quality of thinking; thus, WAIS testing should continue beyond the standard cut-off points even after a specific number of failures. The examiner should proceed as long as the subject still occasionally gives a correct answer and stop when it is apparent the subject has reached his or her limit. This procedure is adopted because disturbed subjects often display a marked fluctuation in ability to perform; they may answer simple questions incorrectly and more difficult ones correctly. Inconsistencies and temporary inefficiencies are important aspects of the thought processes. If a strict cut-off were followed, this fluctuation would be missed.

The Rorschach Test is given in the manner described by Rapaport, Gill, and Schafer (1968). The first card is handed to the subject, who is asked, "What could this be? What does it look like to you?" The subject should be encouraged to give more than one response if he or she stops at the first response or finishes quickly, "Take your time, there may be other things you see or that it might look like to you." On the first card the subject is permitted to give as many responses as desired, although on subsequent cards the examiner should try to limit the subject to about five or six responses. The subject is asked to turn the card over on the desk when finished.

Inquiry into the responses should also follow the recommendations of Rapaport, Gill, and Schafer (1968). The rule is to be brief and nondirective in questioning but to probe for all the information necessary to score the responses adequately. Leading questions should be avoided. The Rorschach inquiry is instituted after each card (following Rapaport) and is directed at obtaining enough information to score the location, determinants, form level, and content and to assess the thinking process that went into the response where indications of thought slippage occur. Deviant verbalizations, pathological percepts, and ambiguous or elliptical responses should be inquired into with a question such as, "Can you say a little more about that?" or "I don't quite understand what you mean by [such and such]." The examiner should be aware that deviant verbalizations may occur during the inquiry itself as well as during the spontaneous perceptual responses on the Rorschach or the specific answers on the WAIS.

It is highly recommended that both WAIS and Rorschach testing sessions be tape recorded and transcribed, because all too often it is not possible to write down accurately the bizarre or deviant verbalizations of an acutely disturbed subject without subtly altering them so that they make more sense. In our procedure the examiner takes notes that are as complete as possible, and then rechecks the accuracy of the final transcript against the tape.

In our experience, valid data on thought disorder from the WAIS can be obtained by administering only its verbal subtests— that is, Information, Comprehension, Digit Span, Arithmetic, Similarities, and Vocabulary—and by limiting the number of Rorschach responses per card to five or six after the first card.

Scoring

For research purposes, scorers can be blind to the identity of the subject, especially with regard to diagnosis. They should, however, be informed of the subject's social class, education, and ethnic background. Acceptable interscorer reliabilities should be obtained and rechecked throughout the course of the scoring.

The scorer uses the scoring sheets presented in Figure 1 in order to record the category and level at which each response is scored; multiple scorings are possible in any response or verbalization. The scorer should attempt to limit scoring to the given categories. However, if a response almost fits the category definition, but should not be scored at as high a level as the category is

Worksheet for TDW score

NAME_____

DATE _____

TDW_____

EXPT_____

WAIS	A - .25										ΣA	B - .50						ΣB	C - .75					ΣC	D - 1.0			ΣD
	Dist	Vague	Pecul	WFD	Clang	Persev	Reln	Comb	Symb	Tendency....		Symb	Queer	Confu	Loose	FabComb	Tendency....		Fluid	Absd	Confab	Aut	Tendency....		Contam	Incoh	Neol	
	1	2	3	4	5	6	7	8	9		ΣA	9	10	11	12	13		ΣB	14	15	16	17		ΣC	18	19	20	ΣD
INFO 1 - 10																												
11 - 15																												
16 - 20																												
21 - 25																												
26 - 29																												
COMP 1 - 6																												
7																												
8 - 10																												
11 - 12																												
13 - 14																												
SIM 1 - 5																												
6 - 9																												
10 - 13																												
VOCAB 1 - 8																												
9 - 16																												
17 - 24																												
25 - 32																												
33 - 40																												
Σ																												

$$TDW = \Sigma\ .25(\Sigma A) + .5(\Sigma B) + .75(\Sigma C) + 1.0(\Sigma D)$$

$$= \Sigma\ .25(\quad) + .5(\quad) + .75(\quad) + 1.0(\quad)$$

$$=$$

Figure 1. Sample Scoring Sheet

Worksheet for TDR score

DATE _____

TDR _____

EXPT _____

CARD	RESPONSE	A – .25										ΣA	B – .5						ΣB	C – .75						ΣC	D – 1.0			ΣD
		Dist	Vague	Pecul	WFD	Clang	Persev	Reln	Comb	Symb	Tendency...		Symb	Queer	Confu	Loose	FabComb	Tendency...		Fluid	Absd	Confab	Aut	Tendency...		Contam	Incoh	Neol	
		1	2	3	4	5	6	7	8	9		ΣA	9	10	11	12	13		ΣB	14	15	16	17		ΣC	18	19	20	ΣD
I	1																												
	2																												
	3																												
	4																												
	5																												
II	1																												
	2																												
	3																												
	4																												
	5																												
III	1																												
	2																												
	3																												
	4																												
	5																												
IV	1																												
	2																												
	3																												
	4																												
	5																												
V	1																												
	2																												
	3																												
	4																												
	5																												
Σ I–V																													
Σ VI–X																													
Σ TOTAL																													

$$TDR = \frac{\Sigma .25(\Sigma A) + .5(\Sigma B) + .75(\Sigma C) + 1.0(\Sigma D)}{R} \times 100$$

$$\frac{\Sigma .25(\quad) + .5(\quad) + .75(\quad) + 1.0(\quad)}{} \times 100$$

Worksheet for TDR score, p.2

NAME _____

DATE _____

EXPT _____

CARD	RESPONSE	A − .25										ΣA	B − .5						ΣB	C − .75					ΣC	D − 1.0			ΣD
		Dist	Vague	Pecul	WFD	Clang	Persev	Reln	Comb	Symb	Tendency...		Symb	Queer	Confu	Loose	Fab Comb	Tendency...		Fluid	Absd	Confab	Aut	Tendency...		Contam	Incoh	Neol	
		1	2	3	4	5	6	7	8	9		ΣA	9	10	11	12	13		ΣB	14	15	16	17		ΣC	18	19	20	ΣD
VI	1																												
	2																												
	3																												
	4																												
	5																												
VII	1																												
	2																												
	3																												
	4																												
	5																												
VIII	1																												
	2																												
	3																												
	4																												
	5																												
IX	1																												
	2																												
	3																												
	4																												
	5																												
X	1																												
	2																												
	3																												
	4																												
	5																												
Σ VI-X																													

defined, the scorer may indicate "a *tendency* to _____ ," which is automatically assigned the next lower score; for example, a tendency to contamination is scored at the .75 level, rather than 1.0.

The final scores obtained are recorded as the TD_W score and the TD_R score.

TD_W = the sum of the TDI scores on the WAIS;

TD_R = the sum of the TDI scores on the Rorschach, divided by the number of Rorschach responses, multiplied by 100.

The frequencies of the scores at each of the four levels are recorded on the scoring sheets for TD_W and TD_R, and the index for each test source is computed according to the formulas

$$TD_W = \sum .25(A) + .50(B) + .75(C) + 1.00(D)$$

$$TD_R = \frac{\sum .25(A) + .50(B) + .75(C) + 1.00(D)}{R} \times 100$$

where A = number of responses scored at level .25
B = number of responses scored at level .50
C = number of responses scored at level .75
D = number of responses scored at level 1.00
R = total number of Rorschach responses.

The Delta Index of Watkins and Stauffacher (1952) reflected the sum of each weighted score (the delta score), using Rapaport's twenty categories, divided by the number of Rorschach responses and then multiplied by 100 (thus correcting for differences in response productivity). Quirk and others (1962) suggested that unusually brief or long Rorschach records might require modified interpretations of the delta score. It is true that some manifestations of thought disorder—such as associative looseness—generally occur in a context of verbal productivity while others may occur in any context. A contaminated response on the Rorschach, for example, can appear in a record with only a few responses. If no account is taken for ideational productivity, the TDI will be low.

In the study reported in Chapters Five and Six, the correlation between the TDI score uncorrected for number of Rorschach responses and the TDI score corrected for the number of responses is quite high: .93 in probands (patients and controls) and .92 in their parents, indicating that about 85 percent of the variance is determined by the Rorschach score uncorrected for number of responses. However, in a record with few responses the ratio score may more adequately reflect the pervasiveness of thought disorder. This representation of prevalence within a record can be particularly important when studying chronic schizophrenic subjects who tend to give fewer responses than do acutely disturbed patients. For example, Table 3 shows the mean number of Rorschach responses produced by several clinical diagnostic groups in the study reported in the following chapters. The chronic deteriorated schizophrenics (that is, those who have been continuously hospitalized at least five years) give significantly fewer responses (mean = 17.4) than any other group, including the recent schizophrenic patients (those who have been continuously hospitalized less than one year) (mean = 26.7). Thus there is empirical justification for using a ratio score for the Rorschach Thought Disorder Index.

Table 3. Mean Number of Rorschach Responses Given by Each Diagnostic Group

		Number of Responses	
Group	N	Mean	Standard Deviation
Chronic deteriorated schizophrenics	20	17.4	0.9
Recent schizophrenics	49	26.7	11.6
a. Chronic	17	23.8	11.3
b. Acute	32	28.1	11.4
Other psychotics	10	31.2	14.7
a. Manic	7	35.0	15.7
b. Depressed	3	22.3	13.2
Nonpsychotics	21	32.5	17.9
Controls	27	25.7	9.2
Parents of schizophrenics	27	26.1	14.8
Parents of nonpsychotics	11	29.0	11.1
Parents of controls	32	23.3	7.3

Note: ANOVA for five index subject groups, df = 4, 122; F = 3.40, p < .01.

The scoring categories of the TDI are listed here and discussed in the following pages.

.25 Level

1. Inappropriate distance
   a. Loss or increase of distance
   b. Tendency to looseness
   c. Concreteness
   d. Overspecificity
   e. Syncretistic response
2. Vagueness
3. Peculiar verbalizations and responses
   a. Verbal combination/condensation
   b. Stilted, inappropriate expression
   c. Idiosyncratic word usage
   d. Peculiar expression
   e. Peculiar response
4. Word-finding difficulty
5. Clangs
6. Perseveration
7. Relationship verbalizations
8. Incongruous combinations
   a. Composite response
   b. Arbitrary form-color response
   c. Inappropriate activity response
   d. External-internal response

Intermediate .25, .5

9. Idiosyncratic symbolism

.5 Level

10. Queer responses
11. Confusion
12. Looseness
    a. Distant association
    b. Loose association
13. Fabulized combinations, impossible or bizarre

.75 Level

14. Fluidity
15. Absurd responses
16. Confabulations
    a. Details in one area generalized to larger area
    b. Extreme elaboration
    c. Tendency to confabulation (.5)
17. Autistic logic
    a. Tendency to autistic logic (.5)

1.0 Level

18. Contamination
19. Incoherence
20. Neologisms

.25 Level

Table 4 presents a schematic relationship among the thought disorder categories. This level is characterized by minor idiosyncracies that would only rarely be noticed in ordinary conversation, although an accumulation of them might result in a lack of clarity. These are the most subtle signs of disorder, and it is on this level that scoring reliability is weakest. One may have the feeling that the speaker is not quite "with" the task, that there is some slight intrusion of an idiosyncratic set, or that the respondent has at least some difficulty in maintaining a clear, unambiguous focus. Category descriptions are given to help the scorer record "minor idiosyncracies," and the definitions include some rules to help make the judgments of the scorer easier.

1. Inappropriate Distance

The subject appears to be off the track, often as a result of undue elaboration of the original idea or percept he or she has been asked to attend to. The associative process seems to be no longer regulated by the original task but rather by some internal set, which dictates that the task or response is either taken as being too real or as having little constraint on thought. Rapaport, Gill, and Schafer (1968) discussed these associative difficulties in terms of the distance maintained by the subject between himself and the task. If the responses show little regard for the task or are over-elaborated associatively, this indicates increase in distance from the task. If the task is taken as too real, or interpreted too literally, then loss of distance has occurred. Category descriptions (lettered headings) are not scored; they are offered simply to aid the scorer in identifying occurrences of the categories themselves (numbered headings).

a. Loss or Increase of Distance

The subject responds with emotionally charged affective elaboration, which results in inappropriate responses; the task is taken as being too real or too personal. At the .25 level, the affective intrusion does not prevent the subject from performing adequately, but the personal associations tend to intermingle with and detract from adequate task completion. If the subject is unable to perform the task, he or she may settle for personalizing it. Sometimes this intermingling causes an originally good response to be spoiled or contradicted. In scoring personally elaborated responses, the scorer must keep in mind how appropriate the final answer is to the task at hand. If there is no attempt to relate the personalizing to the task, this indicates *inappropriate distance*. Some examples from the WAIS follow:

> (Shallow brooks are noisy.) S: You find a person don't know anything makes a lot of noise. [Subject has answered correctly at this point, but continues on to personalize the proverb inappropriately]. Children who aren't occupied enough want attention, who are not given enough attention, not showing enough love. [The original track is lost, an increase of distance.]

> (Why are child labor laws needed?) S: To protect children from very sick parents.

> (Strike while the iron is hot.) S: Get them before they get you.

Table 4. Classification of Thought Disorder Categories

General Thought-Disorder Classification	Level of Deviance			
	.25	.5	.75	1.0
Associative	inappropriate distance	looseness	fluidity	
	tendency to looseness			
	clang			
	perseveration			
	relationship verbalization			
Combinatory	incongruous combination	fabulized combination	confabulation	contamination
		tendency to confabulation		
		tendency to autistic logic	autistic logic	
	idiosyncratic symbolism	idiosyncratic symbolism		

Disorganization	tendency to confusion vagueness word-finding difficulty	confusion		incoherent
Unconventional verbalizations	peculiar	queer	absurd	neologisms

On the Rorschach, a loss of distance can occur during the free association, thus interrupting the associative task and revealing the intrusion of personal concerns that are inappropriate to the task at hand.

> S: These look like crabs . . . I love crabs, did you ever eat crab?

> S: It looks like a vagina because it reminds me of the way my own vagina feels.

> S: Ooh! That's too horrible, take it away, I can't stand looking at it.

In order to be scored as the loss or increase of distance, an association must be a disruption of the task at hand. Sometimes subjects will ask questions about the task itself or make personal comments that are still very much focused on completing the task. Comments about having taken the tests before, remembering prior responses, asking at the end of a response what inkblot tests really mean, social comments that do not occur in the middle of a response, comments about actual "extratest" events (a loud noise, for example) are not scored. Similarly, storytelling or explanations that are clarifications or elaborations in response to the examiner's inquiry are appropriate responses and are not scored, because it is common for many subjects to respond to a question like, "What made it look like that?" by giving personal associations or experiences.

Examples of responses *not* scored:

> (Why does it look like a vampire?) S: Because it looked just like those vampires my kids watch on "Creature Features." When I was a kid, I used to be scared to death of those things.

> (If you were lost in the forest . . .) S: That happened to us once, we found a stream and followed it.

> (Why should people pay taxes?) S: I don't believe they should. [This is a personal opinion, but it is also a clear response to the question.]

b. Tendency to Looseness

The subject responds loosely, or associatively, but in a limited, controlled manner. Looseness is a major category at the .5 level. If the associative train of thought is not controlled and is more free flowing, then it should be scored as *looseness* (.5). Examples of tendency to looseness (.25):

> (Why should we stay away from bad company?) S: A bad company may go bankrupt.
> (Who wrote Faust?) S: The devil, I guess.
> (What does winter mean?) S: Frost, chilly, Fort Campbell.
> (If you were lost in the forest . . .) S: Hm, a book by James Dickey, *Deliverance*.

Rorschach card IX

> S: Well the guy was holding it. It looked like a . . . he could be reaping something, maybe the grim reaper or something like that.

c. Concreteness

The response process on the Rorschach and WAIS with regard to concreteness suggests a loss of perspective in which ideas take on an apparent reality.

> It looks like an x ray and the flesh is not on that card. It'd have to be me or you on the card, blobs of us. If we had real flesh on there.
> (What direction . . . Panama?) S: If you went by airplane. I imagine you would go south.

d. Overspecificity

The subject may attempt to be precise but fail because of excessive obsessionality or compulsivity, resulting in absurdity or bizarreness. It appears that an obsessive disposition has become exaggerated. The scorer should look for arbitrary, irrelevant overspecificity that spoils the response and gives it an overideational quality. This occurs most frequently on the WAIS.

> (Why are people who are born deaf . . .) S: The brain is unable to pick up the message to relay it to their speaking apparatus.

> (How are wood and alcohol alike?) S: There's wood grains and alcohol grains.

An example from the Rorschach:

A bear type of bone.

e. Syncretistic Response

Erring in the opposite direction, the subject may be much too general and overabstract; rather than restricting a conceptual class, he or she includes too much in it. This is the syncretistic response, which is seen most often on items in the Similarities subtest.

> (Air-water) S: Both states of molecular density.
> (Fly-tree) S: They both live in the air.
> (Orange-banana) S: They both contain atoms.

2. Vagueness

The vague response conveys no clear meaning. However, vagueness is sometimes used to mask absence of information. When this is the case, it may not have the same pathological weight as it does when used in a context of confusion and autistic thinking. Because it is difficult to distinguish between the two causes of vagueness, it is scored at a low level, .25. In these responses the subject appears to be attempting *not* to give inappropriate responses (in which he succeeds); nonetheless, he does not succeed in giving any real information. More serious difficulty would result if the subject failed to inhibit the nonrelevant material; the result would be confusion or incoherence, which are scored at higher levels.

Vagueness is essentially a communication disorder, but it also implies an inability to organize and appropriately integrate information. Vagueness .25 can include both long, meandering speeches as well as excessively short, cryptic statements that are too general to carry specific information. Examples of vagueness .25 on the WAIS:

> (Egg-seed) S: birth or hatch, a production.
>
> (Poem-statue) S: could be history.
>
> (Sentence) S: It's something very short in the way of speech or reading.
>
> (What is the Vatican?) S: It's in Rome, Pope. (Explain more.) S: That's all connected together, the Catholic religion.
>
> (Regulate) S: Designate the procedure of work or figuring out a problem.
>
> (Strike while the iron is hot.) S: Well, you would, once you get the momentum up to do something . . . it implies momentum, and when a thing is, it doesn't pay to procrastinate, because you won't have the same person or control.
>
> (. . . a license in order to get married?) S: Legal, legalities. That's a state issue why it's necessary, legality is involved.

On the Rorschach, the subject appears unable to elaborate any clear percept:

> Nothing but two figures on each side. (E: What made them look like that?) I don't know what kind of figures. They don't look like animals or people. They just looked like two smears.

The subject may give a response without clearly communicating what he or she is seeing:

> Picture of like depth and stuff, like of distance . . . where your eye level would be.

3. Peculiar Verbalizations and Responses

We include five kinds of peculiar responses under this category: (a) Verbal combination/condensation responses, (b) stilted, inappropriate expressions, (c) idiosyncratic word usage, (d) peculiar expressions, and (e) peculiar responses. Distinctions among these five types are not firmly established, but the types are presented as heuristic guides to scoring the general class of verbalizations as *peculiar* .25.

Peculiar verbalizations include quaint, idiosyncratic, private terms or expressions in which the meaning may be clear but the expression itself is unusual. There may be an unusual combination of words resulting in strange expressions or incongruous modifiers. Hysterics, in their sloppiness or casualness about word usage, may give several peculiar responses. Generally, the scorer must be alert for stilted, strained, illogical, and unusual expressions that are not part of the conventional modes of response to the various test stimuli. (*Note:* Some pretentious or stilted expressions that are part of a cultural mode of responding are not scored. These exceptions will be noted in the examples.)

a. Verbal Combination/Condensation

Combinatory verbal activity results in a condensation that stands for the original idea but may not appropriately convey it. WAIS:

> (One swallow doesn't make a summer) S: You can't enjoy everything in life just tasting the fruit one time. [Ideas of summer = pleasure; swallow is not only a bird but associated with eating, thus pleasure and eating are combined into "tasting the fruit."]

Rorschach:

> A butterfly. It had very butterfly tipped like on the second wing.

> Maybe a human torso, cage, lung cage.

b. Stilted, Inappropriate Expression

> (Picture Completion: water) S: Optically most strikingly, there's nothing holding the pitcher.

> (Eye-ear) S: Part of your brain's senses.

(Orange-banana) S: Both are female organs of their plant.

(Dark-colored clothes . . . warmer . . .) S: They're opaque to the sun.

(Table-chair) S: Both room settings.

c. Idiosyncratic Word Usage

One example of idiosyncratic word usage is inappropriate metonymy, in which one word is substituted for another of which it may be an attribute or that it may suggest:

I have *menu* three times a day.

Some of these *microfilm* microscopic life.

He's all *clowned* up in some kind of suit.

The entire shape, the perimeter, the *exterior shape*.

(Picture Completion: map) S: No states on the *flag*.

(Dark-colored clothes . . . warmer) S: They *contract* the heat.

Another example of idiosyncratic word usage is when words or ideas that tend generally to occur together are equated and substituted for each other. However, the educational and sociocultural background of the subject should be noted, because lower-class subjects and subjects with low levels of education frequently interchange countries, cities, and continents as well as body parts. Therefore, this kind of interchange should be scored only if the subject gives evidence either of being confused or of blocking on the correct word. Thus, if a subject calls antennae *antlers* at one time and *antennae* at another, the use of *antlers* is scored as peculiar. If *antlers* is the subject's usual term for antennae, it should not be scored.

Thought disorder in subjects of different educational and cultural backgrounds is the subject of studies by Haimo (1976) and by Haimo and Holzman (1979). Some examples of common word interchange occurring in normal subjects follow. *Do not score* unless subject has at least a high school education and indicates confusion about correct terms:

> (Where is Egypt?) S: In Jerusalem.
> (What is the capital of Italy?) S: I was going to say Spain, but Spain is in Portugal.
> Hands = paws = arms
> Feelers = tentacles = antennas = appendages = antlers

Frequently, "word play" sufficiently alters words so that they are no longer real words but are nevertheless still easily understood. At first glance, these may appear to be neologisms because they are invented words; the scorer should keep in mind the education and social class of the subject as well as whether the meaning is clear. Word play that approximates a correct word among subjects who do not know the correct word is not pathological (see Haimo and Holzman, 1979). Idiosyncratic words that are clangs and appear to be the result of an attempt to impress the examiner with pretentious-sounding words or that result from blocking, or slips of the tongue are not as pathological as neologisms. Neologisms reflect fluidity of thinking and a loosening of concern for reality constraints. When scoring verbalizations of lower-class subjects, it is sometimes impossible to know whether a word has been produced from culturally acceptable word play or from neologistic fluidity in thinking. In such cases, the subject should be given the benefit of doubt. Examples of peculiar word usages that are scored at the .25 level follow:
WAIS:

> (Eye-ear) S: They're both *necessity*.

> (Repair) S: Get something wrong with it right . . . *rightened*.

> Because of the *absorbance* of light.

> (Dark-colored clothes . . . warmer) S: They *exorb* the sun.

> (Domestic) S: From some *inalien* source.

> (Sanctuary) S: *Sanctionary*.

(Blood vessels) S: . . . *bussels.*

film (rather than filament)

Rorschach:

It looks like a bear rug . . . because of the *outstretch.*

Could be *a land.*

Two *charged* elephants.

Two *imprint* figures of elephants.

d. Peculiar Expression

Odd combinations of words, perhaps with reiteration or contradiction within a phrase, result in incongruity or a peculiar, inappropriate or anthropomorphic image. '

A reverse reflection.

Ears looking forward.

(Air-water) S: Both are composed of parts of the earth. [Meaning the earth is composed of air and water.]

It certainly has a more *feminine* look, the shape of *him.*

A female womb. [reiteration]

Animals, fish animals.

It could be a piece of topography somewhere in the world.

A frog . . . it sort of reminded you of a leapfrog.

Bearskin rug . . . you know how they scatter out on each side.

Water . . . 'cause it sorta got that blue rainbow look.

Rain . . . looks like little shades of drippings from the cloud.

Fetuses . . . it looked like there was a tightly-bunched organ.

(What made it look like a plane?) S: The pointedness and the fullness of the edges, the sides. It seemed to be very narrow and at other points it seemed to bloom out.

It looks like someone's hand getting ready to snap.

Fountain. (What makes it look like water?) The unity . . . when you see water shooting up like, it's all together, it's not in its parts, you know.

e. Peculiar Response

A peculiar response is more than an idiosyncratic use of words; it is also a particularly distant or unrelated response to a task presented by the examiner. There is an ambiguity that exceeds vagueness. The listener has the feeling that the communication is of some private imagery, outside the realm of common discourse:

Idealized fire. (What do you mean?) It didn't have any blue in it, so it looked like something that had been burning for a long time, or fire that wasn't lit with a match.

And this white space . . . looks like part of a pentagon.

The top part of the spinal column or something.

It could be the underside of a bat.

4. Word-Finding Difficulty

The search for a word that the subject appears to know but on which he is blocking is scored as word-finding difficulty .25. It is important to distinguish this problem of blocking from a simple lack of knowledge of the proper word. Thus, the following scoring rule was adopted: the subject must either give at least two wrong alternatives in his or her search for a word (even if the correct word is then found) or express clearly that he or she knows the word but cannot produce it.

(Blood vessels) S: Capillaries, arteries, and it begins with a v [first try] I won't say ventricle [second try], veins.

What do you call those hard-shelled bugs? Beetle? No, that's not it . . . I'll say beetle, I think that's the name of a bug.

This would be the stem, and the petals flowing out and the, what do you call the things with the seeds on them? Probisc–, no that's nose, uh, stylus?

If a peculiar .25 response is given while the subject is seeking a word, the scorer must choose to score either *word-finding difficulty* or *peculiar,* but not both. In the following example, the overall response reflects word-finding difficulty rather than peculiar use of the word *reverted.*

> There again it seems to be the same picture on the other side, as it is on the other, only *reverted,* or whatever you want to call it, I can't say reverted.

Don't score when the subject does not know a word and simply indicates so:

> It has those, I don't know what you call them, things up there [points].

In the case of blocking on finding the appropriate word, there must be more than a temporary inefficiency. *Don't score* if the subject fumbles only once and then immediately finds the word he or she is looking for:

> That looks like, uh, what do you call it, oh yeah, antenna.

5. Clangs

Clanging is scored at the .25 level if the response is limited to a single, clear-cut usage of rhyming as a means of performing a task. Clanging is commonly found on vocabulary items when the subject is guessing the meaning of the word by defining it as a known word that rhymes with it; thus it should not be scored on the Vocabulary subtest of the WAIS unless the subject is clanging in a loose, bizarre way.

> Not scored: (Tirade) S: [after several failures] A mean old tyrant.
> Scored: (travesty) S: I think of the treasure and the dynasty.

6. Perseveration

Perseveration may occur on both the WAIS and the Rorschach and is revealed by a lingering, unsuppressed, compulsively repeated idea that is forced inappropriately and arbitrarily into a response. Some subjects interpret a difficult task in the light of an earlier task:

> (Tirade) S: Kind of like calamity. [reference to earlier word]
> (Who wrote Hamlet?) S: Longfellow.

An example of a perseverative idea that was carried through several vocabulary items and was scored each time it occurred inappropriately:

> (Remorse) Means whenever you're mourning, whenever your loved ones are dead or something.
> (Sanctuary) Means cemetery.
> (Matchless) Is like whenever someone dies and leaves a match behind. Means they're matchless.

On the Rorschach, perseveration .25 is scored if a response is repeated that does not have good form—that is, when the inkblot does not justify the percept:

> (One subject saw a space ship on six Rorschach cards. On Card X, he had to strain to justify his response.) S: A part of a ship, you can't see all of it.

Repetition of either common responses (such as "butterfly"), which conform to the inkblot, or of vague responses (such as "leaf"), which fit almost any inkblot are not perseverations. To be scored, the responses must be arbitrary; the subject may have difficulty justifying them or may strain to fit the idea to the inkblot.

7. Relationship Verbalization

Relationship verbalization is scored when the subject repeats a response previously given but relates the present response to the former one. The subject is making connections between responses.

> (A patient related each card to the preceding one in a kind of story sequence, carrying the story a bit further with each card.) S: You have the same thing here, except for the pig's being slaughtered . . . Now the devil has destroyed the animal and the butterfly.

> There again you have that expansive thing . . . I find it to be prevalent in quite a few of your pictures.

> An allusion back to an earlier one, that being the mandibles in the very first picture.

> It's in pieces. That's the other part of that [points to previous card], I believe.

8. Incongruous Combinations

Incongruous combination is scored principally on the Rorschach, where contiguous blot details or suggested images are merged into a single incongruous percept. Weiner (1966) described these responses as reflecting inappropriate distance from the Rorschach cards, taking the relationships between images as real, and embellishing them unjustifiably. He described four types: composite, arbitrary form-color, inappropriate activity, and external-internal responses.

a. Composite Response

A composite response combines parts of two separate percepts into a "hybrid" creature. Both parts of the percept are accurately perceived but are combined incongruously into an inappropriate composite:

> The thing on top is a person, with, for some reason, two pairs of arms outstretched.

> It's sort of like a bird and a rodent combination.

> A bear with a duck's face.

Do not score images that are justified in art or mythology (for example, a centaur) or simple descriptions of parts of the blot in which the subject notices the incongruity but does not attempt to link the incongruous parts:

> I don't know what this is. It has a head like a rat and a body like a horse. But there isn't any such animal.

b. Arbitrary Form-Color Response (FCarb)

The FCarb response (see Rapaport, Gill, and Schafer, 1968, pp. 369–370) involves an excessively concrete, *a priori* decision that because the object perceived is a particular color on the card, then it must be actually that color (for example, a pink polar bear). The inkblot is more real than what the subject knows as reality distinct from the inkblot. Composite responses involve combining the form qualities of the blot, while FCarb responses are condensations of two modalities, form and color. The object seen is inconsistent with the color attributed to it. Inquiry can establish whether the subject intended the arbitrary description humorously, had some specific art or literary figure in mind, or can account for it in a strained but realistic manner. FCarb is scored only if the subject does not show awareness of the inappropriateness of the combination.

> This is a little girl right here. She's on fire, too, green fire.

> An orange pelvic bone. Or a small guy with two orange arms.

c. *Inappropriate Activity Response*

This response involves the attribution of an inappropriate activity to an object, usually a human or animal figure. If the resulting image is impossible and distorts reality, it should be scored:

> A beetle crying.

> A man shedding his skin.

d. *External-Internal Response*

This response occurs when both the external and the internal parts of an object are seen at the same time, in a realistically impossible manner.

> This is a woman and down here is her ovaries.

Intermediate .25, .5

This intermediate category is reserved for responses that reflect definite symbolizing activities; some of these activities show ideational control and some of them are unrestrained and reckless. Unlike other thought disorder categories in the TDI, the more controlled response is not merely a tendency to symbolize. Both kinds of responses are definite symbolizing processes.

9. Idiosyncratic Symbolism

Idiosyncratic symbolism is scored either .25 or .5, depending on whether the symbolism is controlled and somewhat legitimate or strained, far-fetched, or bizarre, Weiner (1966) described two types of symbolic Rorschach responses, one involving interpretation of the meaning of the color or shading and the other making use of concrete images to represent abstract ideas. Symbolic responses do not always represent disordered thinking and should be scored only when they take idiosyncratic rather than conventional forms. Holt and Havel (1960) gave examples of conventional color symbolism: black as evil, red as anger, green as envy, blue as coldness, yellow as warmth. Such responses are not scored, nor are simple color responses (where color is used as a primary, secondary, or sole determinant of the response) scored as symbolism (for example, "This is a plant because it's green"). Symbolic color or shading responses are scored when the interpretation is idiosyncratic.

.25 color symbolism:

> This could represent all the different colors that, you know, God created. As far as people.

> And the witch because of the red and the fire . . . and of course the orange also symbolic of Hell.

> This is the blood that was spilled, and it represents the mass death and destruction of war.

.5 color symbolism:

> The red . . . shows action.

> And the fading of this dead world indicates the coming of the new world, which is highly green, symbol of a new world.

The use of concrete images to represent abstract ideas is scored when such symbolism is idiosyncratic and is given with an air of reality (rather than as playfully imaginative).

.25 image symbolism:

> Two men beating the drums . . . like Siamese twins.
> Their hearts would beat at the same time. This would be
> symbolic of their hearts beating together.
>
> These two are different races clashing together.

.5 image symbolism:

> Two objects right here might seem to be horns of
> the devil. Horns might represent evilness.
>
> This picture has a lot of meaning. It means love,
> peace, and happiness.
>
> Looks like a person in the middle and two people
> hanging on the outside. It could be motherhood with her
> two kids on her back, constantly, you know how kids are.
>
> It's a symbolic volcano. It's like a volcano of thought.
> Thought comes from the spirit and goes through the mind,
> the body and just comes out, emotionally.

.5 Level

Many .25 level responses are encountered with moderate
frequency in everyday discourse, but they rarely convey the impression that the subject has lost contact with reality. Rather they
suggest that the subject may have trouble dealing appropriately
with some tasks or that he or she responds idiosyncratically (but not
bizarrely) to some situations. Such a person may be "on the fringe"
but is still in tune with his or her surroundings. An accumulation of
.5 level responses, in contrast, conveys an impression of loss of
mooring, shaky reality contact, emotional overreaction, and distinct
oddness.

10. Queer Responses

These are peculiar responses carried to an extreme. The
subject utters the queer expression with an air of certainty, but the
listener has little idea of what is meant. Queer responses .5 appear
to be the result of a failure to maintain an appropriate set, so that

the subject approaches the task in an idiosyncratic manner and may use stilted and pretentiously pedantic expressions. The queer response lies on a continuum of a particular kind of bizarre expression: *peculiar* at .25; *queer* at .5; *absurd* at .75; and *incoherent* at 1.0. Examples of queer responses:

> Inward type of a photograph of a flower's reproductive cells.

> The outside lookers, the onlookers of the outside.

> Their feet are going together unitedly.

> This so-called sperm-egg combination.

Word misusage, when it appears not to be the result of lack of education, is also scored as *queer* .5 :

> It seemed to appear boneless, just a blob of flesh. There's nothing there to give it any *sternness,* or regularity.

> The *nozzle* for the horse.

> A fly has *branches,* like a tree.

In the description of the .25 level, we discussed the use of pretentious, clanging words by subjects of lower educational levels. Many such words are scored peculiar .25. However, some of these words appear to involve more than pretentiousness, in that there appears to be enough fluidity in thinking so that two words with separate meanings combine, and the resultant word has no clear meaning. Such words might be scored neologisms 1.0, but we believe that they are more a result of social class and education than of a neologistic process. Unless the examiner inquires about the words, it is difficult to know with certainty what process has determined the formation of the word. Because of this difficulty, we have made a compromise rule: Score such words as queer .5, because they seem worse than peculiar, but are perhaps not neologistic:

> *Pestals* on a flower. [Combination of petals, pistil]

> *Tarangula.* [Perhaps a combination of tarantula and orangutan, from the context.]

Domestic *inquility*. [Although this may be a simple peculiar distortion of *tranquility*, it may also have idiosyncratic meaning.]

The lines, the ink *splurges* out.

A little gnome playing a little *fluted* musical instrument. [fluted = flute?]

A *moligamous* society.

11. Confusion

The subject does not appear to be sure what he or she is saying, thinking, or perceiving. Confusion is also scored when the subject appears to be disoriented. Examples of confusion:

This looks like some kind of insect, you know, like under the sea, some type of, not under the sea, some type of crab, yeah, under the sea.

Or a milk-weed butterfly, you know how those milk-weed worms used to look, in the backyard. Oh, you weren't in my backyard.

Somebody could have cut the skin off it and pulled it open and watched it, or looked at it, or something, or stripped it out or something, or pulled it out or something or had it out straight for a minute.

Some people smoking matches and burning cigarettes.

You better call an ambulance to pick me up because I'm gonna die.

Like a backbone, when you listen to an x ray, part of one.

Sometimes a word or expression appears to be a result of a slip. If the slip is limited to a single instance, it is scored as a tendency to confusion, at .25 instead of .5:

(Tranquil) S: Placent, there's no such word as complacent, placid was what I was going to say.

Longsworth, Longfellow.

Like a tulip, they sprout way out and then they droop, when a flower's ready to crick, croak.

12. Looseness

Looseness represents a dramatic loss of cognitive focus. The subject responds to a question or a percept with ideas that seem unrelated, arbitrarily related, or only tangentially related. Associations are embellished in an idiosyncratic manner. In this category, we distinguish between distant and loose associations.

a. Distant Association

A distant association is a partially controlled looseness. The subject loses track of the original task and redefines it in terms of some distant association to the original question. Although the subject is off the track, the scorer can usually identify the unifying distant association that governs the speech. For example:

> It's like these two people stem from the problems of this one man and the other things hanging around, it's like kids, OK, it's like your offspring.

> (Fly-tree) S: A tree doesn't disseminate germs. They both reproduce . . . Seeds have so-called wings.

> (Shallow brooks are noisy) S: Something that is small can cause a great explosion because . . . it causes a building of sediment . . . the water of a shallow stream wears away the rocks beneath, which causes the rocks to move and causes a mudslide.

b. Loose Association

With less control, associations flow rapidly and there is no focus of conversation. The original point is lost; the subject produces free-flowing associations that sometimes involve serial clanging. If the subject limits his looseness to one association, as in loose humor, or to a single clang, then it is scored at the .25 level (inappropriate distance or clang). Free-flowing, uncontrolled looseness is more pathological. We have attempted to distinguish between looseness in language and looseness of perception, which we call fluidity (.75). Examples of loose association:

> Because it's black, dark, darkness, lovemaking.

> I see a reindeer. Rudolph the red-nosed reindeer, and his nose is bleeding . . . because it's snowing and it's cold outside.

It could be a bow for your hair, if you've got any.
Most people do have a lot of hair, it grows, so they should
know how to take care of it.

(Why should people pay taxes?) S: Taxation, we
have representation . . . taxation without representation is
treason . . . It's frightening what Nixon has done now.

(tranquil) S: Peace, pleasant, something pleasant to
listen to or do, or smell. A smile is pleasant. You're a pleasant dummy to be around.

The womb, you know, being the space in there for
the baby. Of course there's no uterus, I don't have any
either.

A little bit of the phallus . . . symbol. That's very
prominent today, for some reason. If you may have read in
the paper the other night, remember when you used to
go to the movies, the saltiest thing in the movies was the
popcorn.

13. Fabulized Combinations:
Impossible or Bizarre

Combinatory thinking makes use of the primary process
mechanism of condensation, in which perceptions and ideas are
inappropriately condensed into conclusions that violate realistic
considerations. Combinatory thinking in language can be seen in
queer and neologistic responses. In the perceptual realm, unrealistic relationships are inferred between images, blot qualities, objects,
or activities attributed to objects and result in incongruous combinations at the .25 level, fabulized combinations at the .5 level, some
confabulations at the .75 level, and contaminations at the 1.0 level.

Many subjects produce fabulized combinations that do not
distort reality constraints (for example, two women holding bowl-
ing balls). These fabulized combinations are not scored because
they result from the combination of two accurately perceived images into a realistically possible whole. Fabulized combination .5 is
scored when the subject forces into an unrealistic relationship two
or more separate and discrete percepts that are contiguous. The
form quality of the separate percepts may be good, but the spatial
relationship between them is taken as immutably real, and the final
combined image is realistically impossible. Impossible combinations

distort reality by involving impossible size discrepancies between objects or blot details, by combining objects that do not occur together in nature, or by mixing natural and supernatural frames of reference. Examples:

> Two crows with Afros and they're pushing two hearts together.

> Two potatoes with eyes and a mouth trying to climb up some kind of pipe or a pole.

> Two women . . . a neck with a chest cavity . . . And it looks like the two women are resting on the chest.

.75 Level

Responses scored at the .75 level represent clear thought disturbances that clinicians have identified with psychotic disruption. Instability of thinking and perceiving, absurdity, and unrestrained combinatory ideation are typical.

14. Fluidity

In verbal looseness .5, the subject's thoughts race and he or she is unable to stick to one focus. In fluidity .75, the impression is that the subject perceives the world in a highly unstable way; something perceived as one thing at one instant will be seen differently at the next instant. Object constancy is gone; things do not exist for very long. It is sometimes difficult to distinguish between *verbal looseness .5* and *fluidity .75* in those disturbed people who speak very rapidly and dart from one percept to the next. In order for a response to be scored as fluidity .75, the subject must verbalize the fluidity and state that one percept appears to be changing into another rather than just following quickly upon the previous percept. Another index of fluidity is the subject's inability to assign an explicit identity to a percept, so that the examiner remains uncertain about what has been described. For example:

> Two people . . . one minute this appears like their eyes and the next this appears like their entire body holding on.

Inability to locate or remember a previously described percept is also scored as fluidity .75, because it appears that the percept is so unstable that it cannot be found again.

> This looks like a picture of, hmm. Oh, at first it looked like a picture of, but I lost that one, so it doesn't look like that any more.

When the subject wavers between two percepts, unable to decide on one or the other—thus evidencing a certain fluidity, though not so indefinite as preceding examples—tendency to fluidity .5 is scored. Examples:

> The two poodles and the two ladies are the same place and I couldn't tell if they were poodles or ladies.
> When I first looked at it, it looked like a bat flying away, then I looked at it again, it looked like a bat coming toward me.
> Just one looks like a bird and one looks just like a, some kind of animal. (What makes it look like a bird?) S: It has like a beak and four feet, legs, it's hairy.

Do not score responses that are given as differentiated, explicit alternatives:

It could be a bird or a flying insect.

15. Absurd Responses

When the examiner or scorer can form no idea about the source of the response, it is scored absurd response .75. It may have meaning in relation to internal events of the subject but not in relation to the question asked or task set for the subject; therefore, it is almost wholly arbitrary.

> (What is the *Apocrypha*?) S: Is that the emancipation and the proclamation?
> (Shallow brooks are noisy) S: That means when it rains, that it's gonna be a shower.

On the Rorschach, an absurd response .75 is one that has no objective support in the inkblot itself. Perseveration and vague per-

cepts should not be scored as absurd. Examples of absurd response
.75 on the Rorschach:

> (Card III, center space): This is a shock of corn or
> wheat that's fastened in the middle, it's a harvest
> shock . . . see the white with the band.

> The whole card looks like a termite's head.

> That looks like a continent that's been doubled over.
> I don't know what continent . . . in Europe, or maybe part
> of Africa, Europe around the Mediterranean Sea.

> It looks like the head of a man with a mountain on it.

16. Confabulations

The subject's original percept is related to the inkblot or test
material, and if he or she had stopped there, all would be well.
Instead, the subject interprets the rest of the blot or material as
though it had to belong to and fit in with the original percept.
Confabulation results from excessive distance from the inkblot or
task. There are two kinds of confabulation, both of which are
scored: (1) overgeneralizations from small to larger Rorschach blot
areas (2) extreme associative elaboration and interpretation of a
percept or a question.

A confabulation is often a manifestation of predicative
thinking that is not explicitly stated; thus, it is sometimes difficult to
distinguish confabulation .75 from autistic logic .75. If the response
process seems to be a result of overgeneralization and elaboration,
it is scored as confabulation .75. Confabulations are more frequently scored on the Rorschach, although the extreme elaboration
can occur on the WAIS.

a. Details in One Area Generalized to Larger Area

This type of confabulation occurs only on the Rorschach
Test. The subject responds to a small area on the blot and over-
generalizes from that area to a larger one in a way that violates
the shape of the larger area, although it may be justified for the
smaller area.

> (Card X): Moustached face. It was in the lower part
> of the picture, and kind of, a headdress, the rest of the
> picture was more or less a headdress on the figure.

(Card I): This one looks like an elephant and that one looks like an elephant. And this, I don't know what it looks like. Say, another elephant. It don't have, it don't have the trunk and everything to be that.

(Card VIII): The player, the basketball player. (What makes it look like a basketball player?) Here's the ball, then, it's not clear where the basketball player is, but I can see the ball, it must be somewhere in there.

(Card II): This could be a vagina and this could be the penis protruding. And this would have to be like a female organs here. And the blood looks like a monthly period.

(Card X): Another bird. Whole thing could be birds flapping. Like a bird . . . different colors, bird hunt.

(Card X): A frame of a body, neck, sides, kidneys, lower part.

(Card X): The digestive system . . . in the stomach. Somebody got ulcers too, got worms in their stomach, got little bugs in their stomach.

b. Extreme Elaboration

In this type of elaboration, the subject carries to an extreme a fabulizing ideational tendency and autistically extends the interpretation of a Rorschach blot area or a question on the WAIS beyond the realm of reality constraints.

(Card II): Somebody's hands were torn to shreds. And that's the knife that cut the hands off. Dogs . . . they're holding the knife in their mouths and that's what cut the hands off.

(Card IX): A god's head. (What made it look like a god's head?) The way like electricity or something just striking out, like, you know, a power or something.

(Card IX): A cow that just kicked you, landed you the other side of a wall, and he got tired and kicked her back.

(Card III): The picture of a man holding his hands in the air, he doesn't have any legs. Like you can see right through his body, as though he's saying, "My mind is an open book."

(Card IX): Two sort of rams . . . light emanating from them, as if their horns and their heads were sparkling out into being rays . . . sort of halos on the rams.

c. Tendency to Confabulation .5

When the percept itself fits the Rorschach card but the elaboration of the percept goes far beyond it, tendency to confabulation .5 is scored. It is scored at .5 because the form level is good, and thus reality constraints have not been lost.

(Card X): Two figures who are blowing bubbles . . . They've blown the bubbles or created all the other creatures.

(Card III): Two men playing drums with all kinds of, sort of heat coming up around them. Or the rhythms of the air being very heavy . . . Seemed to signify that something was going through the air . . . some kind of vibrations.

17. Autistic Logic

The subject attempts to justify a response by saying "because . . ." However, what follows appears illogical or based on private, autistic reasoning processes rather than on commonly acknowledged logical sequences. Autistic logic requires an explicit statement of faulty thinking. Sometimes it is difficult to distinguish ses, from autistic logic itself, and the scorer must look for explicit "because" statements. Do not score explanations of combinatory responses that are given during the process of inquiry. For example, the subject may explain that he has made the center detail on Card VIII a mountain "because the bears looked like they were climbing on it." This may appear to be a positional response (one that involves interpretation solely on the basis of the relative position of Rorschach details) but does not do harm to the form of the detail, and rather than being an expression of autistic logic, is an expression of a lesser tendency for combinatory activity.

(Why does it look like the creation?) S: Because only two. Seems so that this is the forming of the world, so quite naturally men and women would be in it.

I see something rather like an appendix. (What made it look like an appendix?) Looked to me totally useless, then I thought of the appendix.

(Card X: Gold bullion): Everything was pointing up to that gold bullion and so I said it was the most precious metal I could think of.

(How are a poem and a statue alike?) A statue is poetry, but it's not in motion. We have some beautiful statues, anything beautiful, I'd call it poetry. So when you speak of a poem, you put action and feeling to it. So I say that a poem lives.

(Picture completion) I don't see any sails on this ship, so I would say we don't have anyone operating this ship.

Mice in the forest . . . After I saw the animals, I knew it had to be a forest, 'cause they weren't in the zoo. They've gotta have something to eat off of, so they must be in the forest.

a. Tendency to Autistic Logic

Sometimes a response that appears to conform well to the details of the blot is explained autistically in the inquiry. It is difficult to know whether it is this idiosyncratic reasoning that has produced the response, whether the subject is also aware of the form but did not verbalize this awareness, or whether the language of description is itself so peculiar that the scorer cannot be sure how the subject arrived at the percept. In these cases, we score a *tendency to autistic logic .5*.

(Response given to detail on Card IV, which is commonly called a tree): Giant tree, a dead tree, its leaves falling off. (What made it look like that?) . . . looked like something that was dead. So something that towers over you and is dead to me follows it would be a dead tree.

(Card VII, popularly seen as women): Reminds me of old maids because they're far apart, kind of giving each other the eye.

1.0 Level

At the 1.0, or most disordered level, reality contact appears to have broken down completely.

18. Contamination

In the contamination response on the Rorschach, two separate and incompatible percepts merge into one. This is the extreme of combinatory activity, in which neither percept retains its original identity. Two overlapping images, usually of the same area of the inkblot, are fused into a single percept. Rapaport says of contaminations, "We see that in all of them some form of objective spatial contiguity in the card is taken too seriously, with too much reality value; and this loss of distance opens the door for schizophrenic autistic thinking and unrealistic conclusions (Rapaport, Gill, and Schafer, 1968, p. 438).

> (Card I): A butterfly holding the world together. (What makes it look like that?) Because I see on both sides patterns of a map.

> (Card VIII): They're twins. Part of the reproductive system, how they got there. Folded up, in a egg. This is the navel cord, right here. They split, they're twins, they're dancing, because they're happy to get out of their mama's stomach.

> (Card X): It could be artificial plant, because design like animals. Yeah, plant designed like animals. Like a mouth, legs. We do have some plants called elephant leaves

19. Incoherence

The subject's incoherent response is not only unrelated to the task but is completely impossible for the examiner or scorer to understand in any context.

> (What makes it look like a duck?) Their disarrangement. They follow out together, they follow one another. The two toes together, meeting one another. They jacked up in back, like spinal cord being broken.

Tears go up in the air. Blood, and break their neck. You know, reject.

All centered around a compass or a gyroscope or a bottle. Inside the bottle, comes a, inside the bottle, comes all. (What?) It looks like inside the bottle it all came out of.

I don't know what I think of a beaver, might be because it swims.

I was thinking of water, maybe a air-car, I don't know which.

20. Neologisms

Neologisms are invented words, perhaps as a result of verbal condensation, perhaps out of a private language. Sometimes a neologism resembles a verbal contamination, in that two words are combined and a third one emerges from the combination but still carries the meaning of both words. The subject seems unaware of any unusualness in the word uttered—it appears to have meaning to him or her. But the listener may be confused, either because the invented word carries two conflicting meanings, or because it is incomprehensible.

Two people juggling. People *tobbling* like on TV.

The property is more closely *centulated* to the railroads.

A calamity is, in my words, a big *cabangy,* big *cahootsy.*

(Remorse) *Moisterous,* being *moisiful.*

Conclusion

Effective use of the TDI manual increases with experience. Administration and scoring of hundreds of WAIS and Rorschach Tests for a variety of patients sharpen the examiner's sensitivity to deviant verbalizations and responses. Discussing protocols with an experienced diagnostic tester can significantly accelerate the recognition of thought slippage. It is clear that the TDI is not an automatic, self-scoring, easily learned system. It requires training and practice and is best used in the hands of those sensitive to formal characteristics of verbal responses—sensitive not so much to *what* the patient says but to *how* the patient says it. Like other quantitative tests in pathology—radiological or serological, for example—the TDI cannot be used without a training period. We would hope that the manual and the case examples presented in the appendix can provide the basis for training scorers. Working in pairs may also help scorers increase both their reliability and their speed in learning to use the TDI.

In the following two chapters we present our study of the general diagnostic usefulness of the TDI. The TDI scores of several subject groups—including probands (psychiatric patients and normal controls) and relatives of patients—are presented. We believe that our investigation demonstrates a practical and heuristic value for the TDI. The index's main value, however, is not in differentiating diagnostic groups that have been so defined by psychiatric criteria. Rather, its principal value is in assessing and charting both inter- and intra-individual variability of thought disorder. In acutely disturbed patient groups, the TDI can thus be used to assess the effects of therapeutic interventions on the organization of thinking. In nondisturbed subjects, the TDI score may represent a "trait," that is, a quasi-stable titer of thought slippage that is characteristic of the person. Thus, TDI scores may have value in studies of family transmission of thought disorganization.

V

Testing
the Thought Disorder
Index

A valid measure of thought disorder
should be able to distinguish, however grossly, among three population groups: (1) classical schizophrenic patients; (2) acutely disturbed nonpsychotic patients; and (3) normal controls. The purpose of our study was to test how well the Thought Disorder Index
could distinguish among these three groups in an objective, quan-
tifiably replicable manner. It is important that such a measure
distinguish nonschizophrenic disturbed patients from psychotic
patients in order to ensure that what is being defined as "thought
disorder" can be differentiated from general psychiatric disturbance. (An instrument capable of distinguishing among different
classes of psychosis, such as schizophrenia and manic depressive
illness, would be a desirable refinement.)

There is yet a further important consideration in the choice
of groups for studying thought disorder. When the population for

such a study is limited to hospitalized patients, there is the danger that what is being studied is disorganization, or social dysfunction, or perhaps is even a function of hospitalization itself. Thus it is important to study a range of subjects: those who are acutely disturbed, those who are chronically disturbed, and those who manifest some features of schizophrenia (such as thought disorder) but who have never been acutely disturbed. The latter group of subjects is most readily found among the relatives of schizophrenic patients.

This chapter will describe our psychiatric population, how we administered the WAIS and the Rorschach tests to them, and how we recruited their family members for similar testing. When each patient was discharged from the hospital, psychiatric diagnoses were assigned by the patient's psychiatrist, and a number of other rating scales that identify several patient characteristics were obtained from the patient's completed medical record. This information comprised the identifying characteristics of the subjects or independent variables. The TDI scores were the dependent variables.

This chapter also describes the procedures and instruments for collecting and evaluating the independent variables—broadly, the diagnostic information—and reports the distribution of subjects along dimensions of these variables. Chapter Six will describe the results of the validating study with respect to the TDI scores of these subjects.

Research Population

The research population consisted of 227 subjects, divided into the following groupings: twenty long-term chronically hospitalized schizophrenic patients; eighty recently hospitalized psychiatric patients, including forty-nine schizophrenic patients (with diagnoses of acute, chronic, paranoid, nonparanoid, and schizoaffective disorder), ten patients with diagnoses of manic and bipolar depressive disorders, termed "other psychotic," and twenty-one nonpsychotic patients (with diagnoses of neuroses, character disorders, and borderline or latent schizophrenia); twenty-seven normal controls; and 110 relatives of the probands, including forty-five relatives of the recent schizophrenic patients, seventeen relatives of the nonpsychotic patients, and forty-eight relatives of the control subjects.

Except for the twenty chronic deteriorated schizophrenics, the majority of the patients in this study were not long-term hospital patients. Although a number of the recent schizophrenic patients had been hospitalized several times, their cumulative days of hospitalization did not total more than one year, and they had all spent the major part of the previous five years out of hospitals. Some of these recently hospitalized schizophrenic patients, however, had long-standing schizophrenic symptoms, and their conditions were diagnosed as chronic. In contrast, those patients we called "chronic deteriorated patients" had an average total hospitalization of over five years. The composition of the sample thus permits the assessment of differences in thought disorder between short-term and long-term psychiatric patients.

The recently hospitalized psychiatric patients were tested at a university research institute and at a private psychiatric hospital in the course of a larger ongoing research project on schizophrenia. It is noteworthy that the two institutions draw different patient populations. Patients from the former institution were predominantly acute psychotics, generally from lower socioeconomic classes, and were racially mixed. The latter hospital has a predominantly middle- and upper-class white population, with many nonpsychotic and borderline schizophrenic patients as well as some overtly psychotic patients. During the first year of the study, we tested patients admitted consecutively to the two hospital inpatient psychiatric units, but with the following restrictive criteria: (1) that the subject be between the ages of eighteen and fifty; (2) that he or she have no known organic impairment or history of shock treatment; and (3) that each have a WAIS IQ above 80 or a Vocabulary subscale score of 8 or above. After the patient had been tested, the family members (father, mother, and one sibling, ideally the same sex and closest in age to the patient) were asked to participate in a variety of research procedures. We explained to family members that in order to distinguish the psychological and perceptual effects of emotional disturbance, we needed to test people who were not disturbed and that family members were particularly important to the investigation, because we were interested in studying the situations in which some family members had been able to cope successfully while another needed to enter the hospital. Family members and normal controls were paid for participating.

The testing of patients admitted consecutively permitted a wide sampling of different types of psychopathological disturbance, but after one year it became evident that a less random mode of patient selection was necessary in order to increase the possibility of obtaining family members. The selection criteria were then restricted to patients who had at least two family members available for testing or patients in a diagnostic category in which fewer than ten subjects had already been tested. The study admission procedure was altered so that prospective subjects and their families were told about the research and asked to participate, and only those patients with participating family members were tested. This change occurred after sixty patients had already been tested. Chronic deteriorated schizophrenic patients were obtained from a large custodial state hospital. These patients were part of an earlier study of chronic schizophrenics.

Normal controls were obtained from several sources. Fifty percent were recruited from a psychology class in a local college. Subjects in this group were chosen if their MMPI subscale elevations were below 70 (excluding scores on the Masculine-Feminine subscale) and if there were no minor elevations in scales 2 (Depression), 7 (Psychasthenia) and 8 (Schizophrenia)—scales that are typically elevated in schizophrenic disorders. These students and their families were asked to participate as normal controls in a study of psychological and perceptual effects of emotional disturbance. Another 25 percent of the subjects were solicited through news-paper advertisements asking for volunteer families. Black control subjects were found by asking acquaintances, churches, and other agencies to recommend willing and psychologically stable families, preferably in lower socioeconomic classes. All families were screened psychologically, and any having a history of emotional disturbance or of psychiatric hospitalization were excluded. We matched the controls to the patient subjects for educational levels, socioeconomic classes, and race.

Of the 100 patients (20 chronic and 80 recently hospitalized) who served as subjects, 55 were from the research treatment facility, 25 from the private hospital, and 20 (all the chronics) from the state mental hospital. Ten of the recently hospitalized patients were originally designated "other psychotics" (manic and depressed psychotics). However, because this group was so small, and because so few of the "other psychotics'" family members could be recruited for the study's comparison analyses, this group was ultimately dropped from the parametric statistical analyses.

We set out to test families consisting of both parents and one same-sex sibling closest in age to the patient. For this study, a "family" meant that at least two members of the family plus the patient had to be tested, and the presence of a large number of broken families made this goal difficult to achieve. Altogether, twenty-two such families of patients were tested: nine families consisting of two parents and a sibling; six families with both parents; and seven with one parent and a sibling. A total of sixty-two family members of patients were tested. For thirteen probands, only one family member agreed to be tested; no family members were tested for thirty-four patients. Seventy-four normal controls were tested, including probands and their relatives, with sixteen families of three to four members. Table 5 presents this distribution.

Diagnostic Dimensions

There is no single generally accepted behavioral or diagnostic indicator of schizophrenia. Furthermore, different clinicians use different groups of symptoms or assign varying importance to particular symptoms in diagnosing schizophrenia. The majority of studies of schizophrenia have used hospital diagnoses of patients as the criterion for selecting subjects. However, as numerous descriptions have indicated, the diagnosis of schizophrenia is often made on the basis of the occurrence of one or more symptoms that may or may not appear in different patients.

Psychiatric Syndrome Diagnoses

In this study, all newly admitted patients were given physical and neurological examinations in order to rule out toxic psychoses and organic pathology. For the diagnosis of schizophrenia to be

Table 5. Number of Probands with Family Members Tested

Diagnosis of Proband	Family Members Also Tested						No Family Member Tested
	Both Parents and a Sib	1 Parent and a Sib	Both Parents, No Sib	Mother Only	Father Only	Sib Only	
Recent schizophrenic	8	5	3	0	0	5	23
Nonpsychotic patient	1	2	3	1	0	3	11
Control	11	3	2	2	0	2	7

made, more than one of the following symptoms had to be present in the patient:

- delusions and/or auditory hallucinations
- thought disorder with bizarre thinking, autism, or looseness
- blocking or concreteness, derealization, or depersonalization
- flattened or incongruous affect
- paranoid ideation
- confusion
- catatonic behavior

Diagnosis of manic-depressive psychosis was made on the basis of:

- clear-cut cyclical recurrence of mania and/or depression;
- a capacity to return to high premorbid levels of functioning;
- a response, by reduction or disappearance of symptoms, to treatment with lithium carbonate.

Nonpsychotic conditions were diagnosed as either border-line schizophrenic or neurotic. Diagnosis of "borderline" was based on a history of chronic adjustment difficulties without the appearance of any acute schizophrenic symptoms. Neurotic conditions included neurotic depressions, hysteria, obsessive-compulsive disorders, and other personality disorders.

In addition to the diagnoses of schizophrenia, manic or depressive psychosis, or nonpsychotic conditions, distinctions within these diagnostic groupings were also made. Chronic acute and paranoid-nonparanoid patients were distinguished within the recently hospitalized schizophrenic patient group, and the degree of disorganization was specified for all patients. All psychiatric diagnoses, based on symptoms and course of illness, were made by the hospital staff at the time of discharge, in accordance with the American Psychiatric Association's *Diagnostic and Statistical Manual* (American Psychiatric Association, 1968). Table 6 presents the groupings and sources of patients.

Chronic-acute classification. Whereas early studies of schizophrenic patients did not differentiate between chronically and recently ill patients, current investigators realize the importance of

Table 6. Number of Patient Subjects by
Diagnostic Groupings and Hospital

	Hospital		
Hospital Diagnosis	Private	Research	State
Recently hospitalized schizophrenics			
Acute			
Paranoid	2	9	
Nonparanoid	4	12	
Chronic			
Paranoid	1	6	
Nonparanoid	4	6	
Schizoaffective	0	5	
Chronic deteriorated schizophrenics			20
Other psychotic			
Manic	0	7	
Depressed	1	2	
Nonpsychotic			
Borderline or latent schizophrenia	2	2	
Neurotic	11	6	
Total schizophrenics	11	38	20
Total Patients	25	55	20

this differentiation. Within a group of designated chronic schizophrenic patients, there are at least three patient types that differ from each other in important respects:

1. long-term hospitalized patients, confounding the confounding effects of long-term institutionalization with its concomitant social isolation, dehumanization, and frequent long-term, high-dosage levels of neuroleptic medication;

2. patients who have not been hospitalized for the majority of their adult lives and are still able to function outside of a hospital but who have undergone gradual deterioration in adaptive functioning and manifest a moderate amount of impairment and symptomatology, to which they have adapted; and

3. patients who would normally fall into the second category but are currently acutely disturbed; their outward symptomatology

and behavior are more similar to acute schizophrenic patients than to the chronic, nonacute patients.

The present study includes types (1) and (3)—long-term chronic deteriorated patients and recently hospitalized chronic patients, respectively.

In the case of acute disturbance, two outcomes are possible: either the patient will remit and function in a manner comparable to his or her pre-illness functioning or the illness will proceed to chronicity and even deterioration. Prognostic instruments, such as the Elgin and the Phillips scales (Phillips, 1953), are used in order to distinguish between these two prognoses in the patients.

Paranoid-nonparanoid classification. A diagnosis of paranoid was made on the basis of occurrence of fixed, systematized, non-transitory classical paranoid symptoms, including ideas of reference; belief in thought insertion, withdrawal, or control; delusions of persecution; and megalomania. The effects of the presence of paranoia on thought disorder are not known, but because the dimension of paranoid-nonparanoid has been important in research studies of schizophrenia, patients in the present study have been so classified by three means: (1) hospital diagnosis of systematized paranoid symptoms; (2) rating on the Venables-O'Connor Paranoid Rating Scale (Venables and O'Connor, 1959); and (3) psychological diagnosis of presence or absence of paranoid ideation on psychological tests.

State of disorganization. Another problem in the study of schizophrenic disturbed thinking is the great variation of the disorder over time within the individual. Whether the patient is tested during an active acute disturbance, during a partial recovery from that disturbance, or during a remission of symptoms will greatly affect the nature of the behavior observed. Adler and Harrow (1974), for example, found that borderline patients during acute upsets manifested some idiosyncratic thinking, thus sharing characteristics of acute schizophrenic patients; during partial remission, however, they were not particularly bizarre and were similar to the nonschizophrenic group. The present study includes ratings on the Menninger Health-Sickness Rating Scale (Luborsky,

1962), a measure that may give some information about the degree of disturbance at the time of testing.

Patient Classification Scales

We have distinguished among the three groups of patients on the basis of three psychological rating scales—the Phillips Scale for determining acuteness/chronicity and thus predicted outcome; the O'Connor-Venables Scale for assessing paranoid tendencies; and the Menninger Health-Sickness Scale for evaluating degree of disturbance. General descriptions of each measure, together with procedures used and the results obtained for our population, follow.

The Phillips Scale. Phillips' (1953) measure is one of the best means for predicting outcome (and thus chronicity). It consists of five subscales: (1) recent sexual adjustment; (2) social aspects of recent sexual life—patients under thirty years of age; (3) social aspects of recent sexual life—patients over thirty years of age; (4) history of personal relations; (5) and recent adjustment in personal relations. Each subscale has a range of weighted values from 0 to 6, so that the possible total scores range from 0 to 30. Recent investigators have set the scale criteria for designating good premorbid cases (which correspond roughly to reactive schizophrenia) at 12 and below and poor premorbid cases (corresponding roughly to process schizophrenia) at 17 or 18 and above (see Garmezy, 1970). The separation of patients on the basis of the adequacy or inadequacy of their social-sexual premorbid adjustment could reduce the statistical variability of the schizophrenic population. The Phillips subscales, as modified by Epstein and Coleman (Garmezy, 1970), were employed in this study.

Venables-O'Connor Paranoid Scale. This measure rates each patient on a scale of 1 to 5 on the following questions:

1. Does the patient tend to suspect or to believe on slight evidence or without good reason that people and external forces are trying to or now do influence his or her behavior and control his or her thinking?
2. Does the patient tend to suspect or to believe on slight

evidence or without good reason that some people talk about, refer to, or watch him or her?

3. Does the patient tend to suspect or to believe on slight evidence or without good reason that some people are against him or her (persecuting, conspiring, cheating, depriving, punishing) in various ways?

4. Does the patient have an exaggeratedly high opinion of him- or herself or an unjustified belief or conviction of having unusual ability, knowledge, power, wealth, or status?

A rating of 1 indicates no such ideas; 2 indicates the patient will admit such ideas if pressed; 3 that the patient will easily admit ideas; 4 that the patient has explicitly avowed ideas; and 5 that the patient strongly expresses ideas. The lowest score a subject can receive is 4; the highest is 20. This scale is the result of a factor analysis of a series of ratings of long-term hospitalized, chronic schizophrenic patients, and as such it may not be appropriate to a recently hospitalized population.

The primary examiner in this study rated each patient on the Venables-O'Connor and the Phillips scales on the basis of the examiner's own observations, the clinical record, and ward staff consultations (if the rating was in doubt).

The Menninger Health-Sickness Rating Scale (HSR). This instrument obtains a gross measure of degree of disturbance that ranks patients on a scale from 0 to 100, with 100 being the "ideal state of complete functioning integration." The patient is compared with a standard series of patients graded in degrees of health, and there is at least one case description for every five points along the scale. The rater is asked to balance several criteria for healthy functioning to arrive at the single, overall rating:

- the patient's need to be protected by a hospital versus ability to function autonomously
- the seriousness of symptoms (the patient's effect on his or her environment, for example, danger, discomfort, and so on)
- the patient's capacity for utilizing abilities
- the quality of the patient's interpersonal relationships
- the breadth and depth of the patient's interests

Examples of scale points are as follows:

- 99–76, "degrees of everyday adjusting": individuals falling within this range rarely seek treatment
- 75, mild neuroses and character problems: individuals at this point occasionally seek treatment
- 65, clearly neurotic subjects who are functioning moderately well but who have focalized symptoms or lack of effectiveness
- 50, severe neuroses, character disorders, some compensated psychoses: definitely need treatment for adequate functioning
- 35, most borderline schizophrenics, but can include some psychotic depressions
- 25, overt psychoses, unable to function autonomously
- 24–11, increased loss of contact with reality, need for protection from self or for others
- 10, closed-ward patient, little contact
- 0, complete regression, would die without care

Each patient was rated as he or she appeared at the time of testing. Ideally, all patients should be tested at the same stage of their hospitalization. An attempt was made to do this in our study, but logistics made it difficult to do so in all instances. Patients were usually tested as soon after admission as possible, but some severely disturbed patients were not able to do the tasks until weeks or even months after their admission to the hospital. Those patients who were not flagrantly psychotic were generally tested during the first ten days. The majority of patients were tested within one month of hospitalization.

The Health-Sickness Rating was reached by consensus in the following manner: Brief but inclusive clinical descriptions of the patient's behavior and psychological condition at the time of testing were written by the principal examiner, including pertinent information about the past history, presenting symptomatology, and hospital course. These vignettes were read to a group of raters, who then rated the patient on the scale. The final HSR rating was the mean of the separate ratings. This method of consensus rating is the one Lester Luborsky (personal communication, 1974) believes is most reliable. Ten randomly selected vignettes were re-rated after a period of twelve to twenty-four months in the same manner. The rank-difference correlation between the two ratings was .92.

Psychological Test Diagnoses

Before scoring the Rorschach and WAIS protocols for thought disorder, they were analyzed blindly for all patients by an independent diagnostician and diagnoses were assigned, based on interpretation in the manner described by Rapaport, Gill, and Schafer (1968). Without prior knowledge of patient status, the psychological diagnostician wrote short psychological test reports concluding with a diagnostic statement. Three diagnostic classifications were used: schizophrenia, nonschizophrenic psychosis, and nonpsychotic.

The diagnosis of schizophrenia was assigned on the basis of the presence of the following pathognomonic indicators: queer or absurd verbalizations, autistic logic, contaminations on the Rorschach, and content of verbalizations suggesting preoccupations with deterioration and fragmentation. A low F+ percent on the Rorschach, a high range of scatter among WAIS subtests, and lowered comprehension and arithmetic subscale scores were considered contributory but not decisive.

Paranoid features were inferred from occasional occurrences of disorganized thinking in a patient who is generally inhibited, overcautious, litigious, suspicious, hyperalert, and shows a predisposition to reason inferentially.

Manic psychosis was diagnosed when there was an absence of the quality of thought disorder as outlined for schizophrenia but the presence of massive denial, counterphobic recklessness, hyperactivity, playfulness, excitement, overproductivity, and extravagant interpretations leading even to confabulations. Similarly, depressive psychosis was diagnosed if schizophrenic thought disorder features were absent and if strong evidence was present of depressive retardation in motor, perceptual, or cognitive functioning in a setting of self-depreciation, inertia, or potential delusional thinking. Both manic and depressed patients were assigned to the category "other psychotic." The category "nonpsychotic psychiatric patients" was composed of patients with other diagnosable psychiatric impairment—neurotic or character pathology of severe degree—as determined from the psychological tests.

Comparison of Clinical and Psychological Test Diagnoses

Because two independent diagnoses were obtained—clinical psychiatric diagnoses based on symptoms as classified in the Diagnostic and Statistical Manual of Mental Disorders (American Psychiatric Association, 1968), and psychological test diagnoses based on analyses of Rorschach and WAIS transcripts by an experienced clinical psychologist without access to the hospital diagnoses—the relationship of the two becomes a primary matter for investigation.

Table 7 compares the clinical psychiatric diagnoses with the psychological test diagnoses. Our interest in this comparison lay in the congruence of the two diagnoses with regard to diagnosis of (1) schizophrenia, (2) nonschizophrenic psychoses, and (3) nonpsychotic psychiatric conditions.

Of the forty-nine patients labeled recently hospitalized schizophrenics by the clinical psychiatric diagnosis, twenty-two were classified in other categories by the psychological tests: twelve as "other psychotics" and ten as "nonpsychotic." Of the thirty-four patients diagnosed as schizophrenic by the psychological tests, two were called "other psychotics" and five "nonpsychotic" by the psychiatrists. Overall there is 57.5 percent agreement and

Table 7. Comparison of Clinical Psychiatric Diagnosis with Psychological Test Diagnosis

| | | Psychological Test Diagnosis | | | |
		Recent Schizophrenics	Other Psychotics	Non-psychotics	Σ
Clinical Psychiatric Diagnosis	Recent schizophrenics	27	12	10	49
	Other psychotics	2	6	2	10
	Nonpsychotics	5	3	13	21
	Σ	34	21	25	80

Note: Chronic deteriorated schizophrenics and controls are excluded from this table.

42.5 percent disagreement. A coefficient of agreement, a weighted kappa (Cohen, 1968), between the two diagnostic classifications is .36, which although significant is not impressively high.

Schizophrenia was thus diagnosed less often by psychological test interpretation. Whereas the clinical psychiatric interpretation tended to classify more patients as schizophrenic, the psychological test diagnosis classified more patients as "other psychotic" or as "nonpsychotic." When the psychological test method diagnosed the presence of schizophrenia, the hospital psychiatrists tended to agree in 79.4 percent of those cases. The psychological test diagnosis, however, agreed with the psychiatric designation of schizophrenia in only 55.1 percent of the cases (twenty-seven of forty-nine).

The clinical psychiatric diagnosis thus appears to employ a broader definition of schizophrenia than does the psychological test method. In this respect, the results recall those reported by the cross-national study of diagnosis in the United States and the United Kingdom (Cooper and others, 1972), in which British psychiatrists diagnosed schizophrenia in 33.9 percent of their cases, mania in 6.9 percent, and depressive psychosis in 24.1 percent. This contrasted with American psychiatrists, who diagnosed schizophrenia in 61.5 percent of their cases, mania 0.5 percent, and depressive psychosis in 4.7 percent. This study reflected differing diagnostic conceptions of schizophrenia, revealing that the American conception of the illness includes some patients whom the British would place in other diagnostic categories. The issue, however, is not closed as to whether the major functional psychoses—such as manic-depressive illness and schizophrenia—represent discrete pathological entities or whether there is only one major functional illness.

What becomes clear in this comparison of the two methods of diagnosis is that each focuses on different aspects of psychosis. Clinical psychiatric assessments, on the one hand, may overlook subtle signs of thought slippage and emphasize gross behavioral evidence of psychosis. Thus, in the absence of bizarre behavior, the clinical psychiatrist may be unimpressed by mild language peculiarities. The psychologist, on the other hand, who makes a "blind" diagnosis, is unaware of the patient's behavior on the hospital ward and will carefully examine all verbal signs of thought disorder, which then may become amplified signals for the diagnosis of schizophrenia. The clear differences between the two methods of diagnosis required that we discuss the TDI with respect to both (see Chapter Six).

Results of Patient Classification Scales

All recently hospitalized patients in our study were rated on the Venables-O'Connor Paranoid Rating Scale, the Phillips Scale of Premorbid Adjustment, and the Menninger Health-Sickness Rating Scale (HSR). The number of previous psychiatric hospitalizations of each patient, the length of time after admission the patient was tested, and the length of each patient's hospitalization were recorded. The state mental hospital patients (chronic deteriorated) were omitted from these assessments because of insufficient data.

Table 8 presents a summary of patient characteristics with respect to the Phillips Scale, the Venables-O'Connor Paranoid Scale, the Menninger Health-Sickness Rating Scale, the number of hospitalizations, the number of days after admission testing took place, and the total length of hospitalization.

Phillips Scale

There should be considerable overlap between the diagnosis of process or reactive schizophrenia on the one hand and chronicity or acuteness on the other, because the two underpinnings both imply social deterioration and inadequacy. Our data show a significant difference between the patient groups in general on the Phillips Scale (F = 4.7, p < .01). Table 8 shows that the mean Phillips score of the chronic schizophrenics is above the conventional cut-off point of 16 for process schizophrenia, while the acute schizophrenics are in the middle of the range. This difference between acute and chronic schizophrenics on the Phillips Scale is significant (p < .05). The nonpsychotic patients differ significantly from the schizophrenic patients (chronic and acute) on Phillips scores (p < .05). The overlap between the chronic-acute dimension

Table 8. Characteristics of Recently Hospitalized Patient Groups on Independent Measures

Hospital diagnosis	Phillips Scale	Venables-O'Connor Paranoid Scale	Health-Sickness Rating	Number of Hospitalizations 1	Number of Hospitalizations >1	Testing Time[a]	Total length of hospitalization
Recently hospitalized schizophrenics[b] (N = 49):							
Chronic (N = 17)							
Mean	19.0	8.9	30.1	4[c]	13[d]	50.9	114.6
Range	15–25	4–20	11–53			10–120	35–360
Acute (N = 32)							
Mean	13.5	7.5	34.8	20	12	35.7	84.9
Range	6–24	4–16	21–60			3–90	30–195
Other psychotics (N = 10)							
Mean	11.4	5.3	41.8	5	5	30.7	74.7
Range	5–21	4–11	31–56			10–40	26–120
Nonpsychotics (N = 21)							
Mean	13.3	6.6	49.7	17[e]	3	32.7	73.9
Range	5–25	4–13	35–69			1–150	20–210

[a] Number of days from hospital admission to date of testing.
[b] Data not available for chronic deteriorated schizophrenics.
[c] Number of patients for whom research hospitalization was first hospitalization.
[d] Number of patients who had had more than one psychiatric hospitalization.
[e] Data not available for number of hospitalizations of one nonpsychotic patient.

and the process-reactive dimension can be assessed by computing the percentage agreement between the Phillips rating of process and the hospital diagnosis of chronicity. This agreement is 60 percent.

Paranoid Rating Scale

The groups do not appear to differ on the paranoid rating and there is no *a priori* reason to hypothesize group differences. However, when the schizophrenic group is divided into paranoid and nonparanoid according to hospital diagnosis, the difference in the Venables-O'Connor scores is significant: mean score for paranoid schizophrenics = 10.3; mean score for nonparanoid schizophrenics = 6.6 (t = 2.8, p < .01). Although these scores discriminate paranoid from nonparanoid schizophrenic patients when measured against hospital diagnosis at a statistically significant level, the scale disagrees with the hospital diagnosis of paranoid symptomatology in 43 percent of the cases. Likewise, there is 29 percent disagreement between the hospital diagnosis and the psychological diagnosis of paranoid or nonparanoid subclass of schizophrenia. The lack of high correlation between these three indices of paranoia suggests that different criteria have been used to make the diagnostic decision about paranoia.

Health-Sickness Rating Scale

There is a significant difference among the patient groups on the Health-Sickness Rating Scale (HSR) (F = 16.4, p < .01). Schizophrenic patients as a group have significantly lower HSRs than do the nonpsychotic patients (p < .01). Th_____ have significantly higher HSRs than the chronic, recently hospitalized schizophrenic patients (p < .01) but lower HSRs than the nonpsychotic patients (p < .01). This continuum of severity as rated by the HSR scales, which can be seen in Table 8 (from schizophrenics to other psychotic patients to nonpsychotic patients), is not unexpected.

Among the other variables recorded in Table 8, only the difference among the number of hospitalizations is significant, with the chronic (recently hospitalized) schizophrenics having been hospitalized more often. This difference is expected, since the number of prior hospitalizations contributes to a diagnostic decision about chronicity.

None of the variables in Table 8 are significantly interrelated. Health-Sickness Rating and Phillips do not correlate significantly (r = −.02); there is no difference in HSR between those patients hospitalized once or more than once or between those tested less than ten days or more than ten days after admission; and HSR and testing time do not correlate significantly (r = .10).

Demographic Characteristics of Probands

In order to determine whether subjects in the various diagnostic groups could be considered homogeneous and therefore comparable with respect to a number of personal and demographic characteristics, we compared the groups on IQ, sex, ethnicity, age, socioeconomic class, and drug status. These data are presented in Table 9.

There is a preponderance of women among the probands (61 percent of the total, 58 percent of the patients). Black patients accounted for 31 percent of the total patient population, but accounted for a greater proportion of the psychotic patient population (37 percent) than of the nonpsychotic patient population (14 percent). There may be a cultural self-selection factor operating here: lower-class and black families tend to bring only acutely disturbed family members to psychiatric hospitals, while middle- and upper-class families tend to bring less seriously disturbed family members to such hospitals. Significant overall differences in age occur among diagnostic groups (F = 2.7, p < .05). This is expected, because chronic deteriorated patients tend to be older than recently hospitalized patients.

Although there are no significant differences among groups in educational level, the groups do differ significantly with respect to intelligence levels (F = 10.4, p < .001). The schizophrenics and manics have lower full-scale IQs on the WAIS (means 97.7 and 95.7, respectively) than the nonpsychotic patients (mean 112.5, p < .01) and the normal controls (mean 110.5, p < .01). Even within racial and socioeconomic class groupings, significant IQ differences remain between the schizophrenics and the other groups. Despite these differences, the mean IQs of all patient groups are within the normal range.

Several potential interpretations of the IQ differences are possible (none of which can be decided from these data): (1) the schizophrenic patients may have suffered intellectual deterioration as a consequence of their illness; (2) the acuteness of their disturbance may disrupt intellectual performance on the WAIS; (3) people with lower IQ may be more susceptible to schizophrenic illness.

Social class was determined by the Hollingshead-Redlich Two-Factor Index of Social Position (Hollingshead, 1957). In this index, the occupation and education of each subject are ranked and weighted to arrive at a combined score which ranges from 11 to 77. This continuum of scores is divided into five social classes: I = 11-17; II = 18-27; III = 28-43; IV = 44-60; and V = 61-77. Table 9 shows that with the exception of the chronic deteriorated schizophrenics, subjects in the various diagnostic groups are equally dispersed through socioeconomic classes I–III and IV–V.

We based the social class score on the status of the head of the household or of the primary wage earner in the family. Thus, if the subject was self-supporting and living apart from his or her family, the social class score was based on his or her own education and occupation. However, if the subject was supported by a parent or spouse, it was the education and occupation of this supporting person that determined the subject's social class ranking.

Chronic deteriorated schizophrenic patients are distinctly different from the other groups, showing age (p < .001), educational level (p < .02), and social class (they are mostly class V). Although these chronic schizophrenic patients were not tested for IQ, it is likely that their IQs would be significantly lower than those of other patient groups. These differences set this chronic deteriorated group aside as a special group to be considered separately in the comparisons and analyses that follow in the next chapter.

Drug Effects

The prevalent use of neuroleptic drugs has altered research on schizophrenia. It is obvious that patients receiving drugs per-

Table 9. Characteristics of Probands

	Schizophrenic		Other Psychotic			Control
	Recently Hospitalized	Chronic Deteriorated	Manic	Depressive	Nonpsychotic	
N	49	20	7	3	21	27
Sex						
Male	23	9	0	1	9	8
Female	26	11	7	2	12	19
Race						
Black	20	0	2	0	3	10
White	29	20	5	3	18	17
Age						
Median	22	45	26	44	22	20
Mean	25	42.8	27.6	37	23.6	21.1
SD	8.1	9.8	4.7	13.9	7.1	3.2
Range	18–49	22–64	21–36	21–44	18–52	17–28
Educational Level						
Median	12	11	12	12	14	14
Mean	12.7	11.2	13	12.7	13.8	13.6
SD	2	2.5	1.8	1.1	1.6	2.0
Range	4–16	4–18	11–17	12–14	10–16	11–18
IQ (WAIS)						
Median	96	Unknown	95	97	112	114
Mean	97.7	Unknown	95.7	104.7	112.5	110.5
SD	13.2	Unknown	12.7	15.9	9.8	14.2
Range	62–125		76–113	94–123	93–128	78–128

Socioeconomic class[a]						
I–III	23	1[b]	3	1	11	12
IV–V	26	11	4	2	10	15
Drug status						
Neuroleptics	35	20			5[d]	
Antianxiety agents	(3)				3	
Antidepressants	1			1[d]	(1)	
Lithium carbonate	2(1)		6(1)[c]			
None	11			1	9	27

[a] Hollingshead-Redlich Index of Social Position (HRISP).
[b] HRISP was not determinable for eight state hospital patients.
[c] Numbers in parentheses indicate that the subject is receiving a neuroleptic plus other medication so indicated.
[d] One depressed patient and four nonpsychotic are omitted due to lack of information on drug status.

form differently from those not receiving drugs, yet the exact effects of these drugs on various kinds of performance are not known. The ideal solution for this problem would be to discontinue medication prior to testing or to test patients before they have received any drugs. However, removal of all patients from their drug treatment for the sole purpose of research unrelated to patient care would not be ethically proper.

In the present study, a subgroup of the total patient group was kept off medication for a brief period of time (usually about ten days) after admission and were tested during this nonmedicated period. However, patients who were particularly disturbed or caused extreme management problems at admission were put on medication immediately. Therefore those patients who were tested early, free of medication, tended to be less disturbed to begin with than those patients who needed a longer time to become testable. The medical decisions of which drugs to use and whether to use drugs at all in the treatment of a patient depended on the severity and type of disturbance. Thus, many neurotic patients were never on medication or were on the minor tranquilizers. Chronic deteriorated schizophrenics were removed from medication for a period of ten days and were tested during this period.

Table 9 presents the number of patients in each diagnostic group receiving medication. The psychotropic drugs used by the patients in this study have been divided into four groups: the antipsychotic drugs, of which the phenothiazines are the most common; the antianxiety drugs, such as the benzodiazepines; the antidepressant drugs, of which the tricyclics and monoamineoxidase (MAO) inhibitors are most frequently used; and lithium carbonate, used specifically in this group for manic psychoses.

Spohn, Thetford, and Cancro (1971) attempted to develop a drug index in which the potency of a drug in relation to chlorpromazine is computed on the basis of drug levels and the person's weight. Such a drug index is useful only if the drugs being scaled are known to have proportionate effects similar to that of chlorpromazine on the variable in question. In the case of thought disorder, this information is not known. In fact, there are indications that different phenothiazines have differential effects on ideational symptoms (Kurland and others, 1961, 1962), while other drugs have no effects.

In the present study, which investigates differences between schizophrenic and nonschizophrenic patients in nature and amount of thought disorder, it would be impossible to separate drug effects from the effects of schizophrenia if the neuroleptic drugs—and in particular the phenothiazines—functioned to increase thought disorder. However, studies of the effects of phenothiazines on thought disorder indicate the opposite effect. Kurland and others (1962) found that after two weeks on phenothiazines, acutely psychotic patients showed a decrease in conceptual disorganization and global thought disorder, while patients on phenobarbital or placebo remained disorganized. Chapman and Knowles (1964) found that in patients on phenothiazines, although overinclusiveness occurred, the quality decreased, excessive narrowing did not change, and random errors increased. They interpreted the latter finding as reflecting a loss of alertness and intellectual efficiency on drugs. Johnson and Bieliauskas (1971) reported that phenothiazines did not prevent overinclusive thinking from emerging in a sample of actively psychotic schizophrenics.

The majority of patients on phenothiazines are schizophrenic, and the phenothiazines operate to suppress the level of overt pathology. If phenothiazines also act to decrease thought disorder, then the effect of having subjects on phenothiazines will be to reduce the potential variation between the schizophrenic and nonschizophrenic groups.

Characteristics of
Family Members

Table 10 shows that a total of thirty-eight mothers, thirty-two fathers, and forty siblings were tested. Among the siblings, nineteen were women and twenty-one men. One third of the family members tested were black. There were twenty-two patient "families" (at least three family members tested) and sixteen normal control families. Because there were too few family members of the "other psychotic" patients tested (only four), these subjects were omitted from this data analysis. It is difficult to obtain parents of manic patients for research purposes, due in part to the fact that manic patients tend to be older than other patients and to live apart from their parents.

Table 10. Characteristics of Relatives of the Subjects

Characteristic of Family Member	Diagnosis of Proband								
	Schizophrenics			Nonpsychotics			Controls		
	Mothers	Fathers	Siblings	Mothers	Fathers	Siblings	Mothers	Fathers	Siblings
N	14	3	18	5	6	6	19	13	16
Sex									
Male		3	6		6	2		13	13
Female	14		12	5		4	18		3
Race									
Black	5	6	10			1	6	3	5
White	9	7	8	5	6	5	13	10	11
Hospital									
Research	10	11	13	3	3	3			
Private	4	2	5	2	3	3			
Age									
Mean	48.9	51.4	25.3	49.6	53.3	27	47.8	49.8	18
SD	4.7	7.4	9.4	3.8	6.7	11.9	6.6	6.1	2.1
Range	39–55	38–60	17–49	43–55	44–63	17–49	36–58	36–59	15–22
Educational level									
Mean	12.1	12.9	12.9	12.8	13.7	14	11.9	12.8	11.7
SD	2.7	3.4	2.6	3.2	2.9	2.5	2.3	2.7	1.7
Range	6–16	6–19	9–18	8–18	11–19	10–17	7–17	8–17	9–15
IQ (WAIS)									
Mean	104.8	102.8	101.5	111.4	119.2	114	111	109.7	110.9
SD	17.1	13	13	13.5	9.3	9.3	14.5	12.1	9.2

Range	73–12	85–120	78–123	89–125	108–133	96–122	85–131	92–135	96–125
Socioeconomic class									
HRISP mean	36.4	38.8	36.3	36.6	33.7	40.7	47.2	43.1	46.4
I–III	8	6	10	3	3	2	6	6	7
IV–V	6	7	8	2	3	4	13	7	9

The mean age of the seventy parents is 48.9; mothers have a mean age of 47.2 and fathers 50.9. The mean age of the probands is 24.4 and of their siblings 23.6. The mean, range, and standard deviation are given separately for fathers, mothers, and siblings in Table 10. The sibling groups are significantly different in age (F = 4.51, p < .05), with control siblings being younger than the siblings of schizophrenic patients (p < .05).

Educational levels for the groups of mothers, fathers, and siblings are not significantly different (F = .30, n.s. for parents, F = 2.5, n.s. for siblings). The average educational level for all subjects is twelve grades.

The differences in IQ between the groups of parents approach conventional levels of significance (F = 2.9, p = .06). The mean IQ for parents of schizophrenic patients is 104.8, for parents of nonpsychotics 115.4, and for control parents 110.4. The IQ difference between the parents of schizophrenics and the parents of nonpsychotics is statistically significant at less than the 5 percent level of confidence. The nonpsychotic patients and their relatives appear to be somewhat different from the other subjects in their higher educational level and higher IQs. Within socioeconomic classes IV–V, the mean IQ of parents of schizophrenics is 94.8, while that of parents of nonpsychotics is 89.5; this difference is not significant. However, within classes I–III, the parents of nonpsychotics have higher IQs (mean 122.5) than do the parents of schizophrenics (mean 114.2), a difference that is statistically significant (p < .05). Four of the six parents of nonpsychotics in classes I–III have IQs of 125 or above.

There are no significant differences in level of occupation (as scored by the Hollingshead-Redlich ISP) of the fathers of schizophrenics, nonpsychotics, and controls.

These 237 subjects, representing several diagnostic categories, with diverse personal and demographic characteristics, provided Thought Disorder Index scores for analysis. The analysis of these scores is presented in the next chapter.

VI

Test Results and
Substantive Findings

The results reported in this chapter suggest that the Thought Disorder Index can be used for research purposes in the following ways: (1) as a means of assessing severity of thought disorganization in psychotic patients that is not based on observations of symptoms; (2) as a means of studying change in thinking disorganization in the course of a psychosis; and (3) as a means of differentiating types of thought disorder and then addressing the issue of whether schizophrenic thought disorder is different from disordered thinking in other types of acutely disturbed conditions.

Overview of Procedures
and Analysis

Before presenting the distribution of TDI scores among the subjects described in Chapter Five, we will briefly describe some of the administrative procedures followed to obtain thought disorder scores.

Six examiners administered the tests, all of whom were
trained in the administration of the WAIS and the Rorschach by
first watching an experienced examiner give the tests and then
being observed several times giving trial tests. When they reached
acceptable standards, they began testing research subjects.

The greatest variation among subject groups regarding testing procedure occurred in testing the patient population, because
members of this group often required more time and more frequent testing sessions to complete the procedures than did nonpatient subjects. The Rorschach Test was always given in a single
session. Family members and normal controls took both the WAIS
and the Rorschach in a single session; they usually came to the
laboratory together and were tested individually by several
examiners. The chronic schizophrenic patients from the state hospital, however, were administered only the Rorschach Test, because
it was difficult to hold their attention for a long time.

All but a few subjects were tested at the research treatment
facility, the private psychiatric hospital, or the state mental hospital
as part of a larger study of psychological functioning in the major
psychoses. Some relatives of patients and of normal controls were
tested in their own homes when it proved difficult for them to
travel to the testing stations. We followed this procedure particularly when it proved difficult for lower-class black subjects to come
to the laboratory for testing appointments. Following the procedures of Rosenthal, Behrens, and Chodoff (1968) in response to
similar difficulties in getting black subjects to a hospital for
psychological testing, we gave these subjects a choice of test location, and many chose their homes. In these cases, three to four
examiners went to the home and gave the WAIS and the Rorschach
to family members in separate rooms.

Scoring of the TDI

After the testing session, a verbatim typescript of the session
was made by a typist using the examiner's notes and the tape re-
cording of the session. The examiners checked the typescripts for
accuracy and then sent a copy of them to one of the authors who,
without knowledge of the hospital diagnosis or patient status, made
diagnostic statements about the patients' conditions, as discussed in

Chapter Five. Simultaneously, the WAIS and the Rorschach for each subject were separated, coded, and scored blindly according to the TDI manual by two scorers working independently. The scorers were not blind as to social class and race of the subject. Occasionally one of the scorers recognized a record, because each scorer had tested approximately one sixth of the population. For the most part, however, recognition was not possible, because of the many intervening months and testing sessions between test administration and scoring. However, if one scorer was not blind about a particular record, the other scorer always was. After the scorers independently rated a record, they met to compare their separate judgments and then arrived at a consensus about which category and which weight to assign each scorable response.

Reliability

Prior to obtaining consensus, we determined interrater reliability for the WAIS and the Rorschach separately regarding four subject groups: (1) schizophrenic patients, (2) nonpsychotic patients, (3) normal controls, and' (4) relatives of patients. Since the raters had also acted as examiners, the reliability was examined separately for those groups for which neither rater had been the examiner and those for which one of the raters had been the examiner. Since there are no systematic or significant differences between rater-tested and nonrater-tested groups, the groups were combined to yield reliabilities between the two raters' weighted scores, as shown in Table 11.

The interrater reliability correlations for the normal controls are lower, probably because of a narrowing of range of scores. However, the correlation of each rater's scores compared with the final consensus scores is higher than the figures reported here. It is noteworthy that the reliabilities are not a function of a specific test; the raters agree almost equally on both the WAIS and the Rorschach.

We also computed estimates of internal reliability or consistency of the two thought disorder scores, TD_W and TD_R, as estimated from the Spearman-Brown formula (see Table 12). These reliability correlations were computed as follows: the internal consistency of the TD_R score was measured by taking the sum of the

Table 11. Interrater Reliabilities of the TDI

	Product Moment r
Rorschach	
1. Schizophrenic patients	.90
2. Nonpsychotic patients	.93
3. Controls	.82
4. Relatives of patients	.87
WAIS	
1. Schizophrenic patients	.93
2. Nonpsychotic patients	.74
3. Controls	.70
4. Relatives of patients	.85

TD scores for each card, dividing by the number of responses on that card, and correlating these scores on the odd- and even-numbered cards. A similar procedure was followed for the communication deviance (CD) score, which will be discussed later in this chapter. The internal consistency of the TD_W was estimated from the correlation between the TD_W scores occurring on odd- and even-numbered items on the WAIS.

The levels of reliability obtained are sufficiently high to conclude that where scorable incidences of thought disorder occur with a certain minimal frequency, they tend to occur consistently within a test. The consistency across tests—the correlation between TD_W and TD_R, also reported in Table 12—is not as high, suggesting that the two tests, while both measuring thought disorder, differ in the degree to which they elicit the phenomenon in a particular patient. A more reliable assessment of thought disorder should therefore employ both TD_W and TD_R.

Statistical Procedures

In the statistical analyses that follow, scores were transformed into log units because standard deviations for the scores were large relative to their corresponding means, and a log transformation normalized the distribution. The use of a log transformation permitted us to choose among several parametric statistical methods, and we employed a multivariate analysis of variance

Table 12. Intercorrelations of the TD_W, TD_R, and CD Scores

Subjects	N	Correlation Coefficient TD_W and TD_R	Internal Consistencies TD_W	TD_R	CD
Probands	106	.63[a]	.78[a]	.78[a]	.94[bc]
1. Schizophrenics	49	.51[a]			
2. Nonpsychotics	21	.44[a]			
3. Controls	27	.13			
Parents	70	.40[a]	.74[a]	.66[a]	.79[bc]
1. Of schizophrenics	27	.38[b]			
2. Of controls	32	.36[b]			

[a]$p < .001$.
[b]$p < .02$.
[c]The number of subjects used to obtain internal consistencies of the CD scores is less than that used for the other measures, because only a subsample of subjects was scored on CD.

(Finn, 1972). Major parametric analyses were conducted using a single MESA-99 program, and individual comparisons were ordered through the use of Helmert's contrasts. Where the number of subjects was small, as in some special analyses, the data were assessed by nonparametric or distribution-free methods. The Kruskal-Wallis one-way analysis of variance by ranks was used to decide whether the groups being compared were reliably different. When significant differences were obtained, the Mann-Whitney U-Test was used to determine the status of simple effects.

TDI and Diagnosis

In this section we examine first the TDI score differences between all psychotic patients and other groups and then differences between schizophrenic patients and other subject groups. We then focus on the possible influences on TDI scores of all of the patient characteristics detailed in Chapter Five: IQ, sex, ethnicity, social class, premorbid status, paranoid symptomatology, general disorganization, and drug status. From these analyses, inferences about the clinical and research usefulness of the TDI can then be drawn.

Table 13 contains the means and standard deviations of the

TDI of all subject groups classified by clinical psychiatric diagnosis. TDI scores include the summary scores of thought disorder on the WAIS (TD_W) and on the Rorschach (TD_R) and the number of scored occurrences of each of the four levels of thought disorder for the WAIS ($W_{.25}-W_{1.0}$) and the Rorschach ($R_{.25}-R_{1.0}$). Table 14 shows the same data for groups classified by psychological test diagnosis.

The analysis of variance of both the TD_W and the TD_R scores of recently hospitalized schizophrenics, chronic deteriorated schizophrenics, other psychotics, nonpsychotics, and controls showed significant group differences ($p < .001$). The same overall group differences obtained when either clinical psychiatric or psychological test diagnosis was used to define the groups.

In tests for simple effects, recent psychotic patients are significantly different from nonpsychotic patients on TD_W ($p < .03$ for both hospital and psychological diagnoses) and on TD_R ($p < .001$ for psychological diagnosis and $p < .06$ for hospital diagnosis).

TDI and Schizophrenia

When groups were categorized according to clinical psychiatric diagnosis, tests of simple effects showed that the recently hospitalized schizophrenics did not differ significantly from other psychotics or from nonpsychotics on either TD_W or TD_R. The recently hospitalized schizophrenics did, however, have significantly higher scores than normal controls ($p < .001$). Chronic deteriorated schizophrenics differed significantly from all other patient groups with the exception of the recent schizophrenics on TD_R. (The chronic deteriorated schizophrenic group did not receive the WAIS.) Nonpsychotics did not differ from controls on TD_W or on TD_R.

When groups were categorized according to psychological test diagnosis, the recently hospitalized schizophrenics differed significantly from all other patients as a group and from the controls on both TD_W and TD_R ($p < .001$). Nonpsychotics did not differ from controls on either TD_W or TD_R.

It appears, then, that the TDI scores for groups as diagnosed by psychiatric clinical criteria are indeed arrayed on a continuum, with schizophrenics and other psychotics having the high-

Table 13. Means and Standard Deviations of TDI Scores for WAIS (TD_W) and Rorschach (TD_R) for Probands Assigned by Clinical Psychiatric Diagnosis

TDI Score		Recent Schizophrenics	Chronic Deteriorated Schizophrenics	Other Psychotics	Nonpsychotics	Controls
N		49	20	10	21	27
$W_{.25}$	X̄	9.9	—	9.4	5.81	3.48
	SD	5.0	—	5.75	3.57	1.64
$W_{.5}$	X̄	2.7	—	2.10	.86	.41
	SD	3.0	—	2.07	1.28	.62
$W_{.75}$	X̄	.2	—	.10	.048	0.0
	SD	.8	—	.30	.21	0.0
$W_{1.0}$	X̄	.0	—	0.0	.048	.037
	SD	.5	—	0.0	.21	.19
TD_W	X̄	4.9		3.53	1.96	1.11
	SD	3.7		2.55	1.47	.58
$R_{.25}$	X̄	5.4	2.60	3	5.29	2.81
	SD	4.4	2.60	2.45	3.65	3.04
$R_{.5}$	X̄	3.1	1.55	3.3	1.38	.70
	SD	4.6	1.96	2.24	1.67	.89
$R_{.75}$	X̄	2.7	1.45	1.9	1.71	.18
	SD	3.5	1.19	2.12	2.67	.67
$R_{1.0}$	X̄	.4	.70	.10	0.0	0.0
	SD	1.5	1.22	.30	0.0	0.0
TD_R	X̄	17.4	23.79	12.53	9.73	4.46
	SD	15.6	25.70	7.79	7.91	3.72

One-way ANOVA for TD_W; F = 8.?4; df 3, 103; p < .001.
One-way ANOVA for TD_R; F = 8.0?; df 4, 122; p < .001.

Table 14. Means and Standard Deviations of TDI Scores for Each Level of Both TD_W and TD_R for Patients Classified by Psychological Test Diagnosis

TDI Score		Schizophrenics	Other Psychotics	Nonpsychotics
N		34	21	25
$W_{.25}$	$\overline{X}$	9.59	8.86	6.96
	SD	5.69	5.05	4.98
$W_{.50}$	$\overline{X}$	3.91	1.57	.96
	SD	4.61	1.62	2.07
$W_{.75}$	$\overline{X}$	.41	0.0	.04
	SD	.74	0.0	.20
$W_{1.0}$	$\overline{X}$	.15	0.0	0.0
	SD	.44	0.0	0.0
TD_W	$\overline{X}$	4.88	3.07	2.25
	SD	4.15	2.02	2.02
$R_{.25}$	$\overline{X}$	6.12	5.09	3.76
	SD	5.00	3.48	2.83
$R_{.50}$	$\overline{X}$	3.62	3.19	.96
	SD	5.29	2.61	1.15
$R_{.75}$	$\overline{X}$	3.62	2.14	.88
	SD	4.45	2.70	1.56
$R_{1.0}$	$\overline{X}$	.62	.19	0.0
	SD	1.81	.50	0.0
TD_R	$\overline{X}$	20.84	14.70	7.50
	SD	16.17	10.45	6.50

Note: The psychological test diagnosis employed only the three general categories presented in this table.
Note: One-way ANOVA for TD_W; F = 7.09; df 2, 73; p < .001.
One-way ANOVA for TD_R; F = 10.02; df 2, 73; p < .001.

est mean scores, controls having the lowest mean scores, and nonpsychotics occupying an intermediate position. With regard to simple effects, only the two extreme groups—schizophrenics and normal controls—differ significantly from each other, a finding that highlights the existence of noteworthy overlap among the other groups.

    In analyzing the psychological test diagnosis, however, the composition of the nonpsychotic and schizophrenic groups seems to change to the extent that they differ significantly from each other on the TD_R. This finding suggests that the psychological test diagnosis, which provides a more subtle assessment of disturbance of thinking, makes a different discrimination among patients— relying as it does on thought organization and disorganization— than does the clinical hospital diagnosis, which is based on symptoms occurring during the early period of hospitalization. Figures 2 and 3 present a graphic illustration of the distribution of thought disorder scores for TD_W and TD_R using clinical psychiatric diagnoses. Figures 4 and 5 present the distribution of thought disorder scores for TD_W and TD_R using the psychological test diagnoses.

TDI and IQ, Sex, Ethnicity, and Socioeconomic Class

In this study, TDI scores were not related to variables of sex, ethnicity, and socioeconomic position (as measured by the Hollingshead-Redlich Index of Social Position). A fuller analysis of the role of ethnicity and class is contained in the study of Haimo (1976) and Haimo and Holzman (1979), which demonstrated that the TDI

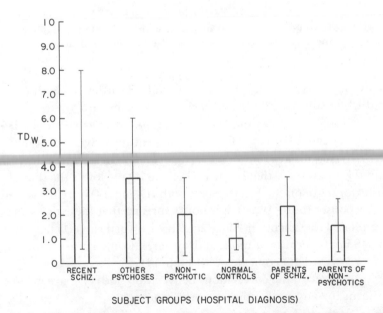

Figure 2: Histogram of TD_W mean scores with ± one standard deviation for six subject groups classified by hospital diagnosis.

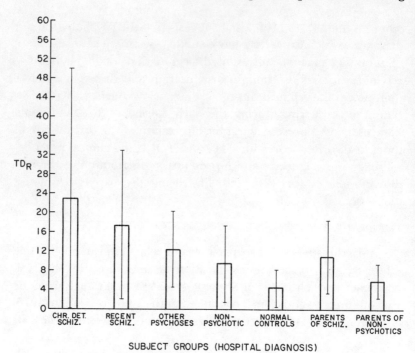

SUBJECT GROUPS (HOSPITAL DIAGNOSIS)

Figure 3: Histogram of TD$_R$ mean scores with ± one standard deviation for seven subject groups classified by hospital diagnosis.

is a valid instrument for assessing thought disorder for both black and white subjects and for all socioeconomic groups.

Table 15 shows the Spearman rank-order correlations between IQ and TDI scores for the various groups. Significant negative correlations are found between IQ and TD$_W$ for the probands and their parents—that is, the higher the IQ the lower the thought disorder score on the WAIS. Since both IQ and TD$_W$ are measured by responses to the WAIS, it is not surprising that these two scores are related to each other. Since acutely disturbed subjects fail many WAIS items because of thought disorder, it would seem reasonable that a lowered IQ coincides with high TD$_W$.

However, the correlations between IQ and TD$_R$ are not significant for any proband or parent groups.

If the different diagnostic groups are divided into those subjects whose IQ is below 100 and those whose IQ is above 100, nonparametric analyses show that the TD$_W$ and TD$_R$ scores signifi-

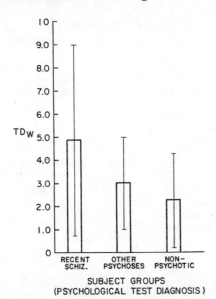

Figure 4: Histogram of TD_W mean scores with ± one standard deviation for three subject groups classified by psychological test diagnosis.

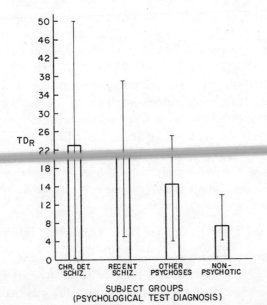

Figure 5: Histogram of TD_R mean scores with ± one standard deviation for four subject groups classified by psychological test diagnosis.

Table 15. Spearman Rank-Order
Correlations of Thought Disorder Index Scores and IQ

Subject Group	N	$IQ\text{-}TD_W$	$IQ\text{-}TD_R$	$IQ\text{-}\#R$ [a]
Probands	97	−.44[b]	−.13	
Schizophrenics	49	−.41[c]	−.15	−.09
Nonpsychotics	21	.06	.34	.31
Controls	27	−.18	.40[d]	.24
Parents	70	−.35[b]	−.07	.43[c]
Of schizophrenics	27	.09	−.13	.41[b]
Of nonpsychotics	11	−.60[d]	.29	
Of controls	32	−.51[b]	.01	.00

[a]Number of Rorschach responses.
[b]$p < .001$.
[c]$p < .01$.
[d]$p < .05$.

cantly differentiate recently hospitalized schizophrenic, nonpsychotic, and control subjects ($p < .001$). When one compares the TD_W of nonpsychotic patients and schizophrenics whose IQs are above 100, the differences between the two groups are significant at only the 10 percent level. Nonpsychotic patients with IQs above 100 have significantly lower TD_R scores than do schizophrenics with IQs above 100 ($p < .05$). Schizophrenic patients with IQs below 100 have significantly higher TD_W than do schizophrenics with IQs above 100, but they do not differ on TD_R.

The WAIS is a structured test that calls for specific culture-influenced responses. It appears that more intelligent schizophrenic subjects are able to structure and limit disordered responses on the WAIS more appropriately than on the Rorschach, in part because the WAIS questions can be answered with over-learned responses. Intellectual level, however, bears no relation to thought-disorder score on the Rorschach.

TDI and Premorbid Status, Paranoid Status, and General Disorganization

The Phillips rating of premorbid adjustment does not correlate significantly with any of the TDI measures, nor are there significant differences in TDI scores between subjects scoring less than 12 or greater than 17 on the Phillips Scale. There are no significant differences in TDI scores between those patients tested during their first hospitalization and those who had been hospitalized more than once prior to testing.

The clinical psychiatric diagnosis of paranoid or nonparanoid status does not differentiate groups on TDI scores, nor did the Venables-O'Connor Paranoid Rating Scale. The degree of acute disturbance at the time of testing, as measured by the Menninger Health-Sickness Rating Scale (HSR), is the only patient status variable that is significantly correlated with thought disorder. The multivariate analysis shows a highly significant relationship between HSR and each of the TDI scores (for TD_W, $F = 29.576$, $p < .01$; for TD_R, $F = 17.757$, $p < .01$). The multiple R between HSR and TD_R and TD_W is $-.427$, a significant correlation.

We interpret this multiple R as indicating that the degree of thought disorder is related to the degree of disorganization, but this relationship is only moderate and accounts for only about 18 percent of the variance—a finding that accords with clinical experience. Some persons with much manifest thought disorder may appear quite disorganized in overt behavior and in need of hospital care. Others, however, may be able to function with a modicum of adjustment and, although requiring hospitalization, they may not be in need of continuous care. Conversely, persons with low levels of thought disorder, such as those with systematized paranoid delusions, may be quite unable to function outside of a hospital and may need continuous care.

TDI and Drugs

In a subgroup of twenty-four recently hospitalized schizo-
phren̶i̶ on phenothiazines alone and eleven were not on medication at all when tested. Although the nonmedicated group tended to have less thought disorder than the medicated group, the difference in amount of thought disorder between the two groups was not statistically significant. The nonmedicated patients were significantly less disturbed (as measured by the HSR) than the medicated patients and were tested within the first ten days after admission, while the medicated group was tested an average of thirty days after admission. These findings should be interpreted with caution because of the confounding effect of nonrandom assignment of patients to medication (the most disturbed

patients were not delayed in being put on medication), as well as the fact that only those patients tested during the first ten days were not medicated and those who could not be tested during that time because of severe disturbance were necessarily in the medicated group.

TDI and Good Form Responses on the Rorschach

Each Rorschach response was scored for accuracy of form perception (F+ percent) by one of the authors without knowledge of the clinical status of the patient. The F+ percent is the percentage of good form responses scored F+ or F± in contrast to F∓ or F−, according to Rapaport's system (Rapaport, Gill, and Schafer, 1968). The correlation between F+ percent and TD_R is negative and significant ($-.29$, p < .05) for all subjects; the correlation is $-.52$ (p < .01) for recently hospitalized schizophrenics. For the parents of schizophrenics the correlation is $-.42$ (p < .01). Low positive correlations approaching significance also appear between F+ percent and IQ in the probands (r = .19, p = .1). F+ percent correlates negatively with the number of responses. It appears that lowered IQ, high TDI, and low F+ percent all reflect aspects of general disorganization.

The Relationship of TDI
Categories to Diagnosis

Thus far we have examined group differences with respect to total TDI scores—composite scores that represent a range of severity of thought disorder in its four levels. At each level or degree of severity of thought disorder there are several categories of responses that are given the same weight. For example, the .5 level is applied to *queer responses, confusion, looseness,* and *fabulized combinations.* In this section we first consider whether subject groups can be distinguished by the frequency with which they produce thought disorder at specific levels of severity. We then examine whether certain categories of response distinguish any of the diagnostic groups.

Table 16 presents the number and percentage of subjects in each group (classified by clinical psychiatric diagnosis) who were scored for thought disorder occurrences at each of the four levels of the TD_W, the mean number of scorable occurrences at each level, and the results of the statistical tests of significance of the use of levels. Table 17 presents the same information for the TD_R levels. The mean number of scorable occurrences at each level for patient groups classified by psychological diagnosis are presented in Table 14.

Number of Scored Occurrences at Each Level

Analyses of variance of the number of scored thought disorder occurrences at the .25 and .5 levels given by the probands (defined by either diagnostic classification) were significant. The analysis of variance of the number of scored .75-level occurrences on the TD_R was also highly significant. The frequency of .75 and 1.0 scores on the TD_W was very low for all groups. At the .75 level, the probability of differences among groups ascertained by clinical psychiatric diagnosis was less than 6 percent, and when ascertained by psychological diagnosis it was less than 1 percent. There were no significant differences at the 1.0 level of the TD_W.

Subjects in all diagnostic groups received scores for thought disorder occurrences at the .25 level, but recently hospitalized schizophrenic subjects produced more of these responses than did any other subject group. The nonpsychotic patients, too, were scored more often for .25-level responses than were the control probands. The chronic deteriorated schizophrenics had fewer .25-level responses than did the recent schizophrenics. All subjects were scored more often at the .25 level on the TD_W than on the TD_R.

The recently hospitalized schizophrenics were more often scored for .5 and .75 responses than were the nonpsychotics and controls, especially on the TD_W. When nonschizophrenics were scored at these higher levels of thought disorder, they had few such responses per subject and had them more often on the Rorschach than on the WAIS. The occurrence of 1.0-level responses was rare for all groups—practically nonexistent on the WAIS and occurring almost entirely in the recently hospitalized and chronic deteriorated schizophrenic groups on the Rorschach. It seems, therefore, that the 1.0-level response may perhaps be pathognomonic of schizophrenia.

Table 16. Number of Subjects Giving Responses Scored at Each Thought Disorder Level on WAIS

Number of Scored Occurrences	Recently Hospitalized Schizophrenics N=49	Other Psychotics N=10	Nonpsychotics N=21	Controls N=27	Parents of Schizophrenics N=27	Parents of Nonpsychotics N=11	Parents of Controls N=32
W.25 responses							
0 (none)	1	1 (D)[a]	0	0	0	0	0
1	0	0	1	4	0	0	3
2–3	5	1 (D)	7	8	6	2	13
4–6	9	0	4	13	6	5	9
7 or more	34	8	9	2	15	4	7
Percentage of subjects using 1 or more W.25 responses	98	90	100	100	100	100	100
Chi-square[b] (each diagnosis vs. recent schiz. and parents vs. parents of schiz.)			6.14*	9.99**			4.84*
Mean number of .25 responses	9.59	9.49	5.81	3.48	7.04	5.45	4.53
t test (each diagnosis vs. recent schiz., and parents vs. parents of schiz.)		.09	3.38**	7.10**		1.49	2.72*
W.5 responses							
0 (none)	14	3 (D)	12	19	10	9	18
1	11	1	4	6	9	2	11
2–3	11	3	3	2	8	0	2
4–6	7	2	2	0	0	0	1
7 or more	6	1	0	0	0	0	0
Percentage of subjects using 1 or more W.5 responses	71	70	43	30	63	18	44
Chi-square[c] (each diagnosis vs. recent schiz. and parents vs. parents of schiz.)			5.14	12.39**		6.27*	2.16

Mean number of .5 responses	2.87	2.10	.86	.41	1.07	.18	.65
t test (each diagnosis vs. recent schiz. and parents vs. parents of schiz.)		.92	3.40**	4.61**	1.07	3.78**	1.58
$W_{.75}$ responses							
0 (none)	40	8 (3D)	20	27	26	11	32
1	6	1	1	0	1	0	0
2–3	2	1	0	0	0	0	0
4–6	1	0	0	0	0	0	0
7 or more	0	0	0	0	0	0	0
Percentage of subjects using 1 or more $W_{.75}$ responses	18	20	5	0	4	0	0
Mean number of .75 responses							
t test (each diagnosis vs. recent schiz.)							
$W_{1.0}$ responses							
0 (none)	45	10	20	26	27	11	32
1	3	0	1	1	0	0	0
2–3	1	0	0	0	0	0	0
Percentage of subjects using 1 or more $W_{1.0}$ responses	6	0	5	4	0	0	0
Mean number of 1.0 responses	.08	0.0	.048	0.0	0.0	0.0	0.0
t test (each diagnosis vs. recent schiz.)[a]	1.68	1.68	.46	.69			

[a] Depressed psychotic patients.

[b] Chi-square for number of index Ss using [...]3, > 3 $W_{.25}$ responses = 11.06, p < .005; for parent groups = 6.52, p < .05.

[c] Chi-square for number of index Ss using [...] > 0 $W_{.5}$ responses = 16.98, p < .005; for parent groups = 6.57, p < .05.

[d] Frequency of occurrences in nonschizophre[...]nic groups was too small to permit valid use of statistical tests of group differences. One-way ANOVA for $W_{.25}$; F = 11.68, df = 3,103, p < .01; for $W_{.5}$, F = 5.50, df = 3,103, p < .01. One-way ANOVA for $W_{.75}$; F = 2.28, df = 3,103, p < .06; for $W_{1.0}$; F = .37.

*p < .05 **p < .01

Table 17. Number of Subjects Giving Responses Scored at Each Thought Disorder Level on Rorschach

Number of Scored Occurrences	Recently Hospitalized Schizophrenics N = 49	Chronic Deteriorated Schizophrenics N = 20	Other Psychotics N = 10	Nonpsychotics N = 21	Controls N = 27	Parents of Schizophrenics N = 27	Parents of Nonpsychotics N = 11	Parents of Controls N = 32
$R_{.25}$ responses								
0 (none)	5	5	1 (D)	2	2	0	1	3
1	3	3	2 (1D)	2	9	3	2	8
2–3	10	7	4 (1D)	3	9	6	1	10
4–6	16	3	2	8	5	9	3	7
7 or more	15	2	1	6	2	9	4	7
Percentage of subjects using 1 or more $R_{.25}$ responses	90	75	90	81	96	96	91	91
Chi-square[a] (each diagnosis vs. recent schiz., and parents vs. parents of schiz.)		8.32**	3.0	.07	9.71**			6.11*
Mean number of .25 responses	5.46	2.60		5.29	2.81	5.18	4.91	2.84
t test (each diagnosis vs. recent schiz., and parents vs. parents of schiz.)		3.30**	2.44*	.16	3.05**		.21	2.78*
$R_{.5}$ responses								
0 (none)	14	7	1 (D)	9	12	11	5	15
1	10	6	1 (D)	3	12	7	5	9
2–3	10	5	4 (1D)	6	2	5	1	7
4–6	9	1	3	2	1	3	0	1
7 or more	6	1	1	1	0	1	0	0

Percentage of subjects using 1 or more $R_{.5}$ responses	71	65	90	57	56	59	55	50
Chi-square[b] (each diagnosis vs. recent schiz., and parents vs. parents of schiz.)		1.51		.39	6.35*			.5
Mean number of .5 responses	3.10	1.55	3.3	1.38	.70	1.52	.64	.90
t test (each diagnosis vs. recent schiz., and parents vs. parents of schiz.)		1.93	.20	2.25*	3.47**		1.95	1.37
$R_{.75}$ responses								
0 (none)	18	6	3 (D)	12	25	14	8	27
1	9	4	4	2	0	7	3	2
2–3	9	10	1	4	2	6	0	3
4–6	7	0	1	1	0	0	0	0
7 or more	6	0	1	2	0	0	0	0
Percentage of subjects using 1 or more $R_{.75}$ responses	65	70	70	43	0	48	27	16
Chi-square[c] (each diagnosis vs. recent schiz., and parents vs. parents of schiz.)				2.5	22.13**		19.09**	7.01**
Mean number of .75 responses	2.75	1.45	1.90	1.71	.18	.78	.27	.25

Table 17. Number of Subjects Giving Responses Scored at Each Thought Disorder Level on Rorschach (Continued)

Number of Scored Occurrences	Recently Hospitalized Schizophrenics N = 49	Chronic Deteriorated Schizophrenics N = 20	Other Psychotics N = 10	Nonpsychotics N = 21	Controls N = 27	Parents of Schizophrenics N = 27	Parents of Nonpsychotics N = 11	Parents of Controls N = 32
t test (each diagnosis vs. recent schiz., and parents vs. parents of schiz.)		2.97*	.96	1.27	4.41**		2.19*	2.47*
$R_{1.0}$ responses								
0 (none)	38	12	9	21	27	26	11	31
1	6	5	1	0	0	1	0	1
2–3	4	2	0	0	0	0	0	0
4–6	0	1	0	0	0	0	0	0
7 or more	1	0	0	0	0	0	0	0
Percentage of subjects using 1 or more $R_{1.0}$ responses[d]	22	40	10	0	0	4	0	3
Mean number of 1.0 responses	.48	.70	.10	0.0	0.0	.037	0.0	.03
t test (each diagnosis vs. recent schiz., and parents vs. parents of schiz.)		2.57*	1.58	2.18*	2.18*		1.19	

[a] Chi-square for number of Ss using 0–3, > 3 .25 responses = 17.22, p < .005.

[b] Chi-square for number of parents using 0–3, > 3 .25 responses = 6.89, p < .05.

[c] Chi-square for number of S using 0–1, > 1 .5 responses = 12.13, p < .01.
Chi-square for number of parents using 0–1, > 1 .5 responses = 8.36, p < .02.

[c] Frequency of occurrences in nonschizophrenic groups was too small to permit valid use of statistical tests of group differences.

[d] Chi-square for number of Ss using 0 or > 0.75 responses = 26.5, p < .001; for parent groups = 7.42, p < .05.

One-way ANOVA for $R_{.25}$; F = 3.99, df = 4,122, p < .01; for $R_{.5}$; F = 3.23, df = 4, 122, p < .05.

One-way ANOVA for $R_{.75}$; F = 3.60, df = 4,122, p < .05; for $R_{1.0}$; F = 2.05, df = 4,122, p < .1.

*p < .05 **p < .01

Number of Subjects Scoring at Different Levels

Chi-square analyses of the number of probands scoring at each level are also included in Tables 16 and 17. The "other psychotic" group was omitted from this analysis due to the small size of this group (expected frequencies within cells were less than 5). Significant overall differences occurred between subject groups on the number of subjects being scored for three or fewer .25-level responses, one or no .5-level responses on the Rorschach, no .5-level responses on the WAIS, and no .75-level responses on the Rorschach. The differences between the groups were similar to those found in the analyses of the number of scored occurrences at each level. That is, responses at the higher levels of thought disorder tended to be given by psychotic subjects, whereas lower levels of thought disorder occurred among all groups, although with greater frequency among psychotic patients.

Categories of the TDI

Each thought-disorder level is made up of several categories. The decision to score a particular response as a specific category—such as *peculiar* or *queer*—is less reliable than the decision to score the level of the response. Nevertheless, some categories appear to discriminate among groups better than others, and it seems important to present these data, taking into account their lesser reliability. Table 18 presents the frequency of scored occurrences of the most important categories for each diagnostic group. This table can be compared with Table 19, which presents a compilation of data from Rapaport, Gill, and Schafer (1968) made by Fred Schwartz (personal communication, 1975).

A comparison of these two tables reveals both similarities and differences between the two studies. The present group of chronic deteriorated schizophrenics appears similar to the group tested by Rapaport, Gill, and Schafer in their use of scored categories of TDI. The recently hospitalized schizophrenics are also similar to Rapaport's "other schizophrenic" groups, though in the present study more of the recently hospitalized schizophrenics gave responses at the higher levels of thought disorder. The present group of nonpsychotics used more scorable categories than did

Table 18. Frequencies and Percentages of Occurrences of TDI Scoring Categories for Each Diagnostic Group (Clinical Psychiatric Diagnosis)

TDI Categories	Schizophrenics Recently Hospitalized (N=49) Freq.	(%)	Schizophrenics Chronic Deteriorated (N=20) Freq.	(%)	Nonpsychotics (N=21) Freq.	(%)	Controls (N=27) Freq.	(%)
WAIS								
1 peculiar	13	(27)			4	(19)	11	(41)
2 peculiar	10	(14)			7	(33)	5	(19)
3–n peculiar	24	(49)			7	(33)	1	(04)
word-finding difficulty	12	(24)			2	(10)	0	
clang	33	(67)			8	(40)	14	(52)
inappropriate distance	41	(84)			15	(71)	17	(63)
vagueness	20	(41)			3	(14)	2	(07)
perseveration	16	(33)			3	(14)	3	(11)
queer	16	(33)			5	(24)	1	(04)
confusion	15	(31)			1	(05)	0	
loose	17	(35)			5	(24)	1	(04)
autistic logic	3	(06)			1	(05)	0	
absurd	8	(16)			0		0	
incoherence	1	(02)			0		0	
neologism	3	(06)			1	(05)	1	(04)
Rorschach								
1 peculiar	7	(14)	5	(25)	3	(14)	9	(33)
2 peculiar	11	(22)	2	(10)	2	(10)	4	(15)
3–n peculiar	21	(43)	2	(10)	11	(52)	3	(11)
word-finding difficulty	13	(27)	4	(20)	3	(14)	1	(04)

clang	1	(02)	0		0		0
inappropriate distance	18	(37)	2	(10)	1	(05)	3	(11)
vagueness	5	(10)	0		2	(09)	2	(07)
perseveration	9	(18)	9	(45)	5	(24)	1	(04)
relationship verbalization	7	(14)	1	(05)	2	(09)	0
incongruous combination	13	(27)	1	(05)	11	(52)	11	(41)
symbolism .25	8	(16)	0		1	(05)	3	(11)
symbolism .5	4	(08)	0		1	(05)	1	(04)
queer	22	(45)	6	(30)	6	(29)	3	(11)
confusion	7	(14)	7	(35)	1	(05)	1	(04)
looseness	15	(31)	5	(25)	5	(24)	0
1 fabulized combination	15	(31)	5	(25)	1	(05)	8	(38)
2 fabulized combination	5	(10)	0		2	(10)	0
3–n fabulized combination	5	(10)	0		1	(05)	0
confabulation	22	(45)	3	(15)	5	(24)	2	(07)
autistic logic	18	(37)	5	(25)	4	(19)	1	(04)
fluidity	17	(35)	4	(20)	4	(19)	1	(04)
absurd	6	(12)	9	(45)	0		0
contamination	8	(16)	1	(05)	0		0
incoherence	3	(06)	6	(30)	0		0
neologism	2	(04)	1	(05)	0		0

Table 19. Frequencies and Percentages of Categories of Thought Disorder for Subject Groups in the Rapaport, Gill, and Schafer (1968) Study

TDI Categories	Recently Hospitalized Schizophrenics Acute N = 29 Freq.	(%)	Chronic N = 33 Freq.	(%)	Chronic Deteriorated Schizophrenics N = 13 Freq.	(%)	Borderline Schizophrenics N = 33 Freq.	(%)	Depression N = 43 Freq.	(%)	Neuroses N = 52 Freq.	(%)	Controls N = 54 Freq.	(%)
DW	8	(28)	10	(30)	2	(15)	6	(18)	4	(09)	1	(02)	0	(00)
1 fabulized combination	3	(10)	4	(12)	4	(31)	8	(24)	1	(02)	2	(04)	1	(02)
2 fabulized combination	0	(00)	0	(00)	0	(00)	3	(09)	1	(02)	1	(02)	0	(00)
3–n fabulized combination	0	(00)	0	(00)	0	(00)	0	(00)	0	(00)	0	(00)	0	(00)
confabulation	6	(21)	10	(30)	4	(31)	7	(21)	1	(02)	1	(02)	0	(00)
contamination	3	(10)	4	(12)	6	(46)	2	(06)	1	(02)	0	(00)	0	(00)
1 peculiar	6	(21)	12	(36)	4	(31)	9	(27)	4	(09)	3	(06)	0	(00)
2 peculiar	6	(21)	7	(21)	0	(00)	3	(09)	0	(00)	3	(06)	2	(04)
3–n peculiar	4	(14)	3	(09)	1	(08)	8	(24)	0	(00)	0	(00)	0	(00)
queer	8	(28)	13	(39)	8	(62)	6	(18)	0	(00)	0	(00)	0	(00)
autistic logic	4	(14)	8	(24)	3	(23)	0	(00)	0	(00)	0	(00)	0	(00)
positional response	1	(03)	6	(18)	1	(08)	1	(03)	1	(02)	0	(00)	0	(00)
absurd	8	(28)	8	(24)	4	(31)	5	(15)	1	(02)	0	(00)	1	(02)
relationship verbalization	2	(07)	2	(06)	3	(23)	2	(06)	1	(02)	1	(02)	0	(00)
perseveration	1	(03)	7	(21)	2	(15)	5	(15)	2	(05)	0	(00)	1	(02)
confusion	5	(17)	2	(06)	0	(00)	0	(00)	0	(00)	1	(02)	0	(00)
incoherence	4	(14)	1	(03)	5	(38)	0	(00)	0	(00)	0	(00)	0	(00)
neologism	2	(07)	0	(00)	3	(23)	0	(00)	0	(00)	0	(00)	0	(00)

Note: This table compiled by F. Schwartz.

the group of neurotics in Rapaport's study. A larger percentage of present control subjects gave fabulized combinations and peculiar verbalizations than did Rapaport's control group.

In the present study, categories that appeared particularly salient in discriminating groups at the .25 level were *vague responses, word-finding difficulties, inappropriate distance,* and *perseveration. Peculiar verbalizations* are frequently used by both patients and nonpatients; however, the occurrence of three or more *peculiar* responses distinguishes patients in all diagnostic groups and relatives of schizophrenics from the controls. It is possible, therefore, that the thought disorder categories that reflect difficulties with words—such as *word-finding problems* (blocking) and *peculiar* expressions—reflect nonspecific psychological disturbances. The salient categories at the higher levels of the TDI (.5 and above) were *confusion, loose associations, queer verbalizations, fabulized combinations, absurd responses, autistic logic, fluidity, confabulations, contaminations,* and *incoherence.*

Several of Rapaport's categories occurred in such low frequencies as to obviate significant discriminating capacities among the groups. Approximately one *incongruous combination* per subject on the Rorschach appeared in all groups and was used by a greater percentage of nonpsychotic than psychotic subjects. Rapaport, Gill, and Schafer (1968) and Weiner (1966) regarded incongruous combinations as an indication of a tendency to combinatory activity on a continuum with *contaminations,* and this category should be further investigated for its capacity to discriminate among groups. *Clang* responses have frequently been quoted to illustrate the loose, bizarre thought disorder of the schizophrenic patient, but clanging was found infrequently in the present groups of subjects. Clanging occurred among normal subjects on the vocabulary subtest of the WAIS, generally in an attempt to define difficult words. There is some indication, however, that clanging may occur more frequently among manic patients (this group has a mean of 1.1 clang responses per subject compared with .8 for schizophrenics and .4 for nonpsychotics); it appears on both the Rorschach and WAIS (and in the latter test not only on vocabulary items). Thus, clang responses should be further investigated for their diagnostic specificity, especially for manic patients, but should not be considered pathological when they occur on the vocabulary subtest in response to difficult words.

Combinatory responses such as the use of *incongruous combinations, fabulized combinations,* and *confabulations* appeared in non-psychotic and manic patients. Such responses do not appear to be specifically characteristic of schizophrenia, but may be characteristic of acute psychological disturbance. It is noteworthy that the manic patients scored higher on the combinatory categories (*fabulized combinations, confabulations, autistic logic,* and *symbolic responses*) than did the schizophrenics. The tendency of this group of manic patients to make connections easily and to elaborate on reality in symbolic, autistic, and bizarrely imaginative ways requires cross-validation on a larger sample.

The categories that best characterize schizophrenic patients (and their relatives) can be termed "thought disorganization." These subjects show not only unusual use of individual words but, more significantly, a loss of focus and an inability to stay on the track. Indications of such disturbances are *vagueness, perseveration, inappropriate distance, confusion, looseness, fluidity, absurd responses,* and *incoherence.* The last two categories particularly characterize the chronic deteriorated schizophrenic group.

A finer-grained analysis with a larger number of non-schizophrenic psychotic patients could more definitely address the issue of whether different psychoses can be identified by specific categories of thought disorder or whether psychotic disorganization invades thought functioning in similar ways regardless of the nature of the functional psychosis.

Thought Disorder Scores
of Relatives

Table 20 presents the means and standard deviations of all of the TDI scores for the relatives of probands (classified by subject's clinical psychiatric diagnosis). The parents of schizophrenics appear to be on the high end of a continuum of TDI scores, with the parents of controls on the low end. Parents of patients have lower TDI scores than do their patient offspring.

Table 20. Means and Standard Deviations of TDI Scores for Relatives of Probands

TDI Score		Relatives of Recently Hospitalized Schizophrenics			Relatives of Nonpsychotics			Relatives of Controls		
		Mothers	Fathers	Sibs	Mothers	Fathers	Sibs	Mothers	Fathers	Sibs
N		14	13	18	5	6	6	19	13	16
$W_{.25}$	$\bar{X}$	6.43	7.69	6.18	5.20	5.67	4.33	4.05	5.31	4.19
	SD	4.13	3.86	3.54	2.59	2.66	1.97	2.30	3.17	2.23
$W_{.5}$	$\bar{X}$	1.29	.85	.71	.20	.17	.83	.63	.69	.44
	SD	1.27	.80	1.10	.45	.41	1.33	.96	1.03	.89
$W_{.75}$	$\bar{X}$	0	.08	0	0	0	0	0	0	0
	SD		.28							
$W_{1.0}$	$\bar{X}$	0	0	0	0	0	0	0	0	0
	SD									
TD_W	$\bar{X}$	2.25	2.40	1.82	1.40	1.50	1.50	1.33	1.67	1.27
	SD	1.46	1.10	1.28	.72	.77	.71	1.06	1.13	.59
$R_{.25}$	$\bar{X}$	5.14	5.23	2.82	4.20	5.50	4.83	2.95	2.69	3.0
	SD	4.04	3.92	1.63	4.09	3.02	4.12	2.39	2.25	2.56
$R_{.5}$	$\bar{X}$	2.07	.92	1.29	.40	.83	.50	.79	1.08	.75
	SD	2.62	1.32	1.36	.55	.75	.55	1.08	1.26	1.06
$R_{.75}$	$\bar{X}$	.57	1.0	.88	.40	.17	0	.11	.46	.31
	SD	.85	1.08	1.37	.55	.41	0	.46	.78	.60
$R_{1.0}$	$\bar{X}$	0	.08	.059	0	0	0	0	.08	0
	SD		.28	.23					.28	
TD_R	$\bar{X}$	9.08	12.59	10.84	4.26	7.69	4.26	4.50	7.99	5.22
	SD	7.27	8.33	11.88	3.07	3.94	2.31	3.82	9.11	4.70

The parents of schizophrenics, of nonpsychotics, and of controls differ significantly from each other on TD_W and TD_R as tested by an analysis of variance ($p < .01$). Parents of schizophrenics score significantly higher ($p < .05$) than do parents of controls. Sibling groups do not differ significantly from each other on any of the measures. The combined group of mothers has significantly more Rorschach responses than does the group of fathers ($p = .01$). Table 16 and 17 presented the number and percentage of relatives responding on each of the four levels of the TDI, the mean number of scorable occurrences at each level, and the results of the statistical tests of significance.

As with the probands, there is very widespread use of the .25 level; the parents of schizophrenics, like their schizophrenic offspring, are more often scored at this level. There are significant overall differences in the number of parents of schizophrenics with one or more .5 responses on the WAIS and two or more .5 responses on the Rorschach as compared with parents of other probands. Very few responses of any parents are scored at the .75 level; these few responses appear almost exclusively on the Rorschach and significantly more among parents of schizophrenics. Only three relatives—a father and a sibling of a schizophrenic patient and a father of a control—gave any responses scored at the 1.0 level. Such responses, therefore, do seem to be largely limited to the schizophrenic patient groups.

These data suggest that parents of schizophrenics show more thought disorder than do parents of normal probands and that many of these parents score higher on the TDI than do the parents of nonpsychotic, psychiatrically disturbed patients.

Table 21 presents the frequencies and percentages of relatives using specific scoring categories. Categories that appear to differentiate the parent groups are *perseverations, word-finding difficulty,* and *looseness* on both the WAIS and the Rorschach, and *confabulations, autistic logic,* and *fluidity* on the Rorschach, all of which tend to be given by parents of schizophrenics.

Relationship Between Parent and Offspring Scores

Do parents with high TDI scores tend to have children who also have high TDI scores? We constructed a two-by-two contingency table in which parent-child pairs are arrayed according to both parent's and child's position above or below their own group median. A chi-square analysis of the TD_W score distributions of such parent-child pairs is statistically significant (chi-square = 4.47, p < .05), with 25 percent of the parent-child pairs sharing positions above the median and 39 percent below the median. The same analysis for TD_R shows similar percentages (30 percent of family pairs sharing positions above the median and 32 percent below the median) but is significant only at p < .10 (chi-square = 3.38). Chi-square analysis of parent-child pairs who share the use of .75 and 1.0 level of responses (21 percent) is highly significant (chi-square = 8.10, p < .01).

Although there is a significant relationship between TDI scores of parents and their children, with thought-disordered parents tending to have thought-disordered children, the relationship is not a strong one. Nevertheless, it can be stated that thought disorder tends to run in families. Among schizophrenic patients with high TDI scores, 87 percent have at least one parent with high TDI scores.

Communication Deviance

In Chapter Three, we discussed the communication deviance (CD) score of Wynne and Singer (1963). We noted that the CD codes presented in Table 2 contained many categories that are not indications of thought disorder (such as subjunctive "if" responses or humor) and some that are indeed congruent with thought disorder (such as clang associations or non sequitur reasoning). Although Wynne and Singer directed their studies at communication difficulties within families, it was not clear whether such communication problems represent thought disorder. In order to investigate the relationship between communication deviance and thought disorder, we compared the Thought Disorder Index scores with CD scores on a subsample of thirty-three families.

Scoring of Communication Deviance

The measure of communication deviance (CD) used in this study is that of Wynne and others (1977). It is computed as the ratio (D/T) of the total number of deviances (D) in the subject's first

Table 21. Frequencies and Percentages of Occurrences of TDI Scoring Categories for Parents of Subject Groups

	Parents of Schizophrenics (N=27)		Parents of Nonpsychotics (N=11)		Parents of Controls (N=32)	
	Freq.	(%)	Freq.	(%)	Freq.	(%)
WAIS						
1 peculiar	6	(22)	3	(27)	9	(28)
2 peculiar	5	(19)	2	(18)	10	(31)
3–n peculiar	9	(33)	3	(27)	4	(13)
word-finding difficulty	8	(30)	1	(09)	3	(09)
clang	13	(48)	4	(36)	20	(63)
inappropriate distance	19	(70)	8	(73)	13	(41)
vagueness	10	(37)	7	(64)	7	(22)
perseveration	9	(33)	2	(18)	2	(06)
queer	1	(04)	0		1	(03)
confusion	3	(11)	0		1	(03)
looseness	6	(22)	1	(09)	1	(03)
autistic logic	1	(04)	0		0	
absurd	0		0		0	
incoherence	0		0		0	
Rorschach						
1 peculiar	6	(22)	3	(27)	8	(25)
1 peculiar	8	(30)	2	(18)	4	(13)
3–n peculiar	9	(33)	4	(36)	8	(25)
word-finding difficulty	7	(26)	2	(18)	3	(09)
clang	0		0		0	
inappropriate distance	10	(37)	3	(27)	7	(22)
vagueness	2	(07)	2	(18)	5	(16)

perseveration	3 (11)	0	2 (06)
relationship verbalization	5 (19)	0	3 (09)
incongruous combination	7 (26)	4 (36)	7 (22)
symbolism .25	3 (11)	0	0
symbolism .5	0	0	1 (03)
queer	4 (15)	0	5 (16)
confusion	3 (11)	2 (18)	0
looseness	6 (22)	2 (18)	1 (03)
1 fabulized combination	6 (22)	1 (09)	7 (22)
2 fabulized combinations	1 (04)	0	2 (06)
3–n fabulized combinations	1 (04)	0	0
confabulation	6 (22)	1 (09)	2 (06)
autistic logic	5 (19)	1 (09)	2 (06)
fluidity	5 (19)	1 (09)	2 (06)
absurd	0	0	1 (03)
contamination	1 (04)	0	1 (03)
incoherence	0	0	0
neologism	0	0	0

response to each of the ten Rorschach cards to the total number of transactions (T). A transaction is defined as a response either to the initial request for an association or to an inquiry about that association. The maximal and usual number of transactions is thus twenty.

Families with three to four members who were tested comprised this subsample. There were thirteen families of schizophrenic patients, four families of nonpsychotic patients, and sixteen families of controls—a total of 116 subjects. The 116 Rorschach protocols were scored blindly for communication deviance by a rater who had no other connection with this research project. The rater used the revised manual for the scoring of the communication deviance (Singer, 1972) and conferred with its author about eight records that had been scored and specific problems in scoring. Although consensus was reached about the scoring of these eight records, we did not obtain interscorer reliability assessments with Singer for the entire sample. The scoring categories were the same as described in Table 2. Table 22 presents the means, medians, and standard deviations for probands, mothers, fathers, and siblings obtained in this study, in Wynne and others' (1977) study, and in the Hirsch and Leff (1975) study. Table 22 shows that the schizophrenic patients and their parents are the highest-scoring groups in our study.

CD Scores of Probands

Schizophrenic subjects and controls differ significantly from each other on CD as determined by a Mann-Whitney U-Test (p < .02). The schizophrenics also differ significantly from controls and nonpsychotics combined (p < .02).

CD in Parents

A Kruskal-Wallis one-way analysis of variance of the CD scores of parents of schizophrenics, parents of nonpsychotics, and parents of controls is significant at the 5 percent level. Parents of schizophrenics score at significantly higher levels of CD than do control parents, as determined by the Mann-Whitney U-Test (p < .01); mothers of schizophrenics have significantly higher CD scores than control mothers (p < .05); fathers do not differ significantly from each other; and siblings of the schizophrenics have signifi-

Table 22. Rorschach Communication Deviance Scores

Diagnosis of Proband	N	Mean	Standard Deviation	Median	Mean Found by Singer and Wynne (1966a)	Median Found by Hirsch and Leff (1975)
Schizophrenic						
Probands	15	1.99	1.23	2.5	1.52, 1.67[a]	
Parents as group	24	1.96	.89	1.8		1.33
Mothers	12	2.12	1.14	2.1	2.42, 2.15[a]	1.26
Fathers	12	1.78	.58	1.6	2.11, 2.85[a]	1.54
Siblings	13	1.42	1.13	1.3	1.26, 1.25[a]	
Nonpsychotic						
Probands	6	.95	.73	.8	.64, 1.11[b]	
Parents as group	8	1.75	1.97	1.4		.88
Mothers	4	1.78	1.33	1.4	.82, 1.23[b]	1.01
Fathers	4	1.73	.96	1.6	.60, 1.47[b]	.75
Siblings	1				.52, .62[b]	
Controls						
Probands	16	.96	1.08	.7	.34	
Parents as group	26	1.35	.87	1.2		
Mothers	14	1.20	.8	1.2	.59	
Fathers	12	1.49	.95	1.4	.49	
Siblings	12	.63	.48	.4	.29	

[a]Remitting and nonremitting schizophrenics, respectively.
[b]Neurotic and borderline patients, respectively.

cantly higher CD scores than do the normal siblings (p < .05).

These results confirm the report of Singer and Wynne (1966b) that the parents of schizophrenics have more deviations in communication on the Rorschach Test than do the parents of controls. In Wynne's (1967) analysis of CD scores, the parents of neurotics and controls combined had significantly lower scores than did parents of schizophrenics. The present study found the same results.

It is noteworthy that the mean values of the CD scores reflect differences between the present sample and that of Wynne and others (1977). Their level of CD for the parents of schizophrenics is about the same as the one we obtained. Although the fathers of schizophrenics in their sample had a higher mean CD score than did the fathers in the present sample, the mean CD values of the mothers in the two samples are very close. The range of CD scores in both studies is also quite similar.

The major differences between the two samples occur in the parents of the nonpsychotic patient group and in the controls; our subjects in those groups obtained higher scores than did those in the Wynne and Singer borderline, neurotic, and normal groups. It is possible that the smaller number of subjects in our study lowered the dependability of our measures of central tendency. It is also plausible that the differences reflect sample differences in the two studies. Our subjects have lower mean educational and socioeconomic levels and probably represent a more heterogeneous population than Wynne and Singer's subjects.

In our sample, the siblings of schizophrenics have higher CD scores than do the siblings of controls. Thus, while the siblings of schizophrenics are not differentiated from siblings of controls by the TDI scores, they do have higher CD scores. Wynne and others (1977) also found higher CD scores in the siblings of schizophrenics than in the siblings of controls.

Comparison with the Hirsch and Leff Study

Hirsch and Leff (1975) obtained differences between the parents of schizophrenics and those of neurotic patients that were significant at the .05 level. Their results, like ours, confirmed the essential finding of Wynne and Singer that parents of schizophrenics produce significantly more communication deviance on the Rorschach Test than do parents of other psychiatric patients. But, as in our results, they obtained an overlap between their two groups that remained even when they transformed their scores to logarithmic units and examined the CD scores of fathers and mothers separately. Although the fathers in the Hirsch and Leff study accounted for the differences between their two groups, in our study it was the mothers who differed from each other significantly.

It is reasonable to assume that the levels of CD obtained by Hirsch and Leff and by us reflect sample differences between the two studies. The parents of our schizophrenic probands had higher CD scores than did those in the Hirsch and Leff study. It would seem that their schizophrenic patients were principally acute schizophrenics, because they excluded any patients whose psychotic symptoms lasted for three or more years and who were hospitalized for a total of two years or more of the past five years. Although our schizophrenic probands were not restricted, they included many who were comparable to both the Hirsch and Leff and the Wynne and Singer population. Scores obtained by the parents of our nonpsychotic and control groups were, however, higher than those reported by Hirsch and Leff, and it seems that these figures also represent differences in sampling.

Hirsch and Leff reported significant positive correlations between verbal productivity and CD. When they removed the effect of word count by an analysis of covariance, the significant difference between the two parent groups with respect to CD disappeared. We repeated the Hirsch and Leff procedure and confirmed that there is a significant positive correlation between word count and CD. Table 23 shows the comparisons between our two studies. In both studies parents of schizophrenics say more than parents of controls or neurotics. The correlations are also quite similar, as are the levels of verbal productivity in both studies. However, when we removed the effect of the word count in an analysis of covariance—although such a use of covariance has an ambiguous acceptability (see Lord, 1960; Woodward and Goldstein,

Table 23. Number of Words Used in First Responses to Rorschach Cards and Correlations Between Word Count and CD in Hirsch and Leff and in the Present Study

| | Number of Words Spoken[a] Parents of | | | | Correlation Between Word Count and CD Parents of | |
| | Schizophrenics | | Neurotics and/or Controls | | Schizophrenics | Neurotics and Controls |
	$\overline{X}$	SD	$\overline{X}$	SD		
Hirsch and Leff	789.4	421.0	612.2	324.3	.57	.76
Johnston and Holzman	832.9	497.0	663.9	267.5	.69	.83

[a]Includes free association plus inquiry.

1977; and Kenny, 1975)—we still obtained a significant difference between the groups (F = 4.58, p < .04). Thus, the differences in CD between the two groups continue to exist in spite of the removal of the effects of verbal productivity. This result obtains whether one considers free-association and Rorschach inquiry separately or combined. Similar results were reported by Wynne and others (1977).

Sampling differences notwithstanding, with the exception of the effects of word count, our results are congruent with those reported by Wynne and others (1977) and Hirsch and Leff: although parents of schizophrenics have more CD than parents of nonschizophrenics, there is an overlap between the two groups. Some nonschizophrenics and their relatives manifest CD, and among some it is manifest to a large extent; conversely, some parents of schizophrenics manifest quite low levels of CD. We would therefore agree with the principal conclusion of Hirsch and Leff that such overlap does damage the view that schizophrenia is transmitted by deviant communication alone. This conclusion would stem from the following reasoning: Both the Hirsch and Leff study and our data showed that some parents of schizophrenics have low levels of CD; therefore, the presence of CD in parents cannot be a necessary condition for schizophrenia in offspring. Further, some parents of nonschizophrenics had a high CD score, so its presence in parents cannot be a sufficient condition for schizophrenia in offspring. A hypothesis more consistent with these data would assign to communication deviance as well as to thought disorder a role as an intermediate variable in the development of schizophrenic disorders, as Wynne and others (1977) suggested.

CD and TDI Compared

Table 24 presents the correlations between the TDI scores and CD scores. There is overlap between these two scores, due in part to the fact that some of the same categories and aspects of disturbed speech are scored in both scoring schemes. The similarities between the two scoring systems were discussed in Chapter Three. Despite the overlap in scoring categories, however, the level of the correlations reflects differences between the two

Table 24. Correlations of Thought Disorder Index Scores and
Communication Deviance Scores

Diagnosis of Index	N	TD_W vs. CD	TD_R vs. CD
Probands[a]	33	.66[b]	.66[b]
Schizophrenics	13	.56[d]	.73[c]
Controls	16	.38	.47[d]
Parents	58	.34[c]	.53[b]
Of schizophrenics	23	.30	.27
Of nonpsychotics	8	−.03	.43[c]
Of controls	27	.28	.57

[a]Includes four nonpsychotic patients in addition to schizophrenics and controls.
[b] = p < .001.
[c] = p < .01.
[d] = p < .05.

scoring schemes. The parent groups have higher CD scores than
do the probands, which is not true of the TDI scores of parents and
offspring. Schizophrenic patients and their relatives have equiva-
lent CD scores, while schizophrenic patients have higher TDI
scores than do their relatives. Nonpsychotic patients and their relatives, however, do not differ from control probands in CD, although nonpsychotic patients do have higher TDI than controls.
It would thus appear that CD primarily reflects communication
problems, and the TDI to a large extent mirrors deviant thought
processes.

Summary

Estimates of internal consistency of the TD_W and TD_R scores are
appropriately high and suggest that thought disorder occurs with a
consistent frequency within a test. TD_W and TD_R scores are moderately
correlated with each other, suggesting that they differ in the extent to
which they elicit thought disorder in a particular subject. More valid
estimates of thought disorder would employ both the TD_W and TD_R.

Thought disorder is moderately related to general disorganization. Psychotic patients have the highest TDI scores, with
recent schizophrenics and other psychotics—as diagnosed by hospital psychiatrists—scoring at about the same level. Chronic deteriorated schizophrenics, however, have significantly higher TD_R

scores than do other nonschizophrenic psychotic patients, although they do not differ from the recent schizophrenics. The psychological test diagnosis yields significant TDI differences between the schizophrenic and nonschizophrenic psychotic patients. The main contributions to the high TDI scores of schizophrenic patients come from the higher level categories of .5, .75, and 1.0.

There are no sex, racial, or SES effects on TDI (see Haimo, 1976; Haimo and Holzman, 1979). IQ is negatively correlated with TD_W and essentially unrelated to TD_R.

Parents of schizophrenics have higher TDI scores than do parents of nonschizophrenic patients and of controls. Sibling groups do not differ from each other. Parents of schizophrenics have significantly higher CD scores than do parents of controls, although there is a noteworthy overlap between the groups in CD scores. CD and TDI scores are correlated with each other, but the differences between them suggest that CD taps primarily communication problems while the TDI principally reflects thought organization. The implications of these results are discussed in Chapter Seven.

VII

Implications for Using the Thought Disorder Index in Research and Clinical Practice

The results of the validation study encourage the use of an index such as the TDI for the assessment of thought disorder. Clear relationships obtain between severity of illness and psychosis on the one hand and level of thought disorder on the other. However, the discrimination of diagnostic groups by thought disorder is equivocal. Even when the psychological test diagnosis is used as the independent variable, overlap among the groups does not disappear. It would seem, then, that the TDI cannot be used to support distinct cut-off points for diagnostic categories or as a sufficient metric for determining diagnosis. The use of the TDI raises several questions, which we shall address in this chapter.

The TDI as a Research
and Clinical Tool

The TDI can be used in research contexts as a means to assess degree of thought disorganization independent of clinical information; that is, blind evaluations can be accomplished. It is important to emphasize, however, that the yield of the TDI is not a diagnostic statement but a quantitative score on a dimension of psychopathology, the extreme of which would be coterminous with psychosis. Psychotic conditions, however, can occur with lesser degrees of thought disorder. Further, the form of the psychosis is not specified by the score, although the TDI can be used as a tool to define further the qualitative differences in thought disorganization among the various psychoses.

For many investigators, thought disorder is a major defining category of schizophrenia (see Bannister, 1960). The diagnostic difficulties in defining subject groups are quite well known, and although standardized interview schedules have begun to make diagnostic assessments more reliable—for example, the Present State Examination (PSE) of Wing, Cooper, and Sartorius (1972), the Research Diagnostic Criteria (RDC) of Spitzer, Endicott, and Robins (1975), and the Schedule for Affective Disorders and Schizophrenia (SADS) of Endicott and Spitzer (1978)—the validity of the diagnoses is not addressed by these standardized interview schedules.

One solution to the diagnostic dilemma is to supplement these new clinical assessments—such as the SADS or PSE—with assessment of thought disorder, which would limit the behavior under study to variations in degree of thought disorganization. Because schizophrenia is a syndrome and may indeed comprise several disorders, our understanding of this psychosis may advance more incisively by focusing on the vicissitudes of thought disorder than by using broad diagnostic categories, which often represent poorly defined disease entities. From this vantage point, the researcher can undertake longitudinal studies of thought disorder in patients and in nonpatients. The TDI can also be used as a dependent variable in studies of therapeutic effectiveness and change and as a monitor of postpsychotic stability in follow-up studies. One can determine the degree of thought slippage in persons presumed to be high risks for various psychoses.

It is possible to work with abbreviated test batteries if frequent testing is to be undertaken and from these brief forms to estimate the index of thought disorder. Hurt (1978), for example, attempted to determine the differential effects over time of two dosages of a neuroleptic, using the TDI as well as other outcome measures. Testing was introduced two days each week. A full battery of the WAIS and Rorschach was administered four times—at the start of the study, at the end of the drug wash-out period, midway through the study, and at discharge. At all other times, the verbal tests of the WAIS and three cards of the Rorschach were administered. The three card sets consisted of one achromatic card (I, IV, V, VI, or VII), one black-and-red card (II or III), and one chromatic card (VIII, IX, or X). Thus, several sets were constructed. The TD_R was prorated for three cards and was an effective measure of change in thought disorder for the groups of subjects.

The TDI can be taught to clinical students as a method of sensitizing them to the nature of thought disorder. Many psychiatrists and clinical psychologists may not have the opportunity to become familiar with the wide range of thought slippage patients can manifest. The use of the TDI in a training context is thus recommended. It would also be highly useful as a method for charting clinical improvement independent of observed behavior. The clinician can retest patients at strategic intervals and compute their TDI scores from the tests.

Is There a Continuum
of Thought Disorder?

Inasmuch as the various groups can be arrayed along a continuum of degrees of thought disorder, the question may legitimately be raised whether thought disorder represents a continuum of thinking from precise, logical, and ordered to loose, illogical, and disorganized. This view would assume a distribution of people along a continuum of thought disorder such that most people would manifest mild degrees of thought disorder at some time, fewer people would display higher levels of thought disorder, and as one reached the extreme end of the continuum, only psychotic persons would predominate. Transition areas would not be sharply defined.

If quality of thinking can be considered to be continuous, then one may assume that the mild slippages, peculiar verbalizations, vague and barely illogical utterances apparent in many people are qualitatively the same as—but milder versions of—utterances that occur in the speech of schizophrenics. To a naive listener, it would indeed be difficult to distinguish qualitative differences between a mild peculiar response given by a psychotic and by a normal person. Nonetheless, the way in which a schizophrenic patient loses the immediate frame of reference, with little recognition that the listener is not following, may differ markedly from the way a normal person would experience a lapse in maintaining his or her frame of reference. The differences may be subtle but real and significant; however, the nature of the TDI does not permit such differentiation. The instrument ranks degrees of thought disorder on a continuous scale, and this process tends not to discriminate qualitative differences within a category.

On the one hand, the idea of thought disorder existing along a continuum may thus be viewed as an artifact of the TDI. The use of the index can, however, pave the way for definitive answers to the question of continuity, first by raising the issue and then by explicitly providing the categories and levels for closer research scrutiny. On the other hand, it can be persuasively argued that the TDI does indeed represent a valid continuum of thought disorder. This argument would observe that thought disorder represents an *interruption* in smooth unfolding of a line of thought. Such interruption can reflect a congeries of processes that include psychotic intrusions of irrelevant preoccupations, organic disturbances of cortical modulation, fatigue, or anxiety. None of these interferences can claim to affect thought processes in one specific way—for example, by concretizing thinking or by shifting the logical base. Yet, all can disrupt thinking, some for more or less indefinite periods and others for relatively short episodes. The severity of the psychopathological process that produces interruption may be related to the severity of the resulting thought disorder. Thus, fatigue and anxiety may provoke peculiar responses, blocking, and fabulations; psychoses or brain pathology may produce autistic logic, confabulations, neologisms, and contaminations.

It is thus reasonable to assume that a continuum of thought disorder exists and that the presence of any degree of thought disorder is an indication of some pathogenic situation that may be trivial or serious, transitory or relatively enduring. In addition to the degree of thought disorder, the duration of the thought disturbance and the person's awareness of the nature of the thought disturbance should also be considered. The TDI could be used as a metric in assigning a weight to the extent of thought disorder; however, severity on the TDI in itself would not at this juncture be a specific diagnostic indicator of schizophrenia (see Harrow and Quinlan, 1977).

Specificity of Thought Disorder

The TDI does provide evidence that a high score is associated with psychosis, although not all psychotic persons produce a high TDI. The issue of whether the TDI discriminates among psychotic persons, however, remains unresolved. That is, acutely psychotic persons, both schizophrenic and manic, will tend to have high TDI scores. Whether the quality of thought disorder differs between these diagnostic groups is not answered by the present study. This lack of specificity on the TDI does not imply that such qualitative differences do not exist. As in the case with IQ, which is a single number that represents an aggregate of cognitive functions—speed of understanding, conceptual thinking, concentration capacity, and breadth of cultural exposure, among many others—a single measure for thought disorder cannot adequately summarize all the complex aspects of thinking that can go awry.

Many clinicians allege that they can distinguish between the grade of thought disorder associated with acute mania and that associated with acute schizophrenia. Qualitative exploration of such differences could be undertaken with the TDI as a tool. The categories of thought disorder in question are described in Chapter Four, and its flexible use permits tests of alleged qualitative differences among groups. We should note, however, that the sharpness of such distinctions in thought disorder depends upon the reality of sharp distinctions among the major functional psychoses. While there seems to be a clinically justifiable difference between a chronic process schizophrenic patient and an acutely excited manic patient (who after recovery returns to a previous high level of competence), there is a large degree of overlap and indistinctness among patients who present themselves with both affective and schizophrenic symptoms.

In our data, moreover, qualitative differences in thought disorder among groups of patients were evident. The recently hospitalized schizophrenics differed from the chronic deteriorated schizophrenics in several aspects. The latter gave fewer lower-level thought disorder responses and the highest rate of thought disorder per response on the Rorschach of any group. Chronic schizophrenics who were not acutely disturbed when tested tended to manifest less anxiety and produce more bizarre and autistic responses, but in a setting of constriction and general impoverishment of communication. Among the recently hospitalized schizophrenics, those who had been chronically ill gave fewer Rorschach responses. The records of acutely disturbed schizophrenic patients who have high TDI scores frequently contain streams of associations revealing disorganization, confusion, and intense anxiety. The manics, in contrast, produce many responses, a general good F+ percent, with many clang responses, combinatory efforts (for example, fabulized combinations and confabulations), rhyming, looseness, humor, and efforts to engage the examiner.

It would be of great interest to study manic and depressed patients further on the TDI. Thought disorder may be an approximate measure of psychotic disorganization, at least in its higher levels, or manic and schizophrenic patients may share a susceptibility to thought disorder that is not shared by other psychotic patients. Furthermore, the stage of the disorder in which the patients are tested may affect the level and quality of thought disorder. The acute phase of both a schizophrenic and a manic psychosis is accompanied by abundant evidence of disorganized thinking. The more chronic phases show considerably less prevalence of disorganized thinking. For example, a study of word associations of seven manic patients during and between phases of acute manic disturbance (Henry, Weingartner, and Murphy, 1971) reported that the patient's associations were highly idiosyncratic during manic phases but essentially normal during nonmanic phases. It would seem that thought disorder—if present at all during post-psychotic periods in manic patients—is present in only subtle forms, while it may persist, only somewhat muted, in remitted schizophrenic patients.

The criteria against which the TDI was validated were the clinical psychiatric diagnosis and the psychological test diagnosis, and overlap of TDI scores among the diagnostic groups was greater when the clinical psychiatric diagnosis was used. Since psychiatric diagnosis of schizophrenia has an interrater reliability of about .70 (see Maher, 1970), the relationship between the TDI and diagnosis would of necessity be limited by that reliability. American psychiatrists tend to apply the diagnosis of schizophrenia to conditions that British psychiatrists would not (Cooper and others, 1972). It seems plausible that in the cohort of subjects used in the present study, schizophrenia was also overdiagnosed by the American psychiatrists—that is, some nonschizophrenics were classed among schizophrenics.

It is likely that the more subtle, less obvious qualities of thought disorder would be recognized through use of the TDI, while they might not come to the attention of a psychiatrist during an interview or during a ward observation. Thus, some persons who might have been schizophrenic may not have been diagnosed as such by the psychiatrist because of the absence of flagrant psychotic symptoms, thus raising the TDI scores of the patients in the nonpsychotic group. These considerations may have merit because the independently evaluated psychological test assessments agreed better with the TDI scores than did the psychiatric diagnosis, a result to be expected, because the psychological test assessment was based on variations in thought organization and not on symptoms.

The difficulties in obtaining valid and reliable diagnoses of schizophrenia notwithstanding, the present study suggests that thought disorder does occur in nonpsychotic people, including those who are not psychiatric patients. Nonpsychotic patients with elevated thought disorder scores showed a pattern of relatively intact performance on the WAIS, with an accumulation of .25-level responses, while on the Rorschach test they produced expansive records and higher levels of thought-disordered responses.

The relatives of the schizophrenics have higher TDI than do the relatives of nonpsychotic patients, who in turn have a higher TDI than do the relatives of controls. This suggests that the TDI may have value for family mapping of schizotypic persons (see Meehl, 1962).

The Nature of
Thought Disorder

Despite the renewed interest in the symptomatology of schizophrenia and in efforts to forge diagnostic units on the basis of typical symptoms (Schneider, 1959; Feighner, 1972; Strauss and Carpenter, 1974), the presence of thought disorder remains the principal defining feature of schizophrenic pathology. Theoretical and descriptive efforts as well as some empirical work (Schafer, 1948; Rapaport, Gill, and Schafer, 1968) even support the notion that thought disorder appears not only in the acute and chronic forms of schizophrenia but also in states of remission and in prodromal periods of schizophrenic psychosis. The TDI can be used to test these assumptions.

The nature of thought disorder may also become somewhat clearer from the use of the TDI. The index assumes that language reflects thought. But because thought cannot be observed by persons other than the thinker him- or herself, it can be assessed only indirectly by observing the thinker's expressive actions. Thus, language use—spoken or written—as well as other expressive actions will convey some of a person's thought processes. The meaning of these expressive actions, of course, is open to interpretation, in the way any text or painting can be analyzed by hermeneutic endeavor.

For the most part, people do make themselves understood. But schizophrenic persons seem to have a harder time in that effort. Their language is sometimes loose or tight, sometimes figurative or literal, sometimes full of logical shifts or almost devoid of logic. In short, their speech makes it difficult for the listener to interpret the thought processes without considerable effort and interpretative leaps. Interruptions, looseness, new words, shifts in direction—all of these modes and more are characteristic of thought disorder. They impart to the speech of the schizophrenic speaker a quality of bizarreness.

Yet a careful listener can decipher and interpret the meaning of such speech, and skilled therapists have demonstrated that ability many times (see, for example, Sechehaye, 1951). Apparently, schizophrenic thought disorder is not either loose or concrete or illogical; rather, it is periodically derailed, intruded upon, or interrupted. Communication by speaking probably involves a more or less constant monitoring of what we say and how we are saying it. This monitoring is automatic and represents an inhibitory function that brakes multiple intrusions as well as maintaining a dominant focus on the regnant task. A number of empirical investigations, for example, demonstrated that hearing oneself speak is required for adaptive behavior and that interfering with such auditory feedback produces measurable changes in behavior, such as temporary impairment of motor efficiency and attention, interferences with speech itself (Broadbent, 1958; Mahl, 1962), and increased disinhibition of speech (Klein and Wolitsky, 1970; Holzman and Rousey, 1971).

Monitoring implies a self-editing function, and probably much self-editing occurs while we are speaking, through perception of exteroceptive auditory stimulation as well as of enteroceptive kinesthetic and vibratory stimuli. Self-editing is also accomplished prior to speech and after speech has been uttered, as in spontaneous corrections of slips of the tongue. From this vantage point it would seem that thought disorder reflects an impairment in the monitoring function that allows expression of otherwise inhibited aspects of thought, such as fringe intentions, subsidiary aims, or inappropriate leaps of logic. The fact of intrusion, rather than the content of the intruding thoughts, suggests a disinhibition of "cognitive centering." This point of view was argued persuasively by Maher (1972), who proposed that the thought slippage of schizophrenic patients could be understood as a consequence of a failure to maintain an attentional focus. This fluctuating attentional focus would, according to Maher, make possible intrusions both of fringe associations into language and of background sensory stimuli into perceptual experience.

Holzman, Levy, and Proctor (1976) offered a similar conception of attentional dysfunction in schizophrenia. On the basis of a series of studies that showed disorders of smooth-pursuit eye movements in up to 86 percent of schizophrenics and in about 45 percent of their first-degree relatives, these authors noted that voluntary attention, motivation, or heedless negligence were not the specific attentional dysfunction in schizophrenia. Rather, the nonvoluntary quality of attention appeared to be disordered, and this dysfunction would manifest itself in a failure to maintain cognitive centering. That is, simple vigilance, activation, or selective attention are probably not central to the impairment; rather, the capacity to focus and concentrate in a consistent and relatively uninterrupted way would be impaired. The failure to maintain a visual-attentional focus that is continuously locked onto a moving target is analogous to Maher's proposal of unstable attentional focus in schizophrenia.

It would thus appear that thought disorder in schizophrenia, like perceptual inconstancy and motor impairment, reflects a failure of central inhibitory mechanisms, which permits ordinarily restrained internal and external stimuli to interfere with behavioral intentions. Thought disorder, in this view, would be one manifestation of a general organismic instability that presents itself as disinhibition in the cognitive, perceptual, and affective spheres. It would not represent a separate domain of impairment.

VIII

Case Illustrations
and Interpretations

In this section we present illustrative case protocols of four patients and the mother and father of one of the patients. The first three protocols are records of patients who were tested while they were hospitalized and actively psychotic; these three patients were tested again two to three years after having been successfully treated for their psychoses and then discharged from the hospital. Their follow-up records are included in this appendix. The fourth protocol is from a nonpsychotic patient for whom follow-up testing was not available. The fifth and sixth protocol are from the mother and father of Case 2; follow-up testing was not carried out in these cases either.

The psychological diagnoses of these four index cases were: Case 1, chronic paranoid schizophrenia; Case 2, schizoaffective psychosis; Case 3, manic psychosis; Case 4, neurotic depression.

These records were selected because they provided particularly good illustrations of the variety of thought disorder within a record and of the variations among subjects. They are not, however, unique. Rather they are representative of the diagnostic category of cases from which they are drawn.

Preceding each protocol we present an abbreviated summary of the symptom picture at the time of admission, during hospital course, and at the time of follow-up. A brief interpretation of test results is included with each case. The following procedures were adopted in the presentation of the verbatim protocols:

Wechsler Adult Intelligence Scale. Responses to those subtests of the WAIS that call for verbal replies are presented, along with the scores given each response and the total raw score for each subtest. The Thought Disorder Index scores (category and scoring level) are noted in boldface immediately following the response to which they apply. At the end of each WAIS record is a summary of the WAIS TDI scores (TD$_W$), the IQ scores, and the scale scores of both verbal and performance subtests. In order to assist the reader, the complete questions are given in parentheses, preceding the responses, for the first case; for subsequent cases, only key words from the question are given. The complete WAIS was administered during the first testing; only selected subtests were administered at follow-up.

The subtests of the WAIS were administered and scored according to the WAIS Manual (Wechsler, 1955) with the following exceptions: (1) Discontinuance rules (stopping a particular subtest after a certain number of consecutive failures) were not followed strictly, in order to permit assessment of the erratic, fluctuating efficiency of some acutely disturbed subjects; however, items were scored strictly according to Wechsler's criteria, so that correct answers occurring past the cut-off point were not given credit. (2) Questioning of incomplete or unclear responses followed Wechsler's criteria but was extended to the investigation of idiosyncratic or bizarre responses. Routine inquiries, such as "Please explain that further" or "How do you mean?" are indicated by the notation "(?)"; other questions by the examiner are written out and enclosed in parentheses. The first items of some subtests are not ordinarily administered; credit given for these questions is indicated at the beginning of these subtests. Typical correct answers, which are simply right or wrong, are not presented for the Information and Picture Completion subtests, but incorrect or unusual responses are quoted. All responses to the Comprehension, Similarities, and Vocabulary subtests are quoted in full, along with the partial (1) or complete (2) credit given them. The amount of

credit given depends on the level of conceptualization and the pre-
ciseness of the reply, according to the general scoring criteria provided in the WAIS Manual. The abbreviation "Dk" is used for
"don't know" replies; "R" indicates that the stimulus was repeated.

Rorschach. The spontaneous associations and the responses
to inquiry are given for each of the ten Rorschach cards. The
examiner's questions appear in parentheses, and the notation "(?)"
indicates routine inquiry such as "What suggested that to you?" or
"How do you mean?" The Thought Disorder Index scores are
noted in boldface immediately following the response to which they
apply. In order to illustrate the similarities and differences between
the TDI and the communication deviance (CD) scoring systems,
CD scores are also given in boldface for cases 2, 5, and 6, with the
numbers indicating the specific score (see Table 2 for details of the
scoring code). Following the instructions of Singer (1972), only the
first responses to each card were scored for CD. The initial reaction
time in seconds is noted for each card. Location, determinants,
form level, content, and populars were scored according to
Rapaport, Gill, and Schafer (1968) and are indicated within parentheses at the end of the spontaneous association. At the end of
the Rorschach is a summary of the TDI scores (TD_R), the Rorschach scoring categories, and the CD scores (when obtained).
The abbreviation "S" is used to indicate "Subject" and "E" indicates
"Examiner;" "V" indicates card turning.

It may be of interest to the reader to examine the TDI scores
of this group of subjects and to note not only the differences
among the subjects but the changes in TDI score level after discharge (second testing) in Cases 1, 2, and 3. Table 25 contains a
summary of these scores.

These test protocols demonstrate that even in psychotic patients, as in Cases 1 and 2, a large portion of the patient's verbalizations is appropriate. Disordered thinking interrupts normal speech
in an erratic and unpredictable fashion. On retesting, instances of
thought disorder may occur on items that earlier did not result in
thought disorder, and conversely, on items where thought disorder
may have occurred on the earlier testing, it may be absent on the
retest. Such occurrences suggest that thought disorder is not necessarily a response to a specific meaningful stimulus.

Table 25. Summary of TD_W and TD_R Scores for Six Subjects. CD Scores for Case II and Her Mother (Case V) and Father (Case VI) are Also Included

Case Number	TD_W	TD_R	CD
I:			
Chronic Paranoid	5.25	31.94	
Schizophrenia	0.75[a]	8.82	
II:			
Schizoaffective	1.00	47.06	4.2
Psychosis	0.25[a]	11.67	
III:	2.25	6.97	
Manic Psychosis	1.00[a]	2.88	
IV:			
Neurotic Depression	0.50	6.11	
V:			
Mother of Case II	4.25	20.83	4.10
VI:			
Father of Case II	1.25	2.50	1.50

Note: The second level of numbers in each of the first three cases are from retests (8.82, for example).

[a]The second or follow-up testing included only selected verbal subtests of the WAIS. Therefore, the first TD_W score (based on the entire WAIS) is not directly comparable to the second TD_W.

Case 1:
Chronic Paranoid Schizophrenia

Historical Notes

    This patient was a 25-year-old single black man with a high school education who worked at unskilled jobs such as janitorial work. He had been hospitalized twice previously and his condition had been diagnosed first as catatonic schizophrenia and then as paranoid schizophrenia. His last hospitalization was two years before the current one. He was a very quiet man who spent most of his time alone. Several weeks prior to admission, his family noticed that he seemed increasingly confused and had become lost on the street, unable to find his apartment. At admission, he was slovenly dressed, moved very slowly, and spoke in monosyllables. On the

hospital ward, he was passive, generally withdrawn, and unrespon-
sive. At times he would smile and laugh inappropriately, apparently in response to his own preoccupations. He spent his time
reading nursery rhymes and children's poems. At the time of testing, three weeks after admission, his Health-Sickness Rating (HSR)
was 25, indicating severe disorganization.

The patient was hospitalized for seventy-four days on a
milieu treatment unit, and was administered trifluoperazine
(Stelazine). He gradually became more outgoing, began participating in group activities, and was described by staff as capable of
warmth and humor. At discharge, the clinical psychiatric diagnosis
was chronic undifferentiated schizophrenia. The psychological test
diagnosis was chronic paranoid schizophrenia.

The patient was contacted for follow-up three years and
four months later. He had had no intervening hospitalizations but
had continued out-patient contacts and medication. He had continued to work in janitorial services and had held his most recent
job for one year. He described himself as having a moderately
active social life, which included drinking and marijuana use.
There had been one period during which he had felt "low," but he
described no current psychotic symptoms as assessed through the
Present State Examination (Wing, Cooper, and Sartorius, 1972).

A year and a half after the follow-up testing (five years after
his discharge), the patient was readmitted to the hospital by the
police. He was actively paranoid, believing that people at work were
conspiring against him, that his thoughts were being broadcast to
others, and that he was in communication with God. He was agi-
tated, sleeping little, and had pressured speech. Increasing excitement, aggressiveness, and grandiosity led to his being committed to
the hospital, with a diagnosis of manic-depressive psychosis.

First Testing

This patient's TDI scores on the WAIS and the Rorschach
are both above the means for schizophrenic inpatients and indicate
significant disorganization of thinking. There is wide scatter within
the WAIS subtests and considerable intrusion of irrelevant, confused, and idiosyncratic responses, all indicative of severe disturbance. The apparent absence of symptomatic anxiety or concern
about the deviant aspects of his performance suggests long-

standing, chronic pathology. The examiner noted severe psychomotor retardation in his speech and motor behavior, as is reflected in the lowered WAIS performance IQ. His responses to the Rorschach represent poor form articulation, and many are absurd and dominated by perseverative, confabulatory sexual responses. Interpersonal aversion and social ineptness are prominent features of his behavior. The disorganization of thinking, poor reality testing, and deterioration of appropriate controls, all of which appear to be blandly accepted, suggest a chronic schizophrenic disturbance.

Second Testing

The retest three and a half years later shows a considerable tightening of controls and improvement of reality testing, reflected in several aspects of the tests: the WAIS subtest scores are elevated, with the Comprehension score having increased 6 points; TDI scores have declined; F+% on the Rorschach has risen from 40 to about 70; and the number of popular responses has increased. He continues to give perceptually inaccurate sexual responses, but is self-conscious and mildly embarrassed about them. Nevertheless, signs of potential disorganization remain in the confabulations, combinatory efforts, tendencies to associative looseness, and sexual preoccupation. The psychological diagnosis remains chronic schizophrenia, with prominent paranoid symptoms.

First Testing

Wechsler Adult Intelligence Scale

Information Subtest:

1.-3. (3 points credited)

4. (What is a thermometer?) (1)

5. (What does rubber come from?) (1)

6. (Name four men who have been presidents of the United States since 1900.)
Abraham Lincoln, John F. Kennedy, L. B. Johnson, Richard Nixon. (0) **[TDI Category: Tendency to confusion; Score: .25]**

7. (Longfellow was a famous man; what was he?)
Henry Wadsworth Longfellow? He was a great poet. (1)

8. (How many weeks are there in a year?) (1)

9. (In what direction would you travel if you went from Chicago to Panama?) (1)

10. (Where is Brazil?)
That's in Asia or Africa? (0)

11. (How tall is the average American woman?) (1)

12. (What is the capital of Italy?) (1)

13. (Why are dark clothes warmer than light-colored clothes?)
Because, I think I ought to skip that one. (?) Because they're dark. (?) I really don't know, it's just a guess. (0)

14. (When is Washington's birthday?)
Twenty-second of January. (0)

15. (Who wrote Hamlet?) (1)

16. (What is the Vatican?)
The Nevatican? (Have you heard of the Vatican before?) I heard of Nevada (0)

17. (How far is it from Paris to New York?)
New York, and Paris is in France. (Take a guess?) I would say about 10,000 miles. (0)

18. (Where is Egypt?)
Egypt is in, let's see, the Pharoahs, pyramids, that's all I know about Egypt. **[TDI Category: Inappropriate Distance; Score: .25]** (What continent?) Eastern hemisphere. (0)

19. (How does yeast cause dough to rise?)
By rising, and it gets damp. (?) It rises when you first mix it, then it rises again when you bake it in the oven. (0)

20. (What is the population of the United States?)
About 50 million people. (0—Five consecutive failures is the cut-off point for this subtest.)

21. (How many senators are there in the United States Senate?)
Two from each state, that would make 104. (0)

22. (What is the main theme of the Book of Genesis?)
In the beginning was the Word and the Word was God and the Word was with God and the earth was void and darkness was upon the face of the earth and God speaking with his face said,

"Let there be Light" and there was light. [**TDI Category: Inappropriate Distance; Score: .25**] (?) It's the Holy Spirit. And he saw that the light was good and then He said, "Let there be light" and the darkness separated, and the light He called day, and the darkness He called night. And he separated the bodies of water. (Can you tell me the theme in short form?) In six days God created the heavens and the earth and on the seventh day he rested. (0—Correct, but past cut-off.)

23. (At what temperature does water boil?) (0—Correct, but past cut-off.)

24. (Who wrote the Iliad?) Dk (0)

25. (Name three kinds of blood vessels in the human body.) Red corpuscles, the white corpuscles, and hemoglobin.(0)

26. (What is the Koran?) Like the Korean war? (0)

27. (Who wrote Faust?) Dk (0)

28. (What is ethnology?) Dk (0)

29. (What is the Apocrypha?) Is that the emancipation and the proclamation? (0) [**TDI Category: Absurd; Score: .75**]

Raw Score: 11

Comprehension:

1.-2. (4 points credited)

3. (What is the thing to do if you find an envelope in the street that is sealed, and addressed, and has a new stamp?) Drop it in the mail. (2)

4. (Why should we keep away from bad company?) Cause it's bad influence. (?) Well, some people like to always fuss and fight and hang around in the wrong places and somebody might get hurt.(2)

5. (What should you do if while in the movies you were the first person to see smoke and fire?) If the management don't see it first? I'd yell (laughs). I would try to be calm while I be making my way to the door. (0)

6. (Why should people pay taxes?)
   I think that they're necessary and useful. (?) Some people, like myself, that not working. (?) It's like myself, I don't feel comfortable, you know, depending upon my family to support me. (0)

7. (What does this saying mean? "Strike while the iron is hot.")
   That means—hit and run. (?) That means that if you hit a person, you shouldn't hang around cause someone might walk up and hit you. Strike in and strike out. (0) **[TDI Category: Loose; Score: .5]**

8. (Why are child labor laws needed?)
   They mean that high school students should be able to have part-time jobs after school and on weekends. (?) To keep them healthy, just to protect them. (1)

9. (If you were lost in the forest in the daytime, how would you go about finding your way out?)
   By looking for the sun. We know that the sun rises in the east and sets in the west. (2)

10. (Why are people who are born deaf usually unable to talk?)
    Deaf mutes? (?) 'Cause some kind of birth defects. (0)

11. (Why does land in the city cost more than land in the country?)
    Because of city taxes and the big, you know, there's more convenience, it's quieter in the country but it's more of a rush in the city. Rush, rush, rush. **[TDI Category: Inappropriate Distance; Score: .25]** (?) Cause of the tall buildings and, you mean a vacant lot? (Could you say more?) That's about it. (1)

12. (Why does the state require people to get a license in order to be married?)
    Because there's a danger that blood might not mix. (?) They could want, the other could have a venereal disease. (0)

13. (What does this saying mean? "Shallow brooks are noisy.")
    To me it means an empty wagon makes a lot of noise. (0)

14. (What does this saying mean? "One swallow doesn't make a summer.")
    It means a somersault, you know, if you turn a flip, or a som-

ersault. **[TDI Category: Clang; Score: .25]** (E repeats question.) That one's a burden, something of a burden to me. We'd better skip that one. (0)

Raw Score: 12

Similarities:

1. (How are an orange and a banana alike?)
   'Cause they're both fruit.(2)

2. (Coat–hat) They're a suit. (?) They're both clothing. (2)

3. (Axe–saw) They both cut. (1)

4. (Dog–lion) They're both animals. (2)

5. (North–west) They're both directions. (2)

6. (Eye–ear) They're both organs. (1)

7. (Air–water) They're both material, like. (?) They both contain oxygen. (1)

8. (Table–chair) One fits with the other. (?) They both have four legs. (0)

9. (Egg-seed) They both produce life. (2)

10. (Poem–statue) They're both, a statue is poetry, but it's not in motion. (?) Well, we have some beautiful statues, anything beautiful, I'd call it poetry, so when you speak of a poem, you put action and feeling to it. So I say a poem lives. (0) **[TDI Category: Autistic Logic; Score: .75]**

11. (Wood–alcohol) Alcohol and what? They're both, you mean, at first, they tell me where alcohol comes from. (E repeats question.) Because alcohol is in the furniture or the paint. **[TDI Category: Peculiar; Score: .25]** (?) Lead or gas, don't they come close to alcohol? (0)

12. (Praise–punishment) Because they both have feelings, they sort of like a prefix and a suffix. **[TDI Category: Tendency to looseness; Score: .25]** Praise is like glorifying a person, punishment is a bawling out. (?) They both have feelings, they're opposite, but they're— (0)

13. (Fly–tree) They both live in the air. They come down. The tree is rooted in the soil and the fly lights down but he mostly lives in a tree. [**TDI Category: Inappropriate Distance; Score: .25**] (?) A fly flies up but he comes down to the earth, so I wouldn't know exactly how they're alike. (0)

Raw Score: 13

Picture Completion:

 1. Knob: (1)
 2. Tail: I would say tits. (What is the most important thing missing?) Tail is missing. (1)
 3. Nose: (1)
 4. Handles: (1)
 5. Diamond: (1)
 6. Water: (1)
 7. Nose piece: Shoulders are missing. (?) Sideburns. (0)
 8. Peg: There's a key missing and the bow. (Most important?) Bow. (0)
 9. Oar lock: The slot that holds it. (1)
10. Base thread: (1)
11. Stars: The flag pole is missing. (0)
12. Dog tracks: The left leg is missing. (0)
13. Florida: That's a map of the U.S., but the outline of the different states is missing, the different parts. (0)
14. Smokestacks: The sail is missing. (0)
15. Leg: One of the tentacles [**Black English, not scored**] is missing, or whatever you call it. (1)
16. Arm image: (1)
17. Finger: There I would say the toe of the shoe. (0)
18. Shadow: The grass is missing on the street that he's walking on. (0)
19. Stirrup: The horn, the stirrup? (Most important?) The stirrup. (1)

20. Snow: Dk (0)
21. Eyebrow: The shoulder I would say. (0)

Raw Score: 11

Vocabulary:

1.-3. (6 points credited)

4. Winter: That's a season of the year that begins in December, and it's always mostly cold and raining. Next word? (2)

5. Repair: To repair means to fix, mend. (2)

6. Breakfast: That means the first meal in the morning. (2)

7. Fabric: That means, a garment, a material, texture of the material. (1) **[TDI Category: Peculiar; Score: .25]**

8. Slice: To cut, split into sections, in half or quarter. (1)

9. Assemble: Means to place together or to build or work a puzzle such as a jigsaw. (2)

10. Conceal: Something that is hidden from the public. Like, you know, conceal a weapon in your pocket. (2)

11. Enormous: Something that is strange, something that is odd, I would say. (0)

12. Hasten: Means to, to get in a hurry or to run for shelter or . . . (1)

13. Sentence: Is a group of words forming paragraphs. (1)

14. Regulate: To gauge or to judge, to set. (?) Like, for instance, if you regulate the flow of water you either turn the tap open all the way, or you turn it halfway. (1)

15. Commence: Means to begin. (2)

16. Ponder: I think that means to, to tangle with someone or to meddle in something, doesn't it? (0)

17. Cavern: Is it like a house or an inn? (0)

18. Designate: Something that's specific such as a radio or TV station output of watts or kilowatts. (?) That they are allowed to operate on only a certain amount of frequency. (0)

19. Domestic: Like an animal, for instance, a horse or a mule that does labor. (1)

20. Consume: Means to use, person that eat food is a consumer. (2)

21. Terminate: Means to fire, or to, you know, from a job. (1)

22. Obstruct: Means to tear down, such as a building or if you, if I wanted to see, you know, over these buildings would obstruct my view. (?) If I wanted to see the wall back here, this wall would be obstructing my view. (How do you mean, tear down?) Well, for instance, what would they call them? The thing that sling the ball that tear down buildings? Isn't that obstruct? (0) **[TDI Category: Confusion; Score: .5]**

23. Remorse: I would have to guess on that one and say that it would mean re-wet something, re-dampen something. (0) **[TDI Category: Clang; Score: .25]** [Remorse = remoist = re-wet.]

24. Sanctuary: A place for birds like in a park where the birds are forbidden to be killed by law. (2)

25. Matchless: Something odd, without a mate. (0)

26. Reluctant: Means that you are, that a person is, struggling about doing something, or that a person regret doing something. (0)

27. Calamity: Means (laughs) something cold and damp. (?) A calamity, calamity, I was thinking of clammy. **[TDI Category: Clang; Not scored on Vocabulary when subject is guessing]** Excuse me, a calamity would be something wild or untamed, I would say. (0)

28. Fortitude: I would think that fortitude means being ungrateful. (0)

29. Tranquil: I would say that that means something like you write with. (0) **[TDI Category: Clang; No score]**

30. Edifice: I would, I wouldn't know, I would guess that has something to do with writing, too. (0)

31. Compassion: That's a feeling, a strong feeling towards something, such as love or hate. (0)

Raw Score: 29

Summary of WAIS Scores:

Verbal IQ: 90	Similarities: 10
Performance IQ: 77	Vocabulary: 8
Full-scale IQ: 84	Picture Completion: 8
$TD_W = 5.0$	Digit Symbol: 3
Information: 8	Picture Arrangement: 7
Comprehension: 7	Block Design: 5
Digit Span: 10	Object Assembly: 9
Arithmetic: 8	

Rorschach Test

Card I (Reaction Time 38 seconds):

1. Looks like a termite. (D F− Ad) **[TDI Category: Absurd; Score: .75]** (?) The whole card looks like a termite's head. The head part. (?) It looks like a bug that I seen on an insecticide can. (Could you show me that?) It looked like a dog and it looked like a cat. (The same part?) Yes. The whole—and it even looked like a cow. **[Fluid; .75]**

2. Looks like a mask. (Ws F± Mask) (?) This would look like the part where you would hold it to your face. It would be like a masquerade—for instance, if you disguised as a cow or something.

Card II (52 seconds):

(S is laughing to himself. E: What's funny?) Nothing's funny.

3. This looks like a couple making love. (W FC′ − Sx) **[TDI Category: Confabulation; Score: .75]** (?) This looks like a vagina and this looks like a penis. There was some red that looked like hair. (Hair?) I guess the color, because it was dark. (Anything else made it look like a vagina?) No, just the way it looked. The a, the split. (S looking around. E: Are you looking for something in particular?) No.

Card III (120 seconds):

4. (S smiles then looks away. E: What does it look like?) This looks like two little lambs, or sheep. (D FC′± A) (Anything else?) No,

that's all I can see on this one. (?) This looks like the head and
these look like hooves or feet. (Sheep?) Well, because it was
black and it looked furry. (Furry?) Like where the lines are
uneven about the nose.

Card IV (90 seconds):

5. (What does it look like?)
   This looks like a vagina. (W F— Sx) (A what?) Vagina, too. (Any-
   thing else?) Well, it looks like a penis being inserted. (Is that
   all?) (Subject is smiling.) These, look like pieces of rubber.
   That's all I can make of that. (Rubber like on a penis?) Yes.
   [TDI Category: Confabulation; Score: .75] (Vagina?) Looked
   like the clitorius [Peculiar; Not scored—Black English]
   (S had trouble locating this percept.)

Card V (50 seconds):

6. This looks like the same thing, only closed this time. (W F— Sx)
   [TDI Category: Perseveration; Score: .25] (What did you
   say?) It seems to be closed this time, looks like. (What do you
   mean, the same thing?) Well, it looked like a, maybe a pork
   steak. [Tendency to Absurd; .5] (?) I guess maybe because of
   the shape of it. Here looks like bones. Yeah. That's all I can
   make out of that one. (Additional: W F— Fd) (But you also
   thought it looked like a vagina?) Well, two lips on either side.

7. (Anything else?)
   Looks like a butterfly. (W F+ A P)
   (That all?) Yes.

Card VI (110 seconds):

8. (What does it look like?)
   This looks like a male's, this looks like the head of a penis.
   (D F+ Sx)
   (Anything else?)

9. This looks like a zipper. (Dr F(C)— Cg)
   (What did you say this looks like?) It looked like a cord. A cord
   like a spinal cord. (Additional: D F+ At)

(Did you say zipper before?) Yes, I'm supposed to say whatever I see, aren't I?

10. This looks like—the testes and this looks like the bag. (Dr F− Sx) (?) Yes. The skin that covers them.

Card VII (140 seconds):

11. (What does this look like?)
    These look like lambs or bunnies. (D F+ Ad) Here, this looks like the hind leg. Here and here. (?) This is the face. This is where the face end up at. Looks more like a smoke signal or something like that. (Additional: D ChF Smoke) It starts down here, that's all I can make out of that one. (Smoke?) No, just because it was hazy or cloudy. (Do the bunnies have ears?) They have teeth.

12. (Anything else?) No, except that it looks — no, I guess not. (What?) Looks like a bra. (W F− Cg,Sx) (Smiles.) These look like tit nipples. And I guess these would be the straps that go over the shoulders. These would be underarm, armpit. (?) This would look like where the clasp hook . . .

13. This looks like a, a girdle. (S F− Cg) **[TDI Category: Absurd; Score: .75]** That's all I can make of that one. (How much of it is the girdle?) (S cannot locate.) I would say just this part here, the white part.

Card VIII (45 seconds):

14. This looks like a—chicken back. (W F− Fd)
    (What did you say?) A piece of chicken such as the back or the breast.
    (?) The whole thing, these look like the bones or the vertebrae.
    (?) 'Cause of the way that it was shaped.

Card IX (110 seconds):

15. This looks like—a kitten. (W F− A) **[TDI Category: Confabulation; Score: .75]** (A what?) Looks like a kitten, shaped like a kitten. (?) It looks like a kitten with a bow tie on—this would be the kitten's ears. This would be the little— (What?) It would

look like a Siamese cat— (?) Because of their outward, you
know, what do you call them that stick out from the cat's nose?
[Word-finding Difficulty; .25] (Whiskers?) Yeah, the little
whiskers. (Where?) They would be about here and here.
(E notes that S responded as if making up parts during the
inquiry.)

16. (Anything else?) It looks like a—vagina and a penis. (W F— Sx)
[TDI Category: Perseveration; Score: .25] This looks like the
penis. This looks like a pelvis. This looks like the testes. (Is that
all? Do you see anything else?) I don't—you mind if I smoke?
(Are you done?) I'm done with that.

Card X (185 seconds):

17. (What do you see there?) This top part looks like a whistle.
(Dd F+ Obj)

18. (Anything else?) No, except that it looks like—looks like sea
food. (D F+ A,Fd) (What kind of sea food?) Like crabs, lobster,
shrimp. (?) This part looks like the head of a crayfish. (And
where is the crab?) (S looks for a long time.) That would be—
that—here, I think.

Summary of Rorschach Scores:

Number of responses (R) = 18 + 3   Populars (P) = 1

$$TD_R = \frac{5.75}{18} \times 100 = 31.94$$

Location:	Deter-minants:	Content:			
Ws 1	FC′ 2	A 4	F% = 83/100	Perseveration	2
W 8 + 1	F(C) 1	Ad 2	F+% = 40/39	Word-finding	1
D 5 + 2	ChF + 1	At + 1	EB = 0/0	difficulty	
Dd 1	F 15 + 2	Cg 3 + 1		Tend.Absurd	1
Dr 2		Fd 1 + 1		Confabulation	3
S 1		Obj 1		Absurd	2
		Smo + 1		Fluid	1
		Sx 6			
		Mask 1			

Follow-up Testing (3 years, 4 months later)

Wechsler Adult Intelligence Scale

Information:

1-4. (4 points credited)
5. Rubber: (1)
6. Presidents: (1)
7. Longfellow: (1)
8. Weeks: (1)
9. Panama: Southwest. (1)
10. Brazil: (1)
11. Height: 5'2". (0)
12. Italy: (1)
13. Clothes: Because the light don't get through as good. (0)
14. Washington: (1)
15. Hamlet: (1)
16. Vatican: I never heard of that. (0)
17. Paris: 4,000 mi. (1)
18. Egypt: Israel. (0)
19. Yeast: By, release little stuff that swells it up. (1)
20. Population: I would say 2 billion. (0)
21. Senators: (1)
22. Genesis: First book, the creation of heaven and earth. (1)
23. Iliad: Dk (0)
24. Temperature: (1)
25. Blood vessels: Vessels, you mean, arteries be one? Different kind of artery, main artery, how many have I named? I'll say red corpuscles and white corpuscles (laughs). (0)
26. Koran: Dk (0)
27. Faust: DK (0)

28. Ethnology: Sounds familiar. (0)
29. Apocrypha: Dk (0)

Raw Score: 18

Comprehension:

1-2. (4 points credited)

 3. Envelope: Drop it in the nearest mailbox. (2)

 4. Bad company: Because it'll make us bad too. (?) Some of
    the badness of the bad company will rub off on you sooner or
    later. (2)

 5. Movies: I know you shouldn't yell fire. You should go to the
    nearest exit and report it to the manager of the theater, I'd
    say. (2)

 6. Taxes: That's something I've been wondering about for 28
    years. To support the government, is that good enough? (2)

 7. Iron: That means—don't beat around the bush. It means
    whatever you have to do, do it while you have a chance. (2)

 8. Child labor: Because some people work a kid pretty hard and
    won't pay him anything. They think he don't know any bet-
    ter. (2)

 9. Forest: I would go by the sun. I know it rises in the east and sets
    in the west, I would think of what time of day it should be and I
    would know my directions. (2)

10. Deaf: Cause they never hear any words spoken so they don't
    know anything to say. They just see your mouth move, but they
    don't hear anything. (2)

11. City land: Because there's more people in the city and the land
    would profit you more. (1)

12. Marriage: That's so you would know which woman belonged
    to which man, without any question about it. (0) **[TDI Cate-
    gory: Inappropriate Distance; Score: .25]**

13. Brooks: That means, the water is low and there's bound to be a
    lot of frogs and things. (0)

14. Swallow: That's a bird, right? I have to pass that one. (0)

Raw Score: 21

Similarities:

1. Orange: Fruit. (2)
2. Coat: Item of clothing. (2)
3. Axe: Both cut wood, both cut. (1)
4. Dog: Both animals. (2)
5. North: Directions. (2)
6. Eye: Organs, human organs, any kind of organs. (1)
7. Air: Both contain oxygen, I guess that's right. (1)
8. Table: Furniture. (2)
9. Egg: Both reproduce, you know what I mean. (?) The egg would reproduce a baby chicken and the seed would reproduce whatever plant it's from. (2)
10. Poem: Let's see, that I don't know. (0)
11. Wood: Alcohol comes from wood. (0)
12. Praise: I don't see how they're alike—one is scolding and one is praising. (0)
13. Fly: I got to tell how they're alike, not how they're different? That one I have to pass up (0)

Raw Score: 15

Vocabulary:

1-3. (6 points credited)
4. Winter: A season of the year that is most time cold. I would say colder than other parts of the year. (2)
5. Repair: To mend or fix. (2)
6. Breakfast: The first meal of the day. (2)
7. Fabric: I know it's sort of like a, cloth, texture. (Texture?) A fabric can be a cloth or plastic, or whatever. **[TDI Category: Peculiar; Score: .25]** (2)
8. Slice: To cut into pieces. (1)
9. Assemble: To arrange. (?) Arrange things in order. (2)
10. Conceal: To hide. (2)

11. Enormous: It's sensitive. (?) A enormous song, a sensitive song. (0)

12. Hasten: To hurry. (2)

13. Sentence: Two different meaning, you mean like a judge sentence or—(Either.) I'd rather say a group of words making a—well, it's a group of words written or spoken, that's what I'd say. (1)

14. Regulate: Means to, to govern or to allow so much. (2)

15. Commence: To begin. (2)

16. Ponder: I did hear that one but I, I don't really remember what it means. (0)

17. Cavern: That's a cave. (2)

18. Designate: Let's see, designate a hitter. (?) It means he's in the game but he hits only, he don't play a position in the field. (0)

19. Domestic: Domestic power, I don't know what that means. That means, like what I'm doing, I do domestic work. (?) Manual labor. (0)

20. Consume: To use up. (2)

21. Terminate: To fire, to expel. (1)

22. Obstruct: Obstructing justice, that means—doing something that you're not permitted to do. (0)

23. Remorse: I don't really remember that one. (0)

24. Sanctuary: I know it's a home for birds. (1)

25. Matchless: If I didn't have any matches in this book (laughs as lights cigarette). (0)

26. Reluctant: I just want to say this, you know it pays to watch television? Because I watched the Reluctant Dragon. [TDI Category: Inappropriate Distance; Score: .25] That means, I don't know what it means (laughs). (0)

27. Calamity: Is that a word, a form of clam, calam? Calam means like cold and lifeless, I guess calamity mean the same thing. Get to some easy ones (laughs). (0) [TDI Category: Clang; Not Scored]

28. Fortitude: Fortitude, forfeit, fortitude. I'd say it means that you're ungrateful, I know it's not right. (0)

29. Tranquil: Tranquil, tranquilizer, that means something that's neutral. (0)

30. Edifice: That one's for college boys, I don't know that one. (0)

31. Compassion: That means that you have a feeling, compassion is a feeling. (?) A warm feeling. (0)

Raw Score: 32

Summary of WAIS Scores:

Prorated Verbal IQ: 105   TD$_W$: 0.75   Information: 11
Comprehension: 13   Similarities: 11   Vocabulary: 9

Rorschach Test

Card I (Reaction Time: 38 seconds):

1. Looks like three bees, three honey bees. (W F± A) (?) I seen then, uh, the middle, emblem, **[TDI Category: Peculiar; No score, black English]** looked like a bee's head and the two outside ones looked like wings, but it looked like more than one bee, so that's why I said three. (?) See this looks like the body and it comes in to your neck and this looks like it could be the head, this looks like the little tentacles.

2. Could be a butterfly or a bat. (W F+ A P) (?) The whole thing, the butterfly spread out. (Bat?) Well, the way the wings drooped.

Card II (33 seconds):

3. Oh boy, I know what I said the last time, and it don't look any different to me. (OK) Well, I won't—but it looked like a vagina to me. (W F− Sx) That's it. (?) Should I show you? See these little lips down here? That looks like, mm, what do you call the lips, the clitorius or whatever? This is like the hair.

Card III (10 seconds):

4. Now this looks like the male's organs. (W F− Sx) This is the, testacles, whatever you call it, test−, and, this is the shaft. That looks incompleted, it should have came on down, you know? And this is the [unclear]. (The what? I didn't hear what you said). This was the hair, I said.

Card IV (8 seconds):

5. Oh, that's like a combination of the two (laughs). (D F± Sx)
   [TDI Category: Tendency to Confabulation; Score: .5] This
   looks like the lips, the clitorius, this looks like the slit.

6. And this looks like a penis again, down here. (D F− Sx) I guess
   I got a one-track mind. **[TDI Category: Perseveration;
   Score: .25]** I never change, they always look like that to me.
   (What do you mean when you say it's like a combination of the
   two?) Well, looks like this top half looks like the lady, and this
   bottom half looks like the man. You should draw a line in
   through here, the top half and the bottom half. (How do you
   explain the fact that they're both there?) I don't know, it just
   looked that way.

Card V (5 seconds):

7. Oh, this is like a butterfly. (W F+ A P) Yep. This looks like the
   head, this is like the wings, and this is like the back part of him.

Card VI (30 seconds):

8. I would say this looks like a flower, from this way. (D F± Bt) (?)
   Well, because the stem was so straight, this is the stem (V). And
   this part down here looks like a little flower, and the top part
   looks it, after growth, **[TDI Category: Peculiar; Score: .25]**
   you know? (The top part looks like what?) Looks like a, well a
   grown flower, a flower after growth, and this looks like a little
   baby flower, here. (Do you mean like, the tip looks more
   open?) Yeah.

9. A leaf. (D F± Bt) I'd say it looks like a flower or an oak leaf. (?)
   Just the shape of it, the top part looks like an oak leaf.

Card VII (20 seconds):

10. This looks like two kids in a stare-down contest. (W M+ H P)
    This is one kid here, like here, and this looks like a rock or
    something that they're standing on. (In a stare-down contest?)
    Yeah. They're standing face to face, looking at each other.
    (Rock?) Oh, it just looked like a solid foundation, this part
    down here, and it looked like they're getting into mischief, and

climbing up there and they're staring at each other. This is his eye, this is his eye, you know. Or it could have been two Indians, see it looks like they got feathers, sticking out.

Card VIII (27 seconds):

11. This looks like a combination of things. This part in here, all this in here, looks like a pirate skeleton. (D F− At) **[TDI Category: Fabulized Combination; Score: .5]** (?) Well, you see how this here might be a shoulders, and the, uh, bottom part, the torso, and it, what made me say a pirate skeleton 'stead of just a skeleton, it looked like the hat is shaped like a pirate's hat.

12. And these two here look like wolverines. (D F+ A P) Or some sort of a rodent, like a rat. How'm I doing? Maybe one day somebody will tell me what they *really* are.

Card IX (23 seconds):

13. That's the liberty bell. V (W F± Bell) (A what?) A liberty bell. (A liberty bear?) A bell, a bell. Liberty bell. This part could be the part that holds it up. This should be filled out a little more, it's in the shape of a bell, and this would be the clapper here, this white part.

Card X (35 seconds):

14. Now I see uh, two crayfish. (D F+ A)

15. Two grasshoppers.
    (D FC+ A) (?) The color green and they looked like a grasshopper perched on a limb or a weed, I might say. And this looked like, here's the antenna.

16. A wishbone. (D F± At)

17. They sort of favor a octopus, these two. (D F± A) That's about everything.

Summary of Rorschach Scores:

R = 17   P = 4 $TD_R = \dfrac{1.5}{17} \times 100 = 8.82$
            Deter-

Location:	minants:	Content:			
W	7	FC	1	H	1	F% = 88/100	Perseveration	1

D	10	M	1	A	7	F+%	= 67/71	Peculiar	1
		F	15	At	2	EB	= 1/0.5	Fabulized Comb.	1
				Bt	2			Tend. Confab.	1
				Sx	4				
				Bell	1				

Case 2:
Schizoaffective Psychosis

Historical Notes

The patient, a 21-year-old college sophomore, was admitted to the hospital in a state of anxiety and tearfulness, complaining that her mind was a void and that she was unable to concentrate. She had had two prior hospitalizations and had not really recovered from the more recent one a year earlier. The patient had long-standing difficulties in social relationships, for which psychiatric assistance had been sought at age eleven. Despite attempts to attend college out of state, she had returned to live with her family.

On the milieu treatment unit, the patient was very demanding and needy; she felt frightened and suspicious. She was tested ten days after admission while she was showing some hypomanic symptoms, such as hyperactivity, inappropriate giggling, and incessant talking. Her Health-Sickness Rating was 29. She was treated with lithium carbonate and trifluoperazine (Stelazine). Soon after she was tested, she became actively confused and delusional and experienced auditory, visual, and tactile hallucinations. This episode may, however, have been a reaction to lithium toxicity; when lithium levels were reduced, she improved. She was hospitalized for a total of eighty-nine days and was discharged with a clinical psychiatric diagnosis of chronic paranoid schizophrenia. The psychological test diagnosis was schizoaffective psychosis.

When followed up three years later, the patient was living with her family and had completed college but had not obtained a job. She was continuing in outpatient treatment with medication of lithium and Stelazine. Though she had not been rehospitalized, she had experienced several periods of acute distress, during which she felt great anxiety that people were against her. Her condition was now diagnosed as manic-depressive. Her therapist described her as continuing to be irritable, having poor relationships with people, being overly suspicious but not delusional, and talking excitably and sometimes tangentially. On the Present State Examination, she described herself as continuing to have symptoms that disturbed her: difficulty with concentration and memory; paranoid symptoms including ideas of reference and persecution; feelings of self-depreciation; and concern that she was in some way damaged internally. She stated that she needed to be on lithium or else she would get "too high" or too depressed.

First Testing

At first testing, this patient shows significant disorganization of thinking on the Rorschach (TD_R is above the mean for schizophrenic inpatients) but manages to contain this disorganization on the WAIS. There is, however, wide variability among her scores on the WAIS, and she appears to have great difficulty in focusing on the task, often giving responses that are vague, spoiled, or only approximately correct. On the Rorschach, there are many indications of confusion and impaired reasoning, with autistic logic, idiosyncratic symbolism, and confabulations that are psychotic in degree and schizophrenic in quality. This patient also shows evidence of a significant affective component—she is verbose, impatient, impulsive, and flighty. Her use of denial as a defense against aggressive urges and depressive ideas is unstable, so that although there are a few early pleasant responses, there is increasing emergence of themes of death, deterioration, and destruction. Her affects are poorly modulated (note her anxiety and failure to respond to Card II, and her difficulty with color).

Second Testing

On retesting, the patient is more articulate and precise and less prone to confusion and disorganization. There are, however, still instances of autistic logic, arbitrariness, and depressive preoccupations. A diagnosis of schizoaffective psychosis seems most appropriate.

First Testing

Wechsler Adult Intelligence Scale

Information Subtest:

1-4. (4 points credited)

5. Rubber: (1)

6. Presidents: Kennedy, Johnson, Garfield, Nixon. (0)

7. Longfellow: (1)

8. Weeks: (1)

9. Panama: (1)

10. Brazil: (1)

11. Height: (1)

12. Italy: (1)

13. Clothes: Dark-colored clothes absorb light. (1)

14. Washington: (1)

15. Hamlet: (1)

16. Vatican: It's in Rome. It's the, a Vatican, is the a, what is the Vatican? That's all I can say. (What's it for?) It's for the religion and politics— **[TDI Category: Vague; Score: .25]** (What religion?) Roman Catholic. (0–1)

17. Paris: Dk, 5,000 miles? (0)

18. Egypt: (1)

19. Yeast: Bubbles, gas bubbles. (Say more?) No, not now. (1)

20. Population: Dk, three million? (0)

21. Senators: 100? (1)

22. Genesis: Dk (?) It's in the Bible. (0)

23. Temperature: 32° it freezes, I don't know when it boils, I forgot. (0)

24. Iliad: (1)

25. Blood Vessels: (1)

26. Koran: It's something to do with India—religion, I don't know. I'm being very vague, I can't help it. (0)

27. Faust: Shakespeare? I don't know. (0)
28. Ethnology: Study of, I forgot. I used to take anthropology, but I forgot ethnology. (0)
29. Apocrypha: Hippocrapha? (R) I forgot that too. (0)

Raw Score: 19–20

Comprehension:

1-2. (4 points credited)

3. Envelope: I'd mail it. (2)
4. Bad company: I don't know. It just makes us feel bad. That's a stupid answer. (0)
5. Movies: I would go tell the manager. (2)
6. Taxes: To support the things that go in the city. (1)
7. Iron: Do something at the right time, I don't know. (2)
8. Child labor: So that children won't be abused. (?) They might have to work too long, long hard hours. (1)
9. Forest: Follow the sun. (?) It would help with directions. (1)
10. Deaf: I had that one before, too. (?) I had these. I answered them much better at that time too. It's because they can't imitate speech, they can't hear it. (2)
11. City land: Dk (?) Not now. (0)
12. Marriage: Dk (?) Can't think of it, just can't think of it. (0)
13. Brooks: Can't think of that either. (0)

Raw Score: 15

Picture Completion:

1. Knob: (1)
2. Tail: (1)
3. Nose: (1)
4. Handles: (1)
5. Diamond: (1)
6. Water: (1)

7. Nosepiece: The glasses are missing the rim. (?) That thing across, the bridge, at the nose. (1)

8. Peg: The eighth one, the violin is missing the bow. (0)

9. Oarlock: The ninth one, the boat is missing the other thing that holds on the oar. (1)

10. Base thread: And the tenth one, the light bulb might be missing a filament. (0)

11. Stars: The flag is missing the, what do you call that thing, the bottom part of the flag? Staff? I can't think of it. (0) **[TDI Category: Word-finding Difficulty; Score: .25]**

12. Dog tracks: The twelfth one, the man's leg or the footprint. (More important?) Both, it doesn't show the leg with the footprint in the snow. (0-1)

13. Florida: (1)

14. Smokestacks: The fourteenth one, the windows, I think those are, portholes on the ship, aren't they? (0)

15. Leg: (1)

16. Arm reflection: The sixteenth one, the lady's missing an arm. (0)

17. Finger: (1)

18. Shadow: The eighteenth one, the man looks like he's walking towards somewhere. I don't know. (?) He's got his hand in his pocket. A sidewalk missing? I don't know. (0)

19. Stirrup: Nineteen, the horse is missing a bridle? No, I'm not sure. (?) Something goes there (points correctly), I don't know what it is. (0)

20. Snow: Twenty—something wrong with the fence around the barn. (0)

21. Eyebrow: Twenty-one—I don't know what she's missing. (0)

Raw Score: 11

Vocabulary:

1-3. (6 points credited)

4. Winter: Season. (?) Cold season. (2)

5. Repair: Fix. (2)

6. Breakfast: Time of day in the morning when you eat. (2)
7. Fabric: Material. (1)
8. Slice: Piece. (1)
9. Assemble: Put together. (2)
10. Conceal: Hide. (2)
11. Enormous: Big, tremendous. (2)
12. Sentence: Group of words put together to have a meaning, convey meaning. (1)
13. Hasten: Speed up. (2)
14. Regulate: Adjust. (2)
15. Commence: Begin. (2)
16. Ponder: Think about. (2)
17. Cavern: Something in a cave, I think. (?) I don't know, I can't remember. (1)
18. Designate: Point to or point out. (2)
19. Domestic: Somebody that's domestic or, domestic is, is something with the household, or like a home, domestic, or uh, I think it comes from like Latin, uh, or like in French—dwelling maybe. (2)
20. Consume: Eat, eat up. (2)
21. Terminate: End. (2)
22. Obstruct: Be in the way of. (2)
23. Remorse: To regret. (2)
24. Sanctuary: A place for uh, safety. (2)
25. Matchless. Unequal, unequaled by, uncomparable, incomparable. (2)
26. Reluctant: Reluctant, somebody that's reluctant, I can't (whispers), hesitant. (2)
27. Calamity: Chaotic event—calamity. (0)
28. Fortitude: Strength. (2)
29. Tranquil: Quietude. (2)
30. Edifice: Edifice is a building structure. (2)
31. Compassion: To have feeling for. (?) Uh, empathy. (2)

32. Tangible: Tangible is something that, is, is live—something, tangible is something that can be touched, that has feeling, that is animated. (0-2)

33. Perimeter: The distance around. (2)

34. Audacious: Bold. (2)

35. Ominous: Threatening. (2)

36. Tirade: Dk (0)

37. Encumber: Dk (0)

38. Plagiarize: Something that's plagiarized is stolen from—uh, plagiarism is to steal from an original, to imitate something that is not one's own. (1)

39. Impale: Dk (0)

40. Travesty: I don't remember. I looked it up. I think travesty is—something to do with, vest? Uh, I'm thinking of relationships with Latin and French. Uh, vesture, something like, something to do with dress I think, like transvestite, relate to, could be related to that. **[TDI Category: Inappropriate Distance (tend. to looseness); Score: .25]** I don't know exactly what it means. (0)

Raw Score: 63–65

Summary of WAIS Scores:

Verbal IQ: 106	Similarities: 9
Performance IQ: 89	Vocabulary: 14
Full Scale IQ: 99	Picture Completion: 8
$TD_W = .75$	Picture Arrangement: 6
Information: 12	Block Design: 10
Comprehension: 9	Object Assembly: 10
Arithmetic: 6	Digit Symbol: 8
Digit Span: 16	

Rorschach Test

Card I (Reaction Time: 5 seconds):

1. OK, it looks like, um, angels. (W M+ (H))

2. Or a butterfly. (W F+ A P) (?) Butterfly, see, it could be like a

butterfly, because that's now the butterfly's wings (thumps on picture).

1. Like twin angels. (?) Uh, it's got, well, like, I just said the first thing off the top of my head **[CD: 110, 196, 312]** but, it's got, uh, they're just, it could be like two little heads there, you know, and they're like flapping their wings—could be Siamese angels, because they're not separated (laughs). **[TDI Category: Fabulized Combination; Score: .5]** (Can you show me where the twin angels are?) Well, see like what I'm doing, I'm just doing a stream of consciousness, I'm just like naming off things very spontaneously, and not really thinking very deeply about it. And a— (Can you just show me where it is?) What do you want to know now? (The twin angels, where they are.) Well, see, like they're Siamese, because they'd be joined together, because they have like two heads, you know. **[213]** (S thumps on picture.) **[220]**

3. Uh, it could also look like a—a woman, with wings. (W F+ (H) P) Huh, I guess that's the same thing. That's all. (?) The woman, see the curves of the body and the feet. Except it's missing a head, would be headless— (mumbles to self).

Card II

OK—This must be a new one. I don't know if I ever saw this before. **[CD: 212]** Ah gee, I don't know what this looks like. It looks like nothing, it looks like a blob. **[192]** It's creepy. I don't know what this is. This makes no sense to me at all. (S turns card over and reads back.) **[220]** Some German shit. **[240]** Printed in Switzerland, huh! Shoobydink! **[312]** No, this doesn't make any sense to me at all. (S gives card back. E: Hold it awhile longer, and see if it looks like anything to you.) There's nothing special about this, it's just, it looked like, it looks like an accident, you know, looks like a child just splattered some paint on a paper and pushed it together. I really, I don't know what this could be. I don't know, I can't do this one, maybe I'll think of something later. (When you said an accident, you mean like—?) Looks like a little child did that. It shows no creativity. And the first one, the first one could maybe, you could make something from it, it had more of a meaning. But that, that shows nothing. [192] It's just a blob, that's just paint, that's just black and red, that's all, that's all it means.

Card III (2 seconds):

4. Oh, these are uh, these are two men washing their hands at wash basins. (W M+ H P)
5. And there's a butterfly between them. (D F+ A P) [TDI Category: Fabulized Combination; Score: .5; CD: 330] And they're effeminate because they look like they have breasts hanging out [Autistic Logic; .75; 331], and they got Pinocchio noses [311] and uh, their ears are sticking out. They're very affected and they're phony, because they're, just the way the, they're standing is just (S sticks her chest out) upright, and the rest of them is just sticking out in the back. That's it (S flings card back to E). [220]
(Where are the men?) In a bathroom. [213] Those things hanging down must be fixtures. [330] (Can you tell me more about, you said they looked affected?) Yeah, their chests are out. And they're outstretched, you know, like that, and then they're bent back like that, you know. (What makes them look effeminate?) At the same time [182], they look like they have breasts. (And that makes them look effeminate?) Yeah, well, they're kind of feminine [331]. You know, they're, they're, they've been emasculated (laughs). That's enough of that one [213]. (What do you mean by the word effeminate?) Don't you know what it means? [212] Effeminate, it means, you know, feminine, lacking masculinity, lacking male characteristics. (And the butterfly?) Right in the middle of them. (Do you mean that the butterfly is like in the bathroom too?) Yeah, it's sort of suspended from the wall, from the ceiling, sort of, it's sort of stiff, it's sort of artificial. It's like Dr. R., stilted, that's what the butterfly is. Dr. R. is the butterfly. [212] Reeking of phoniness and fakery. [Major Symbolism; .5]

Card IV (3 seconds):

6. Oh, Jesus **[CD: 212, 240]**. Oh, this is an ape. Yes, it's an ape that's been struck down dead in the forest. No, it's a bear, excuse me, it's a bear that's been struck down in the forest. **[194]** It's dying **[181]**, it's laying on it's stomach. (W FM·Ch+ A Fab.) (Anything else?) Mm-hmm. Oh, it's got drooping arms. (?) Oh, ape or bear, because it's so big and clumpsy. (What made you decide it was more of a bear?) I don't know, I just named it. **[193]** It looked big and furry, I guess. (Furry?) It just looks like that. The texture of the drawing, see the texture, sort of thick, here, frazzled. **[TDI Category: Peculiar; Score: .25]** (Arms?) The arms are like limp and drooping, that's obvious.

7. It could also be a raccoon. (D F+ Ad) That's it for that one (flings card over onto pile of other cards). (?) The raccoon, the head, you could see the funny head and the ears and the nose sticking out like that. It just suggests a raccoon's head to me, I don't know why, it just does. (S mumbles. E: Is it getting to you?) No, I like it, but I mean, I just like to do a lot of different things. Because those pictures are getting boring. But I'll do 'em. Cause see, I've done these before, and it's a pain.

Card V (38 seconds):

8. This is a—that's a repetition. **[CD: 110, 182]** This is a, uh, I don't know what this is. Um, this could be—this doesn't mean much to me either. (You can say something you said before.) See, this also looks like a blob—has no real definition to it. **[192]**

Umm, it's got, I don't know, it could be like a butterfly, it could be some type of insect. (W F+ A P) Yeah, it must be an insect. Suggests a type of insect. **[260, 320]** (?) Well, it's, there again, it's got, it's got the wings, and it's got like, antlers **[310]**, or, you know, whatever you call it, mm. You know like the spider has the legs? **[182]** Well, this has these things projecting, from its, this is the head **[110]**, and this is the bottom part, I don't know technically what they call those **[TDI Category: Word-finding Difficulty; Score: .25]**. (You said it had no real definition to it.

What did you mean by that?) Well, what I mean is that, it can only, when something doesn't have a definition to it, it's very nondescript, very vague—that could be taken for almost anything. Are we almost through with those things? **[212]** Gee, it looks like there's— (E: 5 more) Oh God **[240]**, I thought there was about 20 more. You know it's just so boring to do the same thing again.

Card VI (8 seconds):

9. Uh, this is, this must be another type of insect. (W F± A) I mean, these are getting to be all the same. Hmm, see it's got a head and it's got these sticking out again. **[CD: 250]** The guy who did these things must have been an entomologist. Must be hung up on bugs. **[TDI Category: Inappropriate Distance; Score: .25; 212, 280]** (S turns card over and reads back.) **[220]** I can't say any more about this one. "Psychodiagno-" **[110]** (?) The same thing again—**[250]** the head and those things sticking out, like wings. It's got like an anterior and an exterior, or whatever you call it, a posterior **[Tendency to confusion (slip); .25; 310]**. (How do you mean?) Well, you know like in biology **[213]**, it's got like a, a, what is it **[170]**, a bottom and a top, or a front and a back. (Which is which?) I don't know. I don't know the, I think this is the anterior and this is the posterior. **[110]**

Card VII (12 seconds):

10. Sleeping Beauty. **[CD: 317]** This is a, I don't know what this is. **[110, 196, 181]**

Two women looking at each other, in the mirror. **[TDI Category: Confusion; Score: .5; 260, 182, 333, 183]** Or it could be a woman seeing herself in, her mirror image (S throws card on pile of cards). **[220]** (First you said it could be two women looking at each other in a mirror?) Mm-hm. (How do you mean?) Just, that's all, looking at each other. There's a mirror here, it's not in the picture, but I'm imagining that there's a mirror there. Could be one woman seeing her image in the mirror. **[250]** (How is it that these two people are looking at each other in the mirror?) Well, I see, I see two possibilities.

First one is there's a mirror in the middle here. They are in a public bathroom, they are in Marshall Fields. Now, there's a mirror on this side, see there's a, you know how it's arranged in Marshall Fields, how they, they have the bathrooms? Well, there's a dividing, there's a sink here **[310, 183]**, you know. And on either side of the sink, there's mirrors. Well, there might be two sinks, with an aisle between. She's at one sink and she's looking at herself, and she's at another sink looking at herself. **[181]** (E: I couldn't understand whether they were looking at each other or looking at—) Well, it could also be one woman that sees her image reflected back to her, see? **[213, 193]**

Card VIII (10 seconds):

11. Umm, this again has, oh yeah, I remember, **[CD: 110, 182]** these are, these are rodents, yes, definitely this is a, rodent here, this is a little rat, and this is a rat. (D FM·F/C± A,Hd P) And it's preying on a, it's eating away at the fingers of a, umm, I don't know what that big thing is, but if it's eating away at something—it's eating away at, at Dr. R, **[212]** yes, because Dr. R. was corrupt. **[331]** So—it's destroying him. **[TDI Category: Confabulation; Score: .75; 330]** Mm-hmm yeah—that's symbolism. Boy, it's getting cold in here. (Rodents?) These little rodents here, see how they're eating away at, they're, they're just getting ready to bite and suck out the blood. **[110]** That's why they're colored pink—**[Autistic Logic, .75; 181, 331]** (Why?) Well, they're colored pink because, that means that their, you know like, their digestive systems are getting all fired up to a—, to prey and to get more blood. They're just like little vampires. They want their food. And they want to get more red and more juicy **[310]** and more healthy and more strong. (Now this is the thing with fingers, right here?) Mm-hm. Right, see these little fingers here. (Symbolized Dr. R.?) Yes. (What about it made it?) Well, you see it, it symbolizes the man, that's all, and all the man contains, the constituents of the man. (What do you mean?) Well, I don't know (laughs). You know, like all his snobbery, fakery. (What about that—) Well, **[211]** I'm just pretending, I'm just pretending, see, because, I'm a—(Yeah, I know you are, I know you're—) Yeah, I'm very bold, right? **[212]**

(—making it symbolism. But what made you think this was a corrupt thing?) Well, just that these are eating at something, see. And, I don't know, I just, it just worked out that way. I don't know why, I just— **[193]** (Was there something about them eating at it?) Yeah, that was the whole thing, just the fact that they, see they are invading, see, destroying, see, that's what did it (laughs).

Card IX (15 seconds):

12. Umm. This is a—mmm, shit **[CD: 110, 240]**, I don't know what this is. I think it's witches, yes, it's two witches. (D M+ (H)) **[260]** Yes, you could tell they have these long, ugly prongy **[TDI Category: Peculiar; Score: .25]** fingers. And they have, wicked witch, two witches. Doesn't mean much to me. **[196]** They look like they're clawing at each other. (?) See, they look like they're going to dig out at each other, and fight. (How much of it is the witch?) Oh. Yeah, that's the hard part. **[193]** Uh, the part that really looks like the witches would be the top parts. Cause, you know, the characteristics of the fingers, the bony hands. The ugly face, like they look like, they have these barbaric animal faces that aren't even human. This is just, represents to me barbarism, violence, you know? It represents what went on at the university when they had all that violence with people going mad and striking out at each other and going crazy, completely losing control. **[TDI Category: Loose; .5; 212]**

Card X (20 seconds):

13. Oh, let's see, this is a, mmm, what is this anyway. **[CD: 110, 170]** I'm getting tired **[212]**, this is, I don't know what this is, it's got a lot of colors in it.

    Oh, I know what this is, it's flowers, yes, it's flowers. (D FC+ Bt) **[260]** These are tulips, these, these yellow things, with the green stems and the green bulbs **[TDI Category: Peculiar; Score: .25]** or whatever you call that stuff around there. (Green stems, did you say?) Mm-hmm, I don't know what you call that in biology, the stuff that's around the flower, encases the flower.

14. Umm, at the top is a big bug. (D FC′+ A) (?) These are both bugs, these are beetles, grey beetles. They represent the mindlessness of people, like Dr. R., that merely follow orders and cannot be humane in their thinking, and care for people and think about their health, but merely destroy them. That's what that represents. **[TDI Category: Major Symbolism; Score: .5]**

15. That's a butterfly. (D F± A) (And the butterfly?) Represents daintiness. (E: Where is it?) Where is the butterfly! Oh no, where did it go! The butterfly is in the center, the blue thing, and it's, yeah. (What makes it look like a butterfly?) Well, it's got wings, and it's got—mm, it could be, the whole thing could be the butterfly, or this could be the sea dragons and this is the butterfly in between. **[TDI Category: Fluid; Score: .75]** And this is the dragonfly up here, the orange thing. (?) Well, it's got, funny little type of wings, it's got like thin wings on top and then on the bottom, it sort of thickens, it's the texture of it, I guess, here. Additional: D F(C)+ A

16. There's sea dragons. (D FC± A) (?) Yeah, this. I don't know. That is just like something you'd see laying around at the aquarium, you see these things in the water. (Describe them more.) You know how you see those beautiful colored things in the aquarium? Do you ever go there? In the water.

17. And these are spiders, the blue things are big—tarantulas, getting ready to spoil all the beauty around them. (D FM+ A P) They're gonna tear away at the flowers, and they're gonna destroy the ecology, upset the balance of nature. The spiders represent cruelty in the world, the barbarism. **[TDI Category: Major Symbolism; Score: .5]**

Summary of Rorschach Scores:

$$R = 17 \quad P = 8 \quad CD = 4.2 \quad TD_R = \frac{8.00}{17} \times 100 = 47.06$$

Location:	Deter-minants:		Content:				
W	8	F/C	1	H	3	F% = 35/100	Peculiar	3
		FCh	1	(H)	2	F+% = 83/89	Word-finding diff.	1
D	9	M	5	Hd	+1	EB = 5/1.5	Tend. confusion	1

FM	1	A	10
FC	2	Ad	1
FC′	1	Bt	1
F(C)	+1		
F	6		

Tend. confusion	1
Inapp. distance	1
Fabulized comb.	2
Confusion	1
Maj. Symb.	3
Loose	1
Aut. Logic.	2
Confabulation	1
Fluid	1

Follow-up Testing (Three Years Later)

Wechsler Adult Intelligence Scale

Information Subtest:

1-4. (4 points credited)
5. Rubber: (1)
6. Presidents: (1)
7. Longfellow: (1)
8. Weeks: (1)
9. Panama: (1)
10. Brazil: (1)
11. Height: (1)
12. Italy: (1)
13. Clothes: (1)
14. Washington: February 12. (0)
15. Hamlet: (1)
16. Vatican: (1)
17. Paris: Dk (0)
18. Egypt: (1)
19. Yeast: (1)
20. Population: 3 billion? (0)
21. Senators: (1)
22. Genesis: Birth of Christ. (0)

23. Temperature: 200° F. (0)
24. Iliad: (1)
25. Blood Vessels: (1)
26. Koran: Dk (0)
27. Faust: Gounod (1)
28. Ethnology: (1)
29. Apocrypha: Dk (0)

Raw Score: 22

Comprehension:

1-2. (4 points credited)
3. Envelope: Mail it. (2)
4. Bad company: Because it's not pleasant. (0)
5. Movies: Alarm everybody and try to open the doors and get the fire extinguisher. (0)
6. Taxes: To support different state activities—paving roads, maintaining public institutions. (2)
7. Iron: Take action while the commotion [**TDI Category: Peculiar; Score: .25**] is going on. (1)
8. Child labor: So children won't be overworked. (1)
9. Forest: Follow the sun. The sun's rays, a direction where I could see a clearing. (1)
10. Deaf: Because speech requires listening and imitation of sound. (2)
11. City land: Land in the city is more densely populated, 'cause more people need the land, so its value is increased. (2)
12. Marriage: To try to ward off any kind of disease by passing on the bad gene. (0)
13. Brooks: People that don't say too much might have more potential than other people realized. (1)
14. Swallow: One thing doesn't make the completed objective. (2)

Raw Score: 18

Summary of WAIS Scores:

Verbal IQ: (Prorated) 109 $TD_W = .25$
Information: 13
Comprehension: 10   Digit Symbol: 10

Rorschach Test

Card I (Reaction Time: 5 seconds):

1. This is a snow angel. (W F+ (H)) (?) The wings, same thing
   with the butterfly. (?) Well, it's just something I pictured like a
   little child laying down in the snow and putting his arms out.
   We learned about this in one of my classes, and they kind of fan
   out their arms and make like a . . .

2. A butterfly. (W F+ A P) (?) Also the whole thing.

3. A princess. (W F(C)± H) (?) The princess just had like an ele-
   gant lace dress on. (?) In just the way it comes around with kind
   of, I thought it would be an extension of her dress. (?) The
   princess is mainly inside, but this dress is kept like a netting
   that's around her other dress, kind of woven around her.

Card II (8 seconds):

4. Two Chinese ladies. (W F$\bar{\text{C}}$ + H) (?) There's just something Oriental about the printing of it, you know, even though it's got
   red hair, if you forget that it's red, there's something about the
   style that's Oriental. (?) You know the way the hair was, it looks
   like the heads, and then there was hair even though it was red.
   (What suggested they were ladies?) The hairdos.

5. Or two bears kind of coming to grips with each other, literally.
   (D FC' + A P) (?) Because they're like two grizzly bears with
   the big hairy, furry coats. (Furry coat?) The big, black blob.

Card III (3 seconds):

6. These are two stuffy men that are at a sink in a lavatory and
   they're both washing their hands. (D M+ H P) And if it isn't
   two men, it could also be one man seeing his reflection in the
   mirror. That's it. (?) Just the way they're positioned—their

posture, the way they're sticking out and they're kind of holding their heads up stiff, you know? (Stuffy?) Well, that's what I just said, the way they're like, they're sticking out their front, and in the back is, it's just the posture. (Men?) Because they were wearing pants, and they've got like these suit jackets on. (Washing their hands?) Their hands are in front of them at the sink, and it looks like two sinks.

Card IV (3 seconds):

7. That's like a big bear that's been shot and it's lying prone down on its stomach in the middle of the forest, and there's its head and there's its tail. (W F+ A P) And there's its legs spread out; just sprawled all over. (?) I just said it, the way it's sprawled out like that and it's just a big giant monster there. (Can you talk more about what suggested that it was shot?) Well, that it just seems so stagnant, **[TDI Category: Peculiar; Score: .25]** so lifeless, 'cause it's just laying there so stilted. (What suggested it's shot?) Nothing in particular, it's just one way of getting killed, I guess. You know, it could have been killed by a hunter or something.

Card V (3 seconds):

8. That's some type of insect also, with wings, like a dragonfly. (W F+ A P) That's all I can say. (?) The way it has wings, and it's got like antlers, so it's an insect.

Card VI (20 seconds):

9. Maybe it's a bird that's been dissected. (W F∓ A) (?) It's got those wings again and same kind of antlers. **[TDI Category: Incongruous Combination; Score: .25]** (Those wings again?) Yeah, just like the other examples. (And the same antlers?) As the other picture had. (Can you describe it? What suggested antlers?) Like, those things on top of the head. Yeah, I don't know. Not my day. (What antlers were you comparing them to?) I forgot, it was another one of those things. (Dissected bird?) It was just like cut down the middle, slit.

Card VII (6 seconds):

10. This is a woman looking at herself in the mirror, there's two faces. (D M+ Hd P) It's over here. And she could have a feather in her head. Maybe she's an Indian maid. Here's the feather and this is the profile. (Woman?) Because of the little tiny features, and the face. (Where?) This is with the feather, it's like a bust. It's not the complete figure.

Card VIII (10 seconds):

11. These are two rats (W FCarb±A P) Two red rats that are preying on some other animal that had died. [TDI Category: Incongruous Comb. (FCarb); Score: .25] And they're at the sides of the animal pulling at his arms. There's the two rats; like little hamsters, but they're more powerful, and they're kind of like going to gnaw at the dead animal that's spread out here. (?) I just told you. Those look like red rats. They just look like rats to me. (Preying?) Well, because they're sticking to it. It just looks like their little claws are sticking and like they're going to eat out of it. (What suggested another animal?) Well, it would just be most likely. (How's that?) It's just a dead thing that they're eating out of. (Dead?) Because, the same reason for the other one, the way it's sprawled out, and it's exposed. You could see part of the ribs or the back spine. And it's got like a mouth that's kind of closed up. It's shut, just looked so inactive.

Card IX (10 seconds):

12. Two monsters with big, huge claws for hands. (D F+ (A)) I don't know what the rest of it is, but these orange things look like monsters. (?) The faces and the claws. (Claws?) Spiny fingers. (Face?) Just like a monster profile. A nose and a mouth, and just the way it looks.

Card X (8 seconds):

13. I think it's a bunch of insects, and these are like tarantulas, spiders—these blue ones. (D F+ A P) (?) Well, just all those different legs, you know, and tarantulas because they're so deadly, and those look just very ominous. (?) Just all the legs

and the position; how it seems to be eating on something. (What did it seem to be eating on?) Another animal. (?) Oh, I don't know, it just looked like another animal. It was attached to it, that's why, it's just eating it. **[TDI Category: Tendency to Autistic Logic; Score: .5]**

14. And then these are venomous flies, poisonous flies. (D F− A) The same reason, the way they're attached to the pink blobs. **[TDI Category: Tendency to Autistic Logic; Score: .5]** (Venomous?) Well, like poisonous, you know. And they could be hanging on to some type of prey near their mouth there. (Poisonous?) I just felt like saying that.

15. And this is like a clam, I think. (D F− A) (?) Well, I think this is what a clam, I'm not sure but it's something like this. (?) It's just the legs, like crustaceans have those legs.

Summary of Rorschach Scores:

R = 15   P = 7 $TD_R = \dfrac{1.75}{15} \times 100 = 11.67$

Location:		Deter-minants:		Content:						
W	8	FCarb	1	H	3	F%	= 60/100	Peculiar		1
D	7	FC'	1	(H)	1	F+%	= 67/80	Incongruous		2
		M	2	Hd	1	EB	= 2/1	combination		
		FC̄	1	A	9			Tend. Aut.		2
		F(C)	1	(A)	1			Logic		
		F	9							

Case 3:
Manic Psychosis

Historical Notes

The patient is a 31-year-old white woman with a high school education. She had been married for eleven years, had two children, and was very active in community projects and volunteer work. Prior to the current hospitalization (her first), she had never experienced psychiatric difficulties. Six weeks prior to admission, she had experienced what was at first a pleasant increase in energy and activity level. She described herself as "happy as a lark," feeling as if she could do anything, having little need for sleep or food. Her mind was racing, and she began organizing projects that she believed could unite the Jewish and Catholic faiths. Increasing disorganization and confusion led to her hospitalization.

The patient was hospitalized for forty-five days on a milieu treatment unit and was administered lithium carbonate. She at first talked incessantly, was unable to listen to others, was easily annoyed, and continued to have grandiose religious ideas. She believed that she heard the voice of God speaking to her. When tested one month after admission, her Health-Sickness Rating was 40. Gradually, she became calmer, more aware of herself, and began talking about marital difficulties. The clinical psychiatric diagnosis at discharge was manic psychosis.

At follow-up testing two years later, the patient had a part-time job which she was conducting from her home. Although she had not been hospitalized since her discharge, she had experienced several periods of extreme highs, which had been dealt with in outpatient treatment. She and her husband had continued in outpatient marital counseling for a year after her discharge. She described no current psychotic symptoms (as assessed on the Present State Examination) but felt full of energy with many exciting ideas.

One year after the follow-up, the patient was again admitted to the hospital for three weeks, prior to the delivery of her third child. She had been feeling nervous and restless and was described as being quite "high."

First Testing

The patient shows significant disorganization of thinking on both the WAIS and the Rorschach, with TDI scores below the mean for schizophrenic inpatients but above the mean for nonpsychotic inpatients. The WAIS scatter (both within and among the subtests) reflects intellectual disorganization, particularly impairment of concentration. She is quite garrulous and emotionally overresponsive, vacillating between a gay, excited, joking manner and an anxious, self-reproaching irritability. Her verbalizations emphasize her distractibility, confusion, and loss of distance from the tasks at hand. Her expansive emotional style and active ideation is appar-

ent on the Rorschach, where she produces a large number of responses with a wide variety of content, determinants, and location
categories. Her responses are embellished and somewhat arbitrary.
The content of her responses suggests prominent affective lability;
unstable projective defenses and denial with emergence of depressive content; and child-like preoccupations, especially with dependency issues. In the midst of her turmoil and confusion, she manages to joke and to convey a flippant, breezy manner. A manic
psychosis is indicated.

Second Testing

At follow-up testing two years later, the patient maintains
her breezy, joking manner. She is much better organized; both TDI
scores are within normal range. She is less confused and better
able to concentrate on the WAIS, although she remains somewhat
loose and garrulous, making many references to herself. The
psychomotor retardation prominent in her low performance scores
on the first testing is not apparent on her retesting score on Digit
Symbol (elevated from 5 to 10). The reduction of Rorschach responses from 61 to 26, as well as the increase in pure form responses, suggests efforts at inhibition and mild constriction in
order to control the fluidity. Her responses have not improved in
perceptual accuracy; they remain somewhat arbitrary and vague
without gross perceptual distortion.

First Testing

Wechsler Adult Intelligence Scale

Information Subtest:

1-4. (4 points credited)

  5. Rubber: (1)

  6. Presidents: Oh, do I have to think real fast? Truman, Eisen-
hower, Johnson, Kennedy. (1)

  7. Longfellow: (1)

  8. Weeks: (1)

9. Panama: I, I can't, you know my mind isn't thinking? I can't even think of the directions right now, that's how, you know, my mind has been. I'll say south. (1)

10. Brazil: My mind is not really, I don't feel like it's really, since all this happened, like to concentrate on it, is what I mean. I know that's a simple question. Where is who, now, Brazil? South America. (1)

11. Height: (1)

12. Italy: It's not Sicily, is it? (0)

13. Clothes: 'Cause they, I have to think about that one too. I know that. They, wait a minute now, is that normal, for my mind not to work as fast? I can see a difference. But I'll think of it. To retain, to retain the heat, they retain the heat. (1)

14. Washington: Oh, I know that. I can't think of it. It's in February. The 22nd? Does every nut go through these? Down at the store, this guy wanted, "How'd you get in a place like that?" (1) **[TDI Category: Inappropriate Distance; Score: .25]**

15. Hamlet: (1)

16. Vatican: Should know that, shouldn't I? It's where the Pope, well, the center of the Catholic Church in Rome. (1)

17. Paris: I don't know. Oh God! I have no idea about that! (0)

18. Egypt: In Cairo? (0)

19. Yeast: By the ingredients in it. (0)

20. Population: About how many millions? Oh, let me think, I knew that at one time. About 100 million? (0)

21. Senators: About 66, I'm not sure. (0)

22. Genesis: The Old Testament. (?) Beginning of time. All this talk about God around this joint. You wouldn't believe it, you'd think it was the Church in here. (0, correct but past cut-off). **[TDI Category: Inappropriate Distance; Score: .25]**

23. Temperature: I knew that one too. 32° (?) What, what was that? Oh, that's kind of cold isn't it, I can't remember (laughs). That is cold isn't it? (0)

Raw Score: 15

Comprehension:

1-2. (4 points credited)

3. Envelope: Put it in the mail box. (2)

4. Bad company: Well, don't we always want to associate with people of the highest caliber? You just, you yourself, people will judge you by that. (?) Well, you're judged by the company you keep. Oh gosh, that seems like a dopey question. Who in the heck would want to hang around with bad people? True? (?) Well, you can get yourself in trouble, like into jail, as bad as this. Oh, that sounds so ridiculous. (1)

5. Movies: Well, you could tell someone in charge. Do they have fire extinguishers in movies? I mean, like around, on the door? They have exits there. (?) You could either open up the exits, or you could get a fire extinguisher yourself, or you could tell, you know, report it to someone in charge. Depends on how bad it is. (2)

6. Taxes: Well, there are many services that the city offers the people, which, you know, it even pays the salaries of the people here, it builds our highways, our libraries. (1)

7. Iron: In relation to what? I'm trying to think what could be hot. I really, right now—(?) No, nothing. I can't think what that would be right at this moment. (0)

8. Child labor: Why are they needed? Well, so parents won't be sending their children out to work at a—before they're ready, and not educating them. Just, I guess there's always some parents that would like to take advantage of their children. Not every parent is a good parent. (2)

9. Forest: Through the sun. **[TDI Category: Vague; Score: .25]** (?) As far as how the sun would set. (?) If I was lost in the, what now, in the forest? Well, how about, as far as even tracing back over the way you came. (1)

10. Deaf: Because they can't hear any sounds. Oh, that would be a terrible thing, wouldn't it? (1)

11. City land: Oh, because of the conveniences we have. (?) Well, they don't have the transportation. (1)

12. Marriage: Well, you're not doing it, you know, doing it a number of times. (?) So they wouldn't be doing it, so they wouldn't be getting married more than once. (1)

13. Brooks: Oh, you can hear the water. (0)

14. Swallow: One what? Oh God! I don't really know what that means. I never heard of it. (0)

Raw Score: 16

Similarities:

1. Orange: You eat 'em. (1)

2. Coat: They're clothing apparel. (2)

3. Axe: Wait a minute, I have to think about what an axe is. They're something. What would you call them? Tools? Is that what you call them? Tools, an axe and a saw, I think so. (2) **[TDI Category: Word-finding Difficulty; Score: .25]**

4. Dog: They're both animals. (2)

5. North: They're directions. (2)

6. Eye: They're parts of the body. (1)

7. Air: Dk (0)

8. Table: You eat off 'em? (0)

9. Egg: Well, I know that, all I have to do is think about it, and I can tell you. Well, a chicken comes from an egg. And a tree could come from a seed. (?) It's the beginning for them. I gotta know how they're alike. (0)

10. Poem: I can't think, right now. (0)

11. Wood: Alcohol is made from wood. (0)

12. Praise: Alike, they're not different? (0)

13. Fly: I can't think of anything. (0)

Raw Score: 10

Picture Completion:

1. Knob: (1)

2. Tail: Not a very happy looking little pig. I guess his tail is missing. (1)

3. Nose: (1)

4. Handle: (1)

5. Diamond: (0—correct but past time limit)

6. Water: Is that water, water glass? I'm curious about what's missing there. Water flow. (?) Is there too, how would I know how much, no, that isn't it. I don't know. (?) Just something about the water. (?) Is there like, enough water in there, for what was in there, but how do I know what's in there? (0)

7. Nosepiece: (1)

8. Peg: Is it the violin bow? (0)

9. Oarlock: That little thing that holds the rowboat. (1) Rowboat. **[TDI Category: Tendency to Confusion; Score: .25]**

10. Base thread: Something about the inside of the light bulb. (0)

11. Stars: Not enough stripes in there. (0)

12. Dog tracks: This crazy dog, what's he doing? Looks more like a bird, with his ears. It doesn't have any footprints. (1)

13. Florida: (1)

14. Smokestacks: As far as, this ship having sails on it. (?) It's got these, oh, I was gonna say what you take off. (0)

15. Leg: (1)

16. Arm image: It's missing part of its leg here. (0)

17. Finger: Dk (0)

18. Shadow: (1)

19. Stirrup: What's wrong with this crazy critter? He's got a long tail, doesn't have a, oh, maybe that's it, doesn't have a saddle. (?) Oh, just got that, whatever it is. (?) I don't know what it's supposed to be. (0)

20. Snow: Oh boy, you aren't talking about that broken-down fence, are you? Oh God, this will drive me crazy all day. I don't know if that's what you're looking for. (0)

21. Eyebrow: What's wrong with this broad? She's got a nose, a mouth—she doesn't have an ear. (0)

Raw Score: 10

Vocabulary:

1-3. (6 points credited)

   4. Winter: It's a season. (?) It's cold. (2)

   5. Repair: To fix. (2)

   6. Breakfast: First thing you eat in the morning. (2)

   7. Fabric: Material. (1)

   8. Slice: To cut. (1)

   9. Assemble: To put together. (2)

  10. Conceal: To hide. (2)

  11. Enormous: Large. (1)

  12. Hasten: To hurry. (2)

  13. Sentence: Putting words together. (?) To make sense. (1)

  14. Regulate: I don't know how to put that in meaning. Uh. I don't know how to put it in meaning, what I want to say about that word. **[TDI Category: Confusion; Score: .5]** I know what I want to say but I can't think what I want to say. (Example?) Like if you want to fix something, to—(?) No. (1)

  15. Commence: To begin. (2)

  16. Ponder: To think. (2)

  17. Cavern: Dk

  18. Designate: To point out. (2)

  19. Domestic: A homebody. (1)

  20. Consume: To devour. (?) To eat it. (2)

  21. Terminate: To end. (2)

  22. Obstruct: A stoppage. Something that's really nonpassable. (1)

  23. Remorse: To regret. (2)

  24. Sanctuary: A place that's peaceful. (0)

  25. Matchless. Dk (0)

  26. Reluctant: Like you don't want to do it. (2)

  27. Calamity: Let's see, how can I put that one? Oh, I know what I want to say, but I don't know how to say it. Oh, like something, something, big happens. (?) Oh like, something like, like some-

thing unexpected, not unexpected, something big. (?) Oh forget that one. (0)

28. Fortitude: Strong. (1)

29. Tranquil: Quiet. (2)

30. Edifice: Dk (0)

31. Compassion: Oh, to have feeling. (?) You could have feeling for another person. (?) Oh, a good feeling, a feeling of understanding. (2)

32. Tangible: Something you can, like a, something you could put your hands on. (2)

33. Perimeter: The rest of these I don't know.

Raw Score: 45

Summary of WAIS Scores:

Verbal IQ: 95	Full Scale IQ: 87
Performance IQ: 77	$TD_W = 2.0$
Information: 10	Picture Arrangement: 6
Comprehension: 9	Picture Completion: 8
Vocabulary: 10	Digit Symbol: 5
Digit Span: 12	Object Assembly: 8
Arithmetic: 7	Block Design: 5
Similarities: 8	

Rorschach Test

Card I (Reaction Time: 10 seconds):

1. Oh, maybe a bat. (W F+ A P) (What else?) There's more things it looks like? That's the only thing I see in it. But I'm supposed to see a bunch of things in it? Maybe a bird. As many things as I think of, as I could see in there? Oh, just a blotch, an ink blotch. (?) Because it had like, looked like it had wings. This isn't too brilliant.

2. A rat. (D FC′− A) (And the rat?) Oh, it just looked kind of ugly. (What made it look ugly?) The whole thing. (What do you mean?) Just looked gloomy like something you'd see in a

spooky castle. (Gloomy?) Mostly because it was black. Black—
(Black what?) Well, a lot of times you associate black with death.

3. Oh, a leaf, it could be a leaf. (W F± Bt) (?) Oh it had a, it just
   had, had a, it just reminded me of that, it had a design. (I have
   9 more of these.) Oh fine, we're going to have fun.

Card II (15 seconds):

4. Oh boy. This could remind me of a, of a cave. (S F± Cave) (?)
   That hole.

5. Or a, a volcano maybe. (D CF·m Volcano) (?) Oh, the same
   reason. (?) Oh, the hole there and then with the red part the
   flames, volcano lava coming up.

6. What else? This reminds me of the sky. (D C'F Cld) (?) Oh it
   was, oh, parts of it were like black when you get before a storm,
   and white—where was a cloud. (And white what?) The white
   part could have been a cloud, yeah.

7. Uh, does it have to be just—can it be parts of the whole thing?
   This reminds me of, a fire (D C Fi) (?) Oh, the red around it, at
   the top.

8. Oh, this reminds me of a, it could be, uh, black people and
   white people, and here, we'll make these Indians. (W C' Abs)
   [TDI Category: Major Symbolism; Score: .5] (?) Well, the
   white people were on the inside and the black people were on
   the outside. (?) Just the colors, just the simulation. **[Peculiar;
   .25]** (Just what?) Just the simulation.

9. This reminds me of an In—, possibly of an Indian tool.
   (Dd F± Obj) (?) On the top of it, oh like a tomahawk.

10. These red dots here remind me of somebody with freckles,
    maybe. (Dr CF Freckles) (OK, when you're done with it, you
    can turn it over) Oh, that's enough.

Card III (15 seconds):

11. Oh, I'm supposed to tell you? This reminds me of a man's bow
    tie. (D F+ Cg) (?) The way it was shaped, it was the perfect
    shape of a bow tie.

12. This reminds me of a (laughs) chest x ray. (DrS F− Xy) (?) It just did. (?) Oh, you could almost see the outline of a person's chest in there. (?) Person's ribs. This part through here, just the outline.

13. And these, they remind me of little babies. (D F± H) (?) The shape of their head and their body. (Where?) I've already lost them, here they are.

14. Uh, this might, kind of reminds me maybe of, oh, of a animal, uh, like a dinosaur-type animal from the sea. (D F− (A)) The legs. (?) Oh, because it had the legs and something strange coming up, you see like in horror movies. Scare everybody.

15. And down here reminds me of two chicken eggs. (D F∓ Eggs) (?) There were two little eggs there. (?) They were round, like eggs.

16. And over here reminds me of two chickens. (D F± A) (?) Oh, they looked like they had hatched the eggs. (?) Well, 'cause they had heads and they looked like they had like wings, and legs. (How much is the chicken?) Uh, how much would it be? About right here. And this piece, no, let me see. I think the whole thing, I'll make the whole thing the chicken. **[TDI Category: Tendency Fluidity; Score: .5]** Here his head, there his wing, and he got a tail, and all the way down. These were one-legged chickens (laughs).

17. And, down here, looks like a couple of fish. (D F± A) (OK, that's good.) OK.

Card IV (12 seconds):

18. Oh, a, a bear. (W FCh+ A) (?) Oh, it was kind of like, looked fuzzy to me, big feet. (?) Just appeared fuzzy. (Fuzzy?) The way it was sha—, uh, was shaded.

19. A tree. (D F+ Bt) (?) Oh, um, the bottom part looked like a tree. (?) Pardon? (?) Oh, it looked like it had a trunk to it.

20. Uh. Arms. (Dd F± Hd) (?) Oh there was two things at the top, two little splotches at the top that looked like arms. (Any particular kind of arms, arms of what?) Oh, they would look like

abnormal arms, they were awful skinny arms. (Like what?)
They were, awfully, awful small, so maybe, someone that,
someone, maybe someone was handicapped.

21. Oh, what else. I guess a, a spider. (Dr F− A) (?) Oh, looked like,
just like a big spider, with the little, like little arms, like they
could be little legs too. (?) Just reminded me of a spider. (?) Oh,
because it had some, those little legs. (Anything else?) Just the
size of it. Looks like a big blob laying there on, like on a desk, or
a chair.

22. A candle. (D F± Obj) (?) Oh, the candle, little bit was also by
the tree trunk, and it looked like it had candle dripping
down.

23. Oh, a, a bee. (Dd F− A) (?) Oh, that was the top there. The
little bee. (?) It just looked like a little bumblebee, the way it was
made. (?) It just was the body shape of a bee. (OK.) OK.
A big toe. (?) Oh, that was part of the bear's foot. (Examiner notes
that it seemed like subject needed to be stopped, as though
responses could go on for a considerably longer time.)

Card V (10 seconds):

24. Uh, a, a, bat. (W F+ A P) (?) The wings. (Anything else?) The,
uh, the head.

25. A, a, oh, a, a rabbit's head. (D F+ Ad) (?) Right at the head
there, like the head of a rabbit.

26. And an alligator. (D F± A) (?) Oh, its feet. (Its feet?) Yeah, it
had feet of an alligator. (Show me where?) At the bottom here.
(Those were like alligator feet?) Should have said alligator
head, but they can be feet too. **[TDI Category: Fluid;
Score: .75]**

27. Uh, two legs. (Dd F± Ad) (?) Oh, the stilts could also have been
legs too, same place. (Any particular kind of legs?) Kind of
skinny legs.

28. Mm, a fur coat. (W Ch•C'F Cg) (Laughs) Oh mercy, did I say,
say the rabbit's ears? (Furcoat?) That whole black splotch. (?)
Looked like it, you could almost see someone wearing that,
color, like a dyed black, you dye a black ranch mink, what do

you call it? Oh what is that called, not ranch. It's something else. **[TDI Category: Word-finding Difficulty; Score: .25]** (A *fur* coat?) Oh, just like the texture that, of the black blotch.

29. Pair of stilts. (Dd F± Obj) (?) At the bottom, those two little parts hanging out. (OK, that's good.) Pardon? (That's good.) Stop? Oh, OK, fine.

Card VI (15 seconds):

30. Oh, it looks like, a, a lion. (W F− A) (?) Its uh, entire body. (?) It had the head, had the feet.

31. And it looks like a rug. (D F± Ad P) (?) Well, it's quite common today to have a skin in your home, use it as a rug. You can put 'em on the wall if you want to. (Skin?) Like a what? 'Cause it looked dead. (How do you mean?) It just looked awful dead. Just the way it was laying, the way it had—it was all sprawled out.

32. Looks like it could be a, also a clothes, uh, clothes hanger. (D F± Obj) (?) Down the middle. You could almost hang your coat on it. Up here. (What kind of clothes hanger do you mean?) Oh, you, have you ever seen them, like a clothes—? (I don't know what you mean, exactly) Oh, they're like a long stick, they have a, little wires, iron things coming out at the top that you can hang your clothes. Have you ever seen, you've seen that, haven't you?

33. Could be a dog's tail down here. (Dr F− Ad)

34. Could be a cat's whiskers. (Dr F+ Ad)

35. This part here could be a, an x ray of a person's spine. (Dd F(C)± Xy) (?) Oh, reminded me, it could have been someone's spine, the back of it, down the middle. (X ray?) Well, it would be how you would picture it, I mean, you've seen pictures of it. And that's, what it reminded me of.

36. And, these two little white dots could be a, bow tie. (Dd F∓ Cg)

37. This part here could be a snake. (Dr F± A) (OK, that's good.)

Card VII (8 seconds):

38. Clouds. (W FC'± Cld) (?) Oh, the way they were shaped,

formed. (How do you mean?) Well, a cloud takes any form, in the sky. (So what especially made them look like clouds?) Just the way they were shaped that's all. (Was there anything besides the shape that suggested clouds?) Anything beside that? Well, the color. (How do you mean?) Well, surrounding it was white, and then the part that I thought would look like cloud was darker.

39. Uh. Cookies. (D F± Fd) (?) It looked like somebody had made cookies and used one of those cookie cutters and came out with different shapes.

40. A, a puppy, couple of puppies. (D F+ A)

41. Oh, a squirrel's tail. (Dd FCh± Ad) (?) It looked like it would have a, like it would be fuzzy like a tail. (Fuzzy?) That picture, it looked fuzzy. (?) Well it—well whoever did the picture, had texture of a fuzzy ta—, had a picture of a fuzzy object there, looked fuzzy.

42. Oh, this looks in here—can we say one thing looks like a, two things? Uh, this one here, a pig's face, pig's nose. (D F+ Ad)

43. A, a teddy bear. Looks like a toy. (D F− Toy) (?) Just looked, in size, large enough for a kid to hold. (Can you say more?) It looked like it, it had, it might be a furry animal. (What made it look furry?) The artist (laughs). You don't think that looks like a teddy bear? (Can you show me what makes it look like that?) Just the size, the size, I feel that it could be something that a kid could hold. (But can you see any parts of a teddy bear?) Oh, maybe down here, these are the feet.

Card VIII (14 seconds):

44. Oh, looks like a mountain. (D F± Lsc) (?) Oh, it looked like it had ledges going up.

45. Looks like a rock. (D F± Na) (?) Oh, down at the bottom looked like a gijantic rock. [TDI Category: Peculiar Verbalization; Score: .25] (Like a what?) Looked like a gigantic rock. (?) Well, it was like a boulder, the form of it, the shape.

46. Looks like a lady's bra. (D F∓ Cg) (?) Just the middle, the green part.

47. Looks like a couple of skunks. (D F+ A P) (?) They were on the side. (?) The way their bodies were formed.

48. Looks like a, like a little cactus plant. (Dds F+ Bt) (?) Oh, there were some, uh, in the middle, there were some, like little sticks coming out.

49. Looks like a, a kind of giant spider at the top. Hmm. (D F− A) (OK?) OK.

Card IX (8 seconds):

50. This looks like ice cream cone, ice cream, without the cones. (D FC± Fd) (?) Uh, it looked like two little, the way it was shaped, into balls. (Anything else?) Color, like strawberry ice cream.

51. This looks like somebody's heart. (D F− Ats) (?) Just from pictures that I've seen. (What about it, though?) I just, to me it just looks like a heart, could be somebody's heart.

52. This looks like two swords. (Dd F± Obj)

53. Down here looks like two windows. (DdS F± Arch) (?) Those two little openings there.

54. This looks like two clowns. (D M+ H fab) (?) Oh, just their, just their form. (?) They looked like they were cutting up. (How do you mean?) Horsing around.

55. And this could be a rock. (D F− Na) (?) Pardon? Oh, the rock. That looks like something you might find if you were out, oh, along the, say near a mountain, it would be a rock that you— (What about it made it look like a rock?) Just the shape. Cause rocks take any form.

56. This could be a witch's hat. (Dd F± Cg) (OK?) OK.

Card X (20 seconds):

Oh, we've got a color one now. Why, all those drab ones and then, now this color one? (Long pause) Oh, I'm supposed to be telling you something.

57. Oh, uh, could represent, all the different colors you see, different colors represent all the different colors that, you know,

God created. (W C Abs) **[TDI Category: Minor Symbolism; Score: .25]** As far as people.

58. And, the yellow could be the, the uh, sunshine. (D C Na) And these two blue thing, uh . . . Oh, God, there's a million.

59. Oh, these brown things look like fish to me. (D F+ A) (What did you say about the blue things?)

60. The blue things? They look like, they, they look like spiders, again, to me. (D FC+ A P) But they're eating the green things, some of the insects, so they're helpful. Oh, I like the colors again, colors, could be colors of the rainbow. And, I like also how they're, each one of them are all, are attached to the other one, as far as helping each other, as far as one, whatever these things are supposed to be, helping the other one. (The spiders were eating the green things?) Yeah. (And what was the green thing, did you say?) Oh, it could be like a harmful insect or . . . (And why did they look like they were helping each other?) Because they were all attached to each other. **[TDI Category: Autistic Logic; Score: .75]** (And what did it mean, that they were attached to each other?) Because, like no one can get along in this world alone, it takes everybody working together. Even the, the animals, where one will kill off the other.

61. Oh, and I, I think, up here, looks like, these two little things up here in the dark, they could be the devil. (W MC'± (H)) And all these other colors are . . . they could even be like human beings all working toward one thing as far as to get to heaven eventually. And these little, like I don't know, like swords, they look like, that's why it makes, it looks like the devil's working and makes it hard for human beings to get there. **[TDI Category: Confabulation; Score: .75]** (?) Down here, this dark thing. Really like devils.

Hm. That's about all.

Summary of Rorschach Scores:

R = 61   P = 5 $TD_R = \dfrac{4.25}{61} \times 100 = 6.97$

Location: Deter-
            minants: Content:

W   10   H   2   F%   = 72/87   Peculiar   2

D	31	M C'	1	(H)	1	F+%	= 70/74	Minor Symb.	1
Ds	1	Ch·C'F	1	Hd	1			Word-finding	
Dd	10	CF·m	1	A	16	Eb	= 2/7.5	Difficulty	1
Dr	5			(A)	1			Tendency to	
Drs	1	M	1	Ad	7			Fluidity	1
Dds	2	C	3	Abs	3			Major Symb.	1
S	1	CF	1	At	1			Confabulation	1
		FC	2	Arch	1			Autistic Logic	1
		C'	1	Bt	3			Fluid	1
		C'F	1	Cld	1				
		FC'	2	Cg	5				
		FCh	2	Fd	2				
		F (C)	1	Fi	1				
		F	44	Lsc	1				
				Na	3				
				Xy	2				
				Obj	5				
				Eggs	1				
				Freckles	1				
				Cave	1				
				Volcano	1				
				Toy	1				

Follow-up Testing (Two Years Later)

Wechsler Adult Intelligence Scale

Information Subtest:

1-4. (4 points credited)

5. Rubber: (1)

6. Presidents: (1)

7. Longfellow: (1)

8. Weeks: (1)

9. Panama: (1)

10. Brazil: (1)

11. Height: (1)

12. Italy: (1)

13. Clothes: (1)

14. Washington: February 12th or February 22nd, I'll let him be born on February 12th. (0)

15. Hamlet: (1)

16. Vatican: (1)

17. Paris: (1)

18. Egypt: Cairo? I know it's somewhere over there. (0)

19. Yeast: I should know that, shouldn't I? All the coffee clatching I do. **[TDI Category: Inappropriate Distance; Score: .25]** I don't really know, I'll just say what's in there, the ingredients, make it rise. (0)

20. Population: I'll say 400 million. (0)

21. Senators: About 52. (0)

22. Genesis: (1)

23. Temperature: 32°. (0)

24. Iliad: (1)

25. Blood Vessels: You must be joking. I'm thinking of something but I don't know how to say it, I don't know how to pronounce it, I'm not sure it would be it, it starts with a c. (0)

26. Koran: Dk (0)

27. Faust: Dk (0)

28. Ethnology: Dk (0)

29. Apocrypha: Sounds familiar. (0)

Raw Score: 18

Comprehension:

1-2. (4 points credited)

3. Envelope: What would I do? I'd put it in the mail box. (2)

4. Bad company: Well, are you for real? (Laughs) Oh, you like to, to, you know, to try to lead a good life, to do the right thing. Being with people, well, you know what I'm, I don't have to elaborate on that, you know. (Elaborate just a little bit.) Elaborate? Well, I don't, I guess most of us, I think the great per-

centage of people, no matter whether they're Jewish or
Catholic, or whatever, or, or Christians, they, they do believe in
God and they try to, well, I think they, basically people are
good and they try to lead, well, no matter what religion you
are, lead, uh lead a good life. (0) **[TDI Category: Looseness;
Score: .5]**

5. Movies: I would go tell the usher. (2)

6. Taxes: Well, supports institutions like this. (1)

7. Iron: I guess if you have a good thought, or an action, or a
   thought, rather than just think about it, this is how I interpret
   this, I don't know if it's right, it's what I would think, you know,
   move on it rather than just think about it. (1)

8. Child labor: Well, there are people that will take advantage of
   others. To protect, protect the rights of children. Cause men
   are bas—, you know you like to think of everybody as good,
   there are people who are greedy. (1)

9. Forest: If I was lost in the daytime, what would I do, how
   would I go about finding my way out, what would I do, what
   would I *really* do? I'd start praying (laughs), hope that somebody found me. What would I do? Maybe I'd try to retrack my
   tracks. (0)

10. Deaf: Because they can't hear the sounds. (1)

11. City land: Well, the city has so many, uh, so many opportunities
    and educational institutions, that are, are available, and trans-
    portation's so readily available. (1)

12. Marriage: Do they still do that? You know what I think?
    (Laughs) Probably why, so they can make a little more money.
    (0)

13. Brooks: There's double meaning behind that? Is, is, there's
    supposed to be a double meaning? You see a double meaning
    there, huh. I never could—that doesn't really mean much, too
    much to me, to be honest. (0)

14. Swallow: You mean a bird? Doesn't make a summer? No, that
    doesn't mean too much to me either, I'm sorry. I'll have to get a
    Ph.D. to get anything out of that. (0)

                                        Raw Score: 13

Similarities:

1. Orange: They're both fruits. (2)
2. Coat: They're both something to wear. (2)
3. Axe: They're both tools. (2)
4. Dog: Both animals. (2)
5. North: Directions, both directions. (2)
6. Eye: Um, is this gonna help you, really? You really think this is gonna help your research? (Laughs) Oh, an eye and an ear, oh, both parts of the body. (1)
7. Air: They're both necessities of life. (2)
8. Table: How they're alike? Well, they kind of go together, unless you like standing at your table (laughs). (0)
9. Egg: How they're alike? Well, they're both, they're both the, they both start from the beginning. **[TDI Category: Vague; Score: .25]** Does that make sense? The poor research, you're gonna be sorry you called me (laughs). You didn't know how well off you were. (Can you explain what you mean?) Well, you want, more specific? I can't seem to get that one together, but I know what I'm thinking. Like all your, all your food comes, you know has to be planted, an egg comes from a chicken. (0)
10. Poem: Well, this is gonna sound corny, they're both (laughs), when I think of a statue, I think of, this is really goofy, but I think that they were both romantic. (0)
11. Wood: Can't you make alcohol from wood? (0)
12. Praise: Alike? Alike! I think they're both different. (0)
13. Fly: I don't think they're too much alike, personally. Maybe you do, probably (laughs). (0)

Raw Score: 13

Vocabulary:

1-3. (6 points credited)
4. Winter: Season of the year. (1)
5. Repair: To fix. (2)

6. Breakfast: Something you eat in the morning. (2)

7. Fabric: Material. (1)

8. Slice: To cut. (1)

9. Assemble: Put together. (2)

10. Conceal: To hide. (2)

11. Enormous: Large. (1)

12. Hasten: To hurry. (2)

13. Sentence: A group of words with a noun and a predicate. (2)

14. Regulate: How would I put that? I know what I want to say but I don't know how to say it. (?) We'll take three hours on regulate, you'll be sleeping (laughs) while I'm trying to think. I keep thinking, I want to say to fix, but I know that's not what I mean. Ooh, to put in order, to get it going. (1)

15. Commence: To begin. (2)

16. Ponder: Wonder, or think. (2)

17. Cavern: Forget that one. (0)

18. Designate: To point out. (2)

19. Domestic: A homebody. (1)

20. Consume: To eat. (2)

21. Terminate: To end. (2)

22. Obstruct: To block. (2)

23. Remorse: Sorry. (1)

24. Sanctuary: Oh, how do I want to say that one? I'm thinking about a quiet place, where it's safe. (2)

25. Matchless: Without matches (laughs), I'm for real! (0)

26. Reluctant: Hesitate. (2)

27. Calamity: Oh, something just terrible. (1)

28. Fortitude: Strength. (2)

29. Tranquil: Peaceful. (2)

30. Edifice: Forget that one. (0)

31. Compassion: A feeling for someone. (?) Oh, there's a word that I'm thinking of, but I can't—empathy. (2)

32. Tangible: Something that you can hold or put your hands on. (2)

33. Perimeter: I think the other ones you could save for the Ph.D.'s.

Raw Score: 50

Summary of WAIS Scores:

Prorated Verbal IQ: 97   Comprehension: 7
$TD_W = 1.0$ Vocabulary: 11
Information: 11   Digit Symbol: 10
Similarities: 10

Rorschach Test

Card I (Reaction Time: 3 seconds):

1. That one to me looks like a bat. (Ws F+ A P) (Else?) A holey bat, he's got holes in him. No, not really. (Most people can usually see more than one thing if they look longer). You really want me to find something else in there, that it reminds me of? All right (sighs), I'll think of something. (?) Oh, the wings, and in the middle there it had a shape like a face. (Show me how much of it was the bat?) Oh, through here, the wings, there, that's part of the wings, listen to me! (Laughs) I'll be back on the nutty ward, calling that the wings. This part right here. And this reminded me of a, it could be a face. (Uh-huh, but this is the wings, right?) Is it wings, is that what you're telling me? (Well, I don't know, I'm asking you if that's what you're telling me). Right, right, that's what I'm telling you.

2. Oh, a painting. (W F∓ Art) (?) Well, some of the, some of your modern art, it could be anything, it's up to your own, imagination.

Card II (5 seconds):

3. That looks like two elephants—I was just at the zoo. (D F± A) (?) Oh, here, right through here. The trunk, here's his ears, up to here, that's his body.

4. Oh, something else? (W F∓ Art) Uh, do you mind if I say a painting again (laughs)? These could all be a painting, just put painting down for all of them. (?) The whole thing could be modern art. (Does it look like a painting of anything?) Just a modern, abstract painting.

5. Oh, this is a—this, kind of, could be a cloud up here on top. (D F∓ Cld) (?) Up here. (Where?) Up here, (laughs) probably thinking where, where's this cloud. (?) The way it, their shape.

6. Or this, I don't know whether you, this could be somebody's mouth. (S F-Hd) Or a donut. I think that's all. I'm done with that one. (?) Just the way it was shaped.

Card III (28 seconds):

7. You know what that reminds me of? (What?) Oh, it reminds me like of, you know sometimes you see pictures of unborn babies. (D F∓ H) That reminds me of that. Oh. I guess that's all. (?) Just the way it was shaped. (How do you see it? I'm not sure I see it the way you see it). Oh, you don't see that? No (laughs), you don't. (I just want you to describe it so I can see it). OK. (Long pause). (It's this part right in here?) Right. (What makes it look unborn?) Is that, do you see that, or no? (I'd like for you to describe it, 'cause I'm just guessing how you see it—) Oh, all right. Just its shape, the whole thing. I don't know why I think that. Do you see that, when I say that, do you see that or no? (I need for you to describe it more). You need for—(Does it look unformed?) No, it looks like it's doing good.

Card IV (5 seconds):

8. That looks like Smokey the Bear's feet. (D F± Ad P) (?) The feet and the legs of a bear. (How come a bear's feet?) Because they're fuzzy. (?) Just the way the art work is done. (But you see just the leg and the foot of the bear?) Mm-hm, uh the, or the, through here, the body.

9. Or a tree. That's about it. (Dd F+ Bt) (?) Oh these. (Look like?) Limbs. (How much of that is the tree?) That's about, or here, right down the middle, could be the, uh, trunk of the tree.

Card V (8 seconds):

10. Let's see. That looks like a bat, or a, yeah. (W F+ A P) Cause of its head, and there's its wings and that's its feet.

Card VI (8 seconds):

11. Hmm. That looks like a, maybe like, a ti—, uh, tiger rug. (W F+ A P) That's been treated perhaps. There's its head, and it's all laid out. (?) 'Cause I've seen them. (Yeah, just tell me how it looks to you). Oh, oh, how it looks. Well, up here on the front is its head. And how it would be like split open and laid completely out. That could be its feet over here.

12. (That's it?) Um. Well, it kind of looks like a coat hanger too. (D F± Obj) There's the hooks. (?) Down the middle here, looks like a pole here in the middle.

Card VII (8 seconds):

13. Oh boy. That to me looks like a cookie design. (Dd F± Fd) (?) Well, when we make cookies, we all get together and make cookies about this time, and we, you know, use those cutters and make different designs, and it just kind of struck me, you know, that way. (What part of it looks like that?) This part here, or either, this up here, this right here. (Anything especially which made it look like cookies?) Well, it did, well, it was, it's just that it struck me. You know, because we have the different shapes and—that's, you know, [**TDI Category: Vague; Score: .25**] and they're long like, and the shapes are long.

14. Or this part could be an animal, or an insect, a flying insect. (D F± A) (?) This part right here, a flying insect, right down here. Like a butterfly, perhaps.

15. And that could be, even like, sometimes you see those prints of, they sell, ah like, for little children's rooms, like a cat, that looks kind of to me like a cat, for a kid's room. (D F∓ A) They, sell a lot of that stuff, prints. (?) This part here, to me, like see its tail here, and feet, head.

Card VIII (15 seconds):

16. Mm. That looks like it could be a chest x ray. (Dd F+ Xy) (?) Right here, through here. (What do you see?) Somebody's ribs.

17. When I first looked at it I thought that could be some lady's girdle (laughs). (D F± Cg) (?) Like a what? A girdle (laughs). Would you believe that when I looked at that whole thing, I thought that? I, guess, more this part here, 'cause, some of those corsets.

18. Oh, when we were at the zoo a couple of, weeks or so ago, some of the animals, looked, coyotes are about the shape of this. (D F+ A P)

19. And down here, it could be a rock. (D F± Na) I think that's about it. (?) We were up in, they had, we were up at Illinois Beach Sunday and a, they had, you know, a lot of rock up there, and I thought of that.

Card IX (11 seconds):

20. Hmm. Well, that could be the horns of a, what, of an antler. **[TDI Category: Peculiar; Score: .25]** (Dd F + Ad) (You said it could be the horns of a what?) Of a deer. Right here.

21. You know the colors kind of remind me of a, of a, Buckingham Fountain, if you've ever been out there at night when they turn the colored lights on. (W CF Fountain) Have you seen it lately? Isn't it lovely? **[TDI Category: Inappropriate Distance; Score: .25]** (?) The coloring.

22. Down the middle could be somebody's cane. (D F± Cg)

23. Oh, down here could be a large cloud. (D F± Cld) (?) Well, you know how they draw pictures of clouds and they're, they're shaped like that.

Card X (11 seconds):

I'll let you get caught up (referring to examiner writing).

24. Mm. Oh, this reminds me of spiders. (D F+ A P) There, I won't go too fast.

25. Oh, and this, this reminds me of the shape of Italy, these two pink things. (D F ∓ Geog)

26. Oh, I know too. Did you ever go to Old Town, you ever seen where they'll uh, put that uh, oh they turn, they put it on a turntable and it, and it, uh goes at a high rate of speed. (W CF Art) And it's paint and it just, you know, spatters. I guess that's about it.

Summary of Rorschach Scores:

$$R = 26 \qquad P = 6 \qquad\qquad TD_R = \frac{.75}{26} \times 100 = 2.88$$

Location:		Deter-minants:		Content:					
WS	1	CF	2	H	1	F%	= 88/92		
W	6	F	24	Hd	1	F+%	= 65/70	Inappropriate	
D	14			A	8	EB	= 0/2	Distance	1
S	1			Ad	2			Peculiar	1
Dd	4			Art	3			Vague	1
				Bt	1				
				Cld	2				
				Cg	2				
				Fd	1				
				Geog	1				
				Na	1				
				Obj	1				
				Xy	1				
				Foun-tain	1				

Case 4:
Neurotic Depression

Historical Notes

The patient was a 23-year-old college-educated white woman who was employed as a community worker. She was concerned that the organization for which she worked was inefficient and even corrupt. During the month preceding hospitalization, she had been "feeling blue" and was subject to episodes of spontaneous crying and severe anxiety. She had difficulty sleeping and was preoccupied with thoughts of suicide, so that she was afraid to be left alone. In college, she had done well academically but had sought brief psychotherapy because of feeling socially inadequate and shy. During the year prior to her hospital admission, she had been involved in an unstable relationship with a boyfriend, had become pregnant, and had had an abortion. She observed that, had she carried her pregnancy to term, she would have delivered the baby around the time of the onset of her depression.

The patient was admitted to a milieu treatment unit, where she was treated without medication. She was tested during the first week of her hospitalization, when she appeared quite depressed, and spoke in a very low, plaintive voice. Her Health-Sickness Rating was 50. She was hospitalized for four weeks, during which time she became more outgoing and expressive of her feelings. Her diagnosis at discharge was neurotic depression. Three years after hospitalization, she had not been rehospitalized.

Interpretative Comments

This patient's intellectual functioning on the WAIS appears intact, although the low Digit Span and Object Assembly scale scores suggest that her attention is impaired by anxiety. Her verbalizations express uncertainty, self-doubt, and self-depreciation. Her TD_W score is quite low. On the Rorschach, she produces an expansive record (45 responses) with accurate form perception (good F+%) and six units of movement, all of which suggest that she is not profoundly depressed. There is, however, much evidence of painful self-examination, passivity, and withdrawal from intellectual pursuits. Suicidal ideation is consistent with her use of color and shading (Appelbaum and Holzman, 1962). Severe anxiety is indicated by her concern with shading and in her curtailment of responses on the first heavily shaded card. Her TD_R score is below the means of both schizophrenic and nonpsychotic inpatient groups but above that of normal controls. Her thinking and verbalizations are mildly arbitrary and peculiar. Her impulsivity, uncritical approach to problems, low tolerance for experiencing anxiety, and need to solicit attention and nurturance suggest prominent narcissistic character features in a neurotic person experiencing anxiety and mild depression.

Wechsler Adult Intelligence Scale

Information Subtest:

1-4. (4 points credited)

5. Rubber: Are you kidding? (S laughs). I don't know any of these kinds of things. Rubber trees. (1)

6. Presidents: (1)

7. Longfellow: (1)

8. Weeks: (1)

9. Panama: (1)

10. Brazil: (1)

11. Height: (1)

12. Italy: Rome, that's not right, is it? (1)

13. Clothes: (1)

14. Washington: (1)

15. Hamlet: (1)

16. Vatican: It's the Pope's headquarters. I don't think that's the word to use. (1)

17. Paris: I have no idea—about 2,000 miles. (0)

18. Egypt: It's in, Asia's up here and then Africa's down here. It's around in there somewhere. It's on the Nile. (Continent?) I think it's Africa, but I'm not really sure. (1)

19. Yeast: I think it has bacteria in it, they're released when the—, when it's in a warm place. (0)

20. Population: (1)

21. Senators: 104, aren't there? (0)

22. Genesis: Dk (0)

23. Temperature: 100—I don't really know. (Scale?) Oh, God, I don't know. (0)

24. Iliad: (1)

25. Blood Vessels: (1)

26. Koran: It's a, like the Bible of the, is it the Moslems? (1)
27. Faust: G-o-e-t-h-e. I don't know how to pronounce it. (1)
28. Ethnology: Dk (0)
29. Apocrypha: Dk (0)

Raw Score: 22

Comprehension:

1-2. (4 points credited)

3. Envelope: Put it in a mail box. (2)

4. Bad company: Because they make you depressed. (0)

5. Movies: Get up and go tell the manager that there's something on fire. (2)

6. Taxes: To run the government. (2)

7. Iron: Do something when you have an opportunity to do it. (2)

8. Child labor: Because—employers could use children for cheap labor. (1)

9. Forest: I'd just look for where there weren't that many trees to find a clearing and listen for noises of traffic to know where a road might be. (1)

10. Deaf: Because they can't hear how to speak. (?) Yeah, because like you learn how to talk from hearing other people and the noise that they make you hear, and then you imitate that, but if you can't hear, you can't imitate that. (2)

11. City land: Because there's no, because there's more industry and lots more things are produced in a concentrated area. (1)

12. Marriage: That's a good question. (?) Because marriage has always been like a couple thing. Like society bases its whole thing on couples. And I think because society's puritanical that, they want people to get married. (0)

13. Brooks: People who really talk a lot—a lot of people who really talk a lot, a lot of the time, don't really have anything to say. (2)

14. Swallow: Well, just because one thing happens, you shouldn't decide right away what's going to happen. Right after that you should wait for more things before you judge. (2)

Raw Score: 21

Similarities:

1. Orange: They're both fruits. (2)
2. Coat: Clothes. (2)
3. Axe: They both cut things. (1)
4. Dog: They're both animals. (2)
5. North: They're both directions. (2)
6. Eye: Parts of the body. (1)
7. Air: They're both parts of the earth. (0) **[TDI Category: Inappropriate Distance; Score: .25]**
8. Egg: They're both things that grow something. (1)
9. Poem: Both artistic works. (2)
10. Wood: They both have to be aged, I guess. **[TDI Category: Peculiar; Score: .25]** (?) Before you can have wood the tree has to grow, and alcohol, I think has to ferment. It's like an aging process for both of them. (0)
11: Praise: Both ways of controlling behavior. (2)
12. Fly: They're both living things. (2)

Raw Score: 19

Picture Completion:

1. Knob: (1)
2. Tail: (1)
3. Nose: (1)
4. Handles: (1)
5. Diamond: (1)
6. Water: (1)
7. Nosepiece: The rest of the frame to cover his nose. (1)
8. Peg: The tuning, the device that's used on this side. (1)
9. Oarlock: On the right side, there's nothing to hold the oars in. (1)
10. Base thread: The rest of the filament in the light bulb. (0)
11. Stars: The rest, that's not right, the flag pole. (0)

12. Dog tracks: Oh, the tracks of the dog. (1)

13. Florida: (1)

14. Smokestacks: You want me to tell you what's wrong with these or? On that type of a boat there shouldn't be sails. These should be a smokestack or something. (What's missing?) Smokestack. (1)

15. Leg: (1)

16. Arm image: (1)

17. Finger: (1)

18. Shadow: (1)

19. Stirrup: There's no, I think they're called pommels on the saddle. Oh, it's a horn. It's called a horn. (0).

20. Snow: Only thing I can think of is that there's no drift around the wood. (1)

21. Eyebrow: (1)

Raw Score: 18

Vocabulary:

1-3. (6 points credited)

4. Winter: A season when it's really cold. (2)

5. Repair: To fix. (2)

6. Breakfast: Meal in the morning. (2)

7. Fabric: Material. (1)

8. Slice: Part—(?) Thinking of a slice of pie, would be a part of it. (1)

9. Assemble: Put together. (2)

10. Conceal: Hide. (2)

11. Enormous: Huge. (2)

12. Hasten: Hurry. (2)

13. Sentence: A statement. (1)

14. Regulate: Watch over. (1)

15. Commence: Start. (2)

16. Ponder: Think. (2)
17. Cavern: Cave. (2)
18. Designate: Name. (2)
19. Domestic: In the surrounding area. (?) I mean, like domestic relations, like U.S. instead of international. (1)
20. Consume: Eat. (2)
21. Terminate: End. (2)
22. Obstruct: Stop. (?) When you obstruct someone, you block their way or something. (2)
23. Remorse: Sorrow. (1)
24. Sanctuary: I don't know exactly the words I want to use, but when someone is, I don't know if that's right or not. I think it's a building where people are, can study or, but I'm not really sure. (0)
25. Matchless: That you can't compare it to something else. (2)
26. Reluctant: That you don't want to do something. (2)
27. Calamity: Tragedy. (1)
28. Fortitude: Strength. (2)
29. Tranquil: Calm. (2)
30. Edifice: I think that's a barrier. (0)
31. Compassion: Understanding. (1)
32. Tangible: Touch, you can touch it. (2)
33. Perimeter: The length around a circle. (2)
34. Audacious: Bold. (1)
35. Ominous: Impending. (?) Like you know something's going to happen, like an ominous sign. (2)
36. Tirade: When someone goes on and on about something. (1)
37. Encumber: To put a burden on. (2)
38. Plagiarize: To copy someone else's work. (2)
39. Impale: Dk (0)
40. Travesty: Dk (0)

Raw Score: 62

Summary of WAIS Scores:

Verbal IQ: 111	Similarities: 13
Performance IQ: 107	Vocabulary: 13
Full Scale IQ: 110	Picture Completion: 13
$TD_W = .5$	Picture Arrangement: 11
Information: 13	Block Design: 12
Comprehension: 13	Object Assembly: 8
Arithmetic: 10	Digit Symbol: 12
Digit Span: 9	

Rorschach Test

Card I (Reaction Time: 10 seconds):

1. A butterfly. (W F+ A P) (E: What else?) Only one way? Mm, I don't know. It looks like a butterfly to me. Let me think.

2. It could be a, like a snow angel that someone made in the snow, except it's black. (W FC′± (H)) (?) Like when you, did you ever make a snow angel? OK, when you, this would be, it's really stretching the imagination—the head here, it's a funny-looking head and someone didn't do that good a job when they were being snow angels. And this is where they put their legs out and this is where they put their arms out, right here. And then maybe they didn't put their head down right, here. They didn't do too good a job. (Snow?) Just because this was white right here and this was different than all the rest of the paper.

3. V (S turns card upside down) It could be some type of machine, when it's upside down, that's spurting out all this liquid. (W C′F Machine) (?) Oil or something that's splurting out right here. (Oil?) Because it was like there were spots out of it, there were black spots that might have looked like something, you know, not just outlined, and drawn, but something that might be, I don't know, like the paint might have been splattered on or the ink or something.

(Addition during inquiry) It could be a, the underside of a bat. **[TDI Category: Peculiar; Score: .25]** (?) Because it looked like it had wings and it looked like you might be looking up at—, but, its head was coming down, real little head. Two little feet coming out. (Underside?) Because you could see, like if it were lying right here. It didn't look like it would be that part, that you saw the whole wing span underneath and then you saw his chest, like you would be looking up at it.

Card II (65 seconds):

4. A rocket. (D FC′± Rocket) Does it have to be the whole thing or just can it be part of it? (?) It's going up. (?) Because it has all the black smoke around it, like it would be, I don't think it's black smoke, but a rocket, I don't really know, but just because it looked like it landed and smoke around it.

5. (S turns card upside down) A woman. (Dd F− H) (?) I just looked at that one part, right here. Hair, feet, arms. (Woman?) It seemed like one, I thought. And it looked like she might have had the hair hanging down, because it was a darker color.

6. Two men looking at each other. (D M± Hd) (?) Nose, mouth, eyes, and I don't know, what this is, horns or something. They're different-looking men. (Men?) Because they were all by themselves and there were two. **[TDI Category: Autistic Logic; Score: .75]** They were sort of outlined. It's not really clear, though. And they wouldn't look like men that you would see walking around, they had, it looked like they had noses, lighter spots where the eyes would be and where the cheek bones might be.

7. An arrowhead. (D F+ Obj) I'm done.

Card III (3 seconds):

8. Two people on a see-saw. (W M+ H P) (?) They just looked like they're sitting. The reason their legs are straight, it's because they're holding themselves on the see-saw, but the see-saw isn't here. This is the round center of it. And they're real close. (Any particular kind of people?) They just looked like they have really formal clothes on and, but their faces don't look like they're people. Looks like it might be chickens dressed up like people.

9. (S turns card upside down) Two old men. (D FC′Ch+ Hd) (Old men?) Because they had the long beards that go under,

they're pretty long. It looked like they might be, it looks like they might be two older black men. Because they have the facial—the blot was not real even, it looked like it was wrinkled. And the facial characteristics looked like they might be that of a person who's black with a shorter nose and I think fuller lips.

10. Two fish. (D F+ A)

11. Two p—, no just one, just one pair of lungs. (D F± At) (?) They were just all by themselves and they were like a kidney-bean shape, and I think that's what a lung looks like, that's what I thought it did. And they had something connecting them like it would be the bone that we have right in there.

Card IV (6 seconds):

12. It's a, it's part of a man sitting on a stool and he's got his feet out. (W M± Hd) I mean, they're not on the floor. (?) It's not all of him. It's cut off right here. (How much?) Toward the bottom right here, about here, his waist. He's sitting on this stool and then he's got, these are his feet and he's got them up like he doesn't want to put his feet on the floor. I don't know what these are, right here.

13. It's part of a, part of it is a flower. (Dr F± Bt)

Card V (15 seconds):

14. That's a bat. (W F+ A P) (?) That's what it looks like. It's like you're looking at it, but it's flying down here. So you're seeing the top part of it, and these are its wings and these are the feet. I don't think that bats have horns or anything like that. This part doesn't look like it, but this part right in here does. I don't know what this is, but this part of it looks like a bat.

15. And I see two chicken legs. (Dd F+ Fd) (?) Because they were shaped like they were sort of out there, they didn't belong to the bat, though. They were all by themselves, and outlined, and were like drumsticks that you would eat. They were shaped like that.

16. And two men with beards and they, but they don't have any

eyes. (De F+ Hd) I don't know, they could have eyes, either
they have no eyes or they have bushy hair, they have like hair
coming out this way. I look at that one way and they could have
no eyes, but if I look at them, they could have hair coming out
(S gestures to forehead) here, then they have eyes. (?) Two men
with beards, where were they? Oh, I know. If you look at them
like this, this was their forehead, then this would be bushy hair
right there, eye, and there's the nose. And there's the mouth
and their beard. And it's the same over here.

17. A part of two legs of a, of a, of a cat. (Dd FC′∓ Ad) (?) It would
be like you would be looking at the underside of, and that's the
stomach right here. But that's all. There's no head or anything.
(Cat?) I started to say dog, but cat legs are sort of stubby, they
don't have as much shape, those are straighter—different colors, like it might have been a spotted cat.

18. Two snakes looking at each other. (Dd FM± A) (?) On little
sand hills. And they came out to talk, it looked like it might be
in a cartoon or something, and they're just up and looking at
each other and talking.

Card VI (20 seconds):

19. It could be a bird. (D F+ A)

20. Or a worm. (D F+ A) (?) All the way down, just the dark part.

21. Or a tunnel. (D FC′± Tunnel) (?) It would start here and then
you would have to go through here and then these would be
two rocks or something that you would have to squeeze
through. And then go clear up to the top. (Tunnel?) Because it
was dark in the middle, darker than the rest, and it went all the
way up the picture. But you could always see the dark places
even through the two white places.

22. Or a coat. (D FCh+ Cg) V (?) V-neck. This little, some kind of
design here, and this would be the zipper and these would be
the arms. It's like an old furry coat. (Furry?) Because the spots
weren't even and fur would be sticking out here. It would be an
old furry coat. (Old?) It looked like it's been used a lot, maybe
some of the fur had been pulled out. And that would be why all
the spots were uneven.

23. Or two snakes. (Dd F(C)± A) (?) Right here, one is going this way. This is his head. And then there's one, this is right against his stomach, and they're right—this is the profile of both of them. And then they're like on top of each other, their stomachs are together. They're like going sideways. (Snake?) They were sort of spotted like rattlesnakes are, they both had like the spotted coloring and they were big. Just the shape made it look like they had faces.

Card VII (17 seconds):

24. It's two women sitting together. (W M+ H P) (?) Their faces, and they have their hair up. It's sticking straight up in a kind of pony tail or braid. And then this is their stomachs and they have their arms backwards and they're sticking backwards out. **[TDI Category: Peculiar; Score: .25].** And then there's their dresses. They have long dresses, sitting with their knees together and they're talking and looking at each other, or she might be looking in a mirror.

25. And two bears. (D F± Ad) (?) I don't know if they really look like bears, they don't have that long of ears, though.

26. And a butterfly. (D F± A)

27. And two men. (Dd F− Hd) (?) Did I have it this way, when I saw it? I didn't know I said it. I was thinking about it, but—he also has his hair way up, on both sides.

28. And icicles. (Dr FC'± Icicles) (S turns card upside down) (?) 'Cause it looked lighter than the rest of the picture. It looked like the ink had dripped, looked like they might have been hanging down. It wasn't even or anything.

29. And two strange looking animals. (D F± A)

Card VIII (25 seconds):

30. There's two, I think they're rats. (D F+ A P)

31. And a butterfly. No, it looks like there are three butterflies. (D FC(C)± A) (?) They all had a center which is the darker place, and they all had colors that were not the same, and they were in sort of a fan shape. (?) They look like they're all pull-

ing each other. (?) They're all connected so they might be fly-ing together or something, [**TDI Category: Fabulized Com-bination; Score: .5**] they look like they would be connected, because they're holding on to each other. [**Tendency to Autis-tic Logic; .5**]

Card IX (12 seconds):

32. Two unicorns. (D F+ A) (?) Here's the horn on top of their head. This is part of their body, but it stops here.

33. Two, a pair of hands. (Dd F± Hd) (?) It's really just the fingers, I guess.

34. And two Oriental men. From the Orient. (Dr F− Hd) (?) They have the long beard, and they have that, just sort of a sq—(?) Yeah, but these are their beards coming down here. Real skinny, long beards or goatees coming down. Do you see it? And there are their eyes, nose, and they have um, just sort of a squinty look.

35. And a butterfly. (D FC(C)− A) [**TDI Category: Perseveration; Score: .25**] (?) 'Cause it was darker in the middle and it had the color and an outline.

36. And two men that look like Mark Twain. (D F+ Hd) (?) Moustache.

37. And two a, look like, sort of like, a ghost on a cartoon char—, on a cartoon show. (S FC′±(H)) (?) They have a little horn and there's their mouth. (Ghosts?) Because they were white. But they didn't look like a ghost that you might see. They looked sort of silly.

Card X (20 seconds):

38. There are two, a, insects. (D F± A) (?) Tentacles.

39. Two birds. No, I see a lot more birds, four birds. (D F± A) (?) Just looked like birds. They were in the shape of them. They looked like they might have been flying.

40. Two worms. (D FC+ A) (?) The dark green was all of one color, and it was long.

41. A man diving. (Dd M+H)

42. Two fish. (D F± A)

43. Two, ah, babies and they're sucking onto **[TDI Category: Peculiar; Score: .25]** something. (D M± H) (?) It's sucking onto something. I don't know what, it's just that they looked like they weren't developed that well, like it could have been a picture of a fetus or something, and their faces looked like a babyish type of thing.

44. Two lungs. (D F∓ At)V (?) 'Cause they were in the shape and they had something connecting them that looked like it might have been bones or something, different lines.

45. And a wishbone. (D F+ At)

Rorschach Summary:

$$R = 45 \quad P = 5 \qquad\qquad TD_R = \frac{2.75}{45} \times 100 = 6.11$$

Location:		Deter- minants:		Content:						
W	7			H	5	F%	= 56/98	Peculiar		3
D	25	FC'Ch	1	(H)	2	F+%	= 84/86	Perseveration		1
Dd	8	M	6	Hd	8	EB	= 6/1.5	Fabulized		
Dr	3	FM	1	A	17			Comb.		1
De	1	FC	1	Ad	2			Tend. Aut.		
S	1	FC(C)	2	At	3			Logic		1
		FCh	1	Ay	1			Autistic		
		FC'	6	Bt	1			Logic		1
		C'F	1	Cg	1					
		F(C)	1	Fd	1					
		F	25	Icicles	1					
				Machine	1					
				Rocket	1					
				Tunnel	1					

Case 5:
Mother of Case 2

Historical Notes

Mrs. A., a 48-year-old housewife with two children, was college educated and taught ceramics out of the A.'s home. She was a

flamboyant, somewhat bizarre-appearing woman who talked incessantly in a pressured, intensely anxious manner. In her interactions
with her daughter and with the hospital staff she was intrusive,
manipulative, and sometimes hostile. She was deeply disappointed
that her eldest child had had so little success either academically or
artistically. While she was demanding and had high expectations,
she was also overprotective and clearly had difficulty permitting
her daughter to separate from her.

Interpretative Comments

Mrs. A. shows significant disorganization in her thinking on
both the WAIS and the Rorschach. Her TDI scores are quite high,
especially for a nonpatient. Despite her difficulty in cognitive focusing and the spottiness of her performance, she attains a verbal IQ
score of 119. Her characteristic style of responding is jerky, with
anxious, spasmodic starts and stops, often beginning incorrectly or
tangentially but eventually arriving at the correct response. There
is a striking amount of scatter within the WAIS subtests, indicative
of uneven intellectual interests. Her verbalizations are peculiar,
with odd overspecifications, word-finding problems, and a proneness to rambling in a vague, confused manner. Her communication
deviance score on the Rorschach was the highest CD score obtained
in the study. Although the CD scores overlapped the TDI scores in
scoring peculiar word usage, the majority of her CD scores were for
sentence fragments, contradictory and inconsistent references, disqualifications, reiterations, interruptions, extraneous remarks, and
temporary card rejections.

The Rorschach suggests a fluid, labile, unsettled woman who
struggles with strong aggressive impulses, feelings of fragmentation, and bizarre sexual concerns, which intrude inappropriately
into her responses on the WAIS as well as the Rorschach. Mrs. A. is
aware of her inappropriateness; she comments on the "roundabout
way" in which she responds and worries that the examiner may
think she has a "hang-up with sexual organs." Although Mrs. A.
does not appear to be overtly psychotic, she does appear to interpret reality in a fluid, idiosyncratic manner.

Wechsler Adult Intelligence Scale

Information Subtest:

1-4. (4 points credited)

5. Rubber: (1)

6. Presidents: (1)

7. Longfellow: Longfellow was a famous American poet. (1)

8. Weeks: (1)

9. Panama: (1)

10. Brazil: (1)

11. Height: (1)

12. Italy: (1)

13. Clothes: Could it have been something to do with the dye? The texture of the warmer dyes to the skin, **[TDI Category: Peculiar; Score: .25]** to the human skin? (0)

14. Washington: (1)

15. Hamlet: (1)

16. Vatican: The seat of the Pope, you know, the seat of the Catholic Archdiocese, the home, located in Rome, Italy. (1)

17. Paris: I'd say it's about 1,400 miles. I'm guessing. This is bad, I don't know. (0)

18. Egypt: Egypt is in Middle Africa, Africa. Do you have to state where, south or not? Africa. (1)

19. Yeast: Gee, I don't know. The combination of the yeast with the flour causes the other ingredients, causes it to expand, you know, expands, and blows the flour up, some element of the yeast. (1)

20. Population: I'd say now about 140 million, 150, no, yeah, does that seem out of line? (1)

21. Senators: 48 states—100 senators, 50 states. (1)

22. Genesis: The main theme. I don't know. Love. The book of Genesis. It's in the Bible, no? Let's say love, I'm just guessing. You wouldn't say religion? No, no, it's got to be a special thought. Just guessing now. (0)

23. Temperature: 98.5, no, more than that? Over 100? Well, either one, Fahrenheit or Centigrade? I'll say 100, I don't know. (0)

24. Iliad: Homer. Ask me questions like that, I'm good. (1)

25. Blood vessels: Oh no! Three kinds, what do you mean? How do you mean that? We have three kinds! You don't mean like the white corpuscles? I can't answer that, I'd just be guessing. Red corpuscles, no, no, no. (0)

26. Koran: The Koran is the Bible of the Mohammedan, of the Mohammedan world, the Mohammedan Bible. Certain things that I don't know, does it seem to be common, depending on knowledge or background, if you've had them or is it—? I should know the three—, but I would be curious, if you'd tell me after this is over, of the bussels. [TDI Category: Peculiar; Score: .25] of the— (1)

27. Faust: I'm thinking of the music—Gounod. Dante? Gounod wrote the opera Faust, Dante wrote the story Faust. I'm thinking Mephistophiles, but that's a character in Faust. (1)

28. Ethnology: The study of various ethnic groups, or race, you know. (1)

29. Apocrypha: What? I don't know what that is. What do you mean? Is this based on a Greek legend? How is that spelled? Oh, I didn't understand you. No, I don't know what that is. (0)

Raw Score: 23

Comprehension:

1-2. (4 points credited)

3. Envelope: I would mail it. I've had that happen. I would mail it in the mailbox. (2)

4. Bad company: It's not a good influence for us, for a person, socially or otherwise. We could easily become brainwashed. You would always seem to be fighting to keep yourself together. (2)

5. Movies: Well, my first reaction would be to warn the audience and try to get to the nearest, but without hysteria, try to get to the closest exit, in some sort of order. The main thing I would

do would be to not alarm, but to make the audience, the people around me, aware that there is smoke and fire. Should try to keep as orderly as possible. (0)

6. Taxes: Taxes is an obligation as citizens of our country. To our nation, to this country the United States. As a citizen, I think we have an obligation. I think that's carried to an extreme. Within reason, taxes within reason. Taxation, we have representation, so therefore we should have taxation. For we formed our constitution, it was taxation without representation is treason. **[TDI Category: Loose; Score: .5]** (E: What are they for?) Obligation, maintenance, and it acts as payment for our legislators, our representatives in our state and federal government, paying for our schools, roads, highways, etc. bettering the welfare of our country, for the welfare of our country it says. But you know different, when it goes into the pockets of the wrong people. Whatever I'm saying now is going to go in there (S points to tape recorder, begins whispering). It's frightening what Nixon has done now, it's terrible. He's put a freeze, you know, I mean—a lid. (2)

7. Iron: In other words, do something while you have the opportunity. Go at something while the opportunity is there. Don't procrastinate, don't wait. (S mutters to herself:) Three kinds of blood vessels. Could it be like, in the stomach, vessels, arms, no? I never took anything. (2)

8. Child labor: To control the age of children starting to work. Primarily I would say at the factory or industrial level because there was so much of that at the turn of the century. Children were put to work at nine, ten, eleven. Now there's definitely a law that states that no youngster can go to work before the age of sixteen technically. (Why is that law needed?) Well, so they can't be taken advantage of as far as, payment-wise. Also they have to be in school for a number of years. There's a law in this country they must have school until the age of sixteen. I mean there was a time when they were out of school, they didn't go to school and just put them to work. For their own welfare, I'd say. (2)

9. Forest: I would, well I would try to, this happened to us, we

had a frightening experience in the Smokey Mountains. We were going around in circles. We tried to find the, we tried to sort of, picture the direction I would think from whence, I came in and try to either circle back or just go out straight from that direction. And not circle around because we'd only be going around in circles. Try to head forward or by trying to establish in my mind in which direction, north, east, or south would be. (How would you do that?) I don't know. By following the rays of the sun or whatever. Following the rays of the sun or trying to see in which, yeah, or if I could follow some sort of path. (1)

10. Deaf: They don't hear. The hearing is not there to establish the sounds that should come from the voicebox, **[TDI Category: Peculiar; Score: .25]** so this has to be developed by therapy. Am I right? (2)

11. City land: The value is much greater in the city because of industrial value and the demand for population. There's much more demand for living in an urban area than in the rural and the land which will build high-rises or tremendous buildings will realize much profit from what's going onto the land. And the footage, areawise, although in the country it can be bad too. (1) **[TDI Category: Vague; Score: .25]**

12. Marriage: Oh, it's just a law; also it has a lot to do with the health of either parties, having to have a blood test made, and also it's some sort of a tax on the two individuals. It's some sort of payment to the state, to the city. And I think you have to apply because you have to be registered that you are filing for a marriage so that there's some sort of registration of the marriage in public files, or in city. I seem to go about these things in a roundabout way. I have nothing to go by—there's no way of studying what you're gonna ask. It's a way of, you know of keeping records of marriage, for statistical purposes too, I'd say, yeah. (2)

13. Brooks: It would mean putting it toward human or people. **[TDI Category: Peculiar; Score: .25]** One who chatters a lot or talks much, much of it is just a lot of noise and there isn't much to it. There isn't much too deep thought. A lot of light-hearted chatter or conversation or, could pertain to children. A lot of

careless, light-hearted conversation. It's a lot of noise, but it really means nothing. There isn't much depth, in other words, there isn't much depth to the thoughts. (2)

14. Swallow: One experience, having a certain experience does not create the whole idea, the whole way of life. Just because you accomplish in one little area does not mean that you have conquered the whole thing. It's just a beginning, there's more to it, to success or whatever you mean, to achievement. (1)

Raw Score: 23

Similarities:

1. Orange: They're both fruit. (2)
2. Coat: Clothes. (2)
3. Axe: They're both carpenter tools, you know, tools. (2)
4. Dog: Animals. (2)
5. North: Directions. (2)
6. Eye: Parts of the body, the head. (1)
7. Air: Atmosphere. (0)
8. Table: Furniture. (2)
9. Egg: Fertilized egg, or how can you say it. An egg is the end result of the planting of the seed. Oh, how would you say that. Fertilization, planting. (?) A result, an egg is a result of fertilization, of an implantation, of an implanation. **[TDI Category: Word-finding Difficulty; Score: .25]** (0)
10. Poem: Pieces of art. (2)
11. Wood: For fire or for heat? Fire or heat, combustion, I don't know, fire or heat. (1)
12. Praise: Means of a, you know, thoughts of, accomplishment or expression, expression of accomplishment, either good or evil, well, they're not the same, evil or good. Expressions of human behavior. (?) Well, types of human accomplishment or behavior. (0)
13. Fly: Nature, I don't know. Elements of nature, yeah. Outdoors, you know. (1)

Raw Score: 17

Picture completion: ·

1. Knob: (1)

2. Tail: Pig, his little thing is missing. What do you call that, his tail. (1) **[TDI Category: Word-finding Difficulty; Score: .25]**

3. Nose: (1)

4. Handles: (1)

5. Diamond: (1)

6. Water: The pitcher is in mid-air. It should be held by a hand conducting it to the glass, to pour the water. (0)

7. Nosepiece: Part of the man's nose is missing, right? (0)

8. Peg: I should know that one. One of the pegs is missing on the violin. I play the violin. (1)

9. Oarlock: One of the rests on the boat for the oar is missing. (1)

10. Base thread: One of the fagments, **[TDI Category: Tendency to Confusion (slip); Score: .25]** or filaments, is missing in the bulb. Something is wrong with the filament in the bulb. (0)

11. Stars: This is stupid. We don't make the flag like that. It does not have those lines like a staff. It's not a staff. That's not the way it's supposed to be. It's wrong, not right. (0)

12. Dog tracks: Part of the man's foot. The step **[TDI Category: Peculiar; Score: .25]** is not right. It's missing as he's walking, I don't see it. (0)

13. Florida: The map is wrong because they've got the state of Florida in the middle of the country. It should be at the southeastern, the most southeastern part of the map. (1)

14. Smokestacks: This boat looks like there's a boat on a boat, within a boat. Can't have a sailboat over a steamer, within a steamer. Doesn't look right. The masts are not right. (0)

15. Leg: (1)

16. Arm image: She's powdering her nose, but you don't—, it doesn't show in the mirror. She's just sitting and looking at herself. The, you know, the illusion **[TDI Category: Peculiar; Score: .25]** is wrong. What else could be missing? (1)

17. Finger: (1)

18. Shadow: This is kind of nasty. He's walking into, it's not right, the sun does not set in the, could it be, the sun comes up, it does not rise, I can't see what's wrong here. Or is it the fact that he's missing his hand. He's got it in his pocket. And he's facing in the wrong direction. **[TDI Category: Peculiar; Score: .25]** I can't see that. That wasn't right. (0)

19. Stirrup: Horse has two reins? Should only have one around his mouth? Connected back to the saddle? There's something wrong there. Could that be it? (0)

20. Snow: This is a barn, something wrong with the stack, the pile of wood there. (What?) It can't be it's piled in the snow, it should be, where, inside the house instead of outside, for heat. (0)

21. Eyebrow: (1)

Raw Score: 12

Vocabulary:

1-3. (6 points credited)

4. Winter: A season, a time of the year. (1)

5. Repair: To fix. (2)

6. Breakfast: First meal of the day, in the morning, morning meal. (2)

7. Fabric: Material. (1)

8. Slice: Piece of something, piece of bread. (1)

9. Assemble: Put together. (2)

10. Conceal: Hide. (2)

11. Enormous: Big, gigantic. (2)

12. Hasten: Make fast, fast, hurry. (2)

13. Sentence: Group of words in a paragraph. (1)

14. Regulate: To control. (2)

15. Commence: To start. (2)

16. Ponder: To think about. (2)

17. Cavern: Big hole, big cave. (2)

18. Designate: To start, to confront, to, I don't know, we designated that project, recognized. (0)

19. Domestic: Product that is made here, made in this country, not foreign. (2)

20. Consume: Take in, to eat, to take over. (2)

21. Remorse: To feel sorry, sad. (1)

22. Terminate: To end, to stop. (2)

23. Obstruct: To get in somebody's way such as obstructing traffic or, an obstruction is something in the way. (2)

24. Sanctuary: A place of, to think, to ponder, sort of a little haven, away from, a place of tranquillity, away from excitement, sort of a quiet place. (2)

25. Matchless: There's nothing like it, it can't be matched. Perfect, superb. (2)

26. Reluctant: Do not wish to do something. Do not want to go, reluctant, uncertain. (2)

27. Calamity: Catastrophe, a terrible happening. (2)

28. Fortitude: To be tough, to be brave, stick-to-it-iveness. (2)

29. Tranquil: Quiet, at peace. (2)

30. Edifice: A building. (2)

31. Compassion: To have feeling for another, feeling of anxiousness, a feeling for another one's problems. Compassion, having a feeling of warmth towards another person. (1)

32. Tangible: Means object is an obvious object, it's there, it's physically seen. (1)

33. Perimeter: Surface or area. Perimeter around the circle has to do with area. (?) A way of measuring area of a circle, or a certain type of uh, I can't think, styles, different forms. (?) Area or how you measure the, around, the surface of a circle? How you measure the surface of a circle. (0)

34. Audacious: Nervy, audacious person is forthright, belligerent, very outspoken. (2)

35. Ominous: Something impending, bad, to foretell something sad that is coming on, or bad. (2)

36. Tirade: A temper tantrum, a complete lack of control of temper. (0)

37. Encumber: To encounter, to encounter **[TDI Category: Clang; Score: .25]**, to come to, to have to hassle with, to have to do with. (0)

38. Plagiarize: To copy or to steal someone else's work, just copying, stealing another one's ideas, thoughts. (1)

39. Impale: To do damage to part of the body. I would say, to the sex organs, **[TDI Category: Inappropriate Distance; Score: .25]** to impale, create injury to something. (?) To cut or to do harm. To cut. (0)

40. Travesty: That's a travesty on death, a soliloquy, a thought, a philosophical thought, an idea, such as a travesty on death. Am I on the right track, or—? (0)

Raw Score: 60

Summary of WAIS Scores:

Verbal IQ: 119	Similarities: 12
Performance IQ: 104	Vocabulary: 13
Full Scale IQ: 113	Picture Completion: 9
$TD_W = 4.0$	Picture Arrangement: 9
Information: 14	Block Design: 9
Comprehension: 15	Object Assembly: 8
Arithmetic: 13	Digit Symbol: 9
Digit Span: 11	

Rorschach Test

Card I (Reaction Time 13 seconds):

1. It looks like a blob of nothing. **[CD: 192]** It could be a part of a vagina, of a uterus, of a womb. **[260, 181]** (D FCh ± Sx) This part here could be the vulva or the vagina tract, or the woman's female organs. **[320, 312, 182]** Could have inside, uh, a fetus—baby growing inside of the womb. Baby developing inside the womb of a woman's, uh, womb, of a woman's womb, a female womb. **[TDI Category: Peculiar; Score: .25; 310]**

Otherwise just a blob, I don't know. (Vagina?) The part there
that was, looked like a little cut, like, you know, little roundish,
and a little split. It would look like a woman's, the in—, [314]
you know, the lip of the vagina. (Fetus?) It looked, there was
like a sort of a hazy uh, it showed, sort of a, within the drawing,
almost the beginning of the shaping of a baby. [110, 310] (What
made you—) Fetus. (Think of a fetus?) I don't know, I just sort
of had that feeling of a, of a womb, the fuzziness, [183] the uh,
especially the shaping of the, of that, what I think's a vagina,
that's part of it, and then it's kind of coming—(Can you show
me that?) Here (S laughs), I know you see it different [212], and
then here would be the start of a baby developing inside, here,
the shape of the legs. I don't know what this could be, could be
nothing more than a flower. [260, 181, 250] (The split is
where?) Right there. It's wrong, am I way off? [194, 170]

Card II (15 seconds):

(S laughs) You're gonna think I have a hang-up with sexual
organs. [CD: 212]

2. This could look like two little animals, two little, tiny little dogs
kissing, touching each other with their noses and their, I don't
know, [CD: 181, 320, 110] could be like two little uh, two little
pigs, with their uh, you know, I don't know what the red could
designate. Or they're coming together and they've hurt each
other and there's blood spouting from their, from their feet
and their heads. They're fighting. And I see sort of, look like
two little pig eyes, you know, (S mumbles) each other.
(W FM+ A P; D CF Bl, Fab, Aggr.) That's about all I can make
out of it. This sort of thing has to do with perception, or what?
(?) That would be like the two snouts coming together, and,
kind of in combat, or they're trying to hurt each other, and
here's just the blood coming from their, wherever they may
have hurt themselves, the blood is spurting out from the head,
and here's the little feet, or their paws, and more blood coming
out from there. (OK, and the—) I see the two little eyes, right
there, one eye on each of them, gives me that feeling. [211]

Card III (27 seconds):

3. This, too, has a feeling of movement. Actually, looking at it now, I can see a, it's part, I could say a part of a drawing, of an immovable object, **[TDI Category: Peculiar; Score: .25; CD: 181, 319]** it's an object, and I would say it's part of a vase, or a bowl. And it's unfinished, unfinished. Or, it, yeah. **[110]** And the red could be just, maybe decoratitive, **[315]** of the bowl. (W F/C± Obj) (Drawing?) Uh, the way it was set, it was shaped at the bottom like it was set on a **[110]**, like a bottom of a vase, it was quite obvious there, as a, like a, like something that would rest on something, you know. **[140, 213]** Part of the vase was like cut off. I would say the red, in that, thinking of it as a vase, is, is uh, is the color that it could be painted on the front of it. **[320, 311]** Then I, sense two creatures going at each other. **[250]** (Before you get to that, you said it looked like it was unfinished?) Because the whole shape was not, it just looked like part, it looked like this should keep going up.

4. Or you could think of two mammals, and also, on either side, uh, going at each other, and they've hurt each other in combat, and there's blood, squirting. (W F± A Fab; D CF Bl, Aggr.) And like their paws or their legs are detached from their bodies. Blood is squirting up into the air. And there's blood in the middle. They seem to be going around something, or something like, spiraling around uh, each one's, one foot or one paw is around something, it seems to be turning around. I could picture that much, these two different things. Actually, it's pretty much shaped in proportion. I could make out of it (S mumbles). That's all. (?) Two animals, yeah. (Where?) On either side. (How much—) They seem to be going, huh? (How much of it is the animal?) Not much, just their bodies, and a head, one foot, one of their legs, each one has a leg, they're facing each other, and they seem to have been in anger or something, combat, there could be spurts of blood in between, spurting of blood on the outer side of their head, their feet are detached, and they seem to be going around, spiraling around this, you get a feeling of motion from this bottom part here. (What do you—) They're circling, they're circling around on a,

on a—(They—) Yeah, yeah. (What makes it look like that?) It's
turning around, the way it, the uh, the drawing, the, the m—,
the uh, direction, the direction of the drawing at that point
there. **[TDI Category: Vague; Score: .25]**

Card IV (8 seconds):

She was surprised to see me, today (referring to daughter).
[CD: 212]

5. And this could be, heh, heh, heh, I'll tell you what it is, it looks
   like the bottom of a man, a big furry creature, and two big feet.
   [CD: 182] (W FCh± (H),Sx) Two big feet and looks like a long
   penis hanging out there (laughs), can't, **[110]** big furry object,
   some furry creature. Something peculiar hanging down. I
   could think of a male creature, I'd say like part of a gorilla or
   something, you know. Kind of grotesque, very grotesque, I'd
   think of something very grotesque. **[320]** Two big feet like,
   stretched apart. Like cut off, I don't know, I can't picture what
   the rest of this could be, like part of a, part of a body **[260, 181]**,
   these things hanging on the sides, with some grotesque creature **[311]**, I would say, with this big male organ hanging down.
   [120] (You said part of a body, you mean like, what's cut off?)
   Like, the, like you've got like half of the stomach and then the
   rest of it is, the chest is cut off, like part of the stomach. **[TDI
   Category: Queer Response; Score: .5]** (So all of it isn't there?)
   No, I'd say it was part of something. (Furry?) The uh, to me it
   looks furry. **[110]** (?) The uh, shadings, and the way the ink
   drawing is, uh, the blendings, you get a feeling of uh, I don't
   know, furriness, animalness.

Card V (12 seconds):

Can I think of anything here? Let's see.

6. It could be two dead creatures, lying side by side. Their heads
   are hidden like down in the distance. Could think like of two
   deer, two deers who were maybe struck down in a road or in a
   highway, you can see like part of a leg of each animal, on either
   side. I don't know why I say two **[CD: 193]**, I just feel like
   there's, I feel like there's two parts, something is like in jux-

taposition [310], I think you'd say. Or you could say it's just two objects, two objects of the same [311] that are lying side by side. But I can sort of visualize it looks like a dead object, could be a dead animal, or as I said, two dead deer. I don't know why I said that. (W F∓ A Fab., Aggr.) (?) These could be this, one side, could be a foot, you know. And then they're laying on the other part of their body, this could be the other, other leg or something of each one, you see. They're like coming together, their heads are like spread out, in death, I don't know. Kind of weird, but, I don't know where I got that idea (laughs). [193] (Dead?) There's something so final, so—, there's something abjective [315] or, flat, so—, it's laying there so, still. The shape of the way the, the legs are sprawled out, like they had been pounced upon or hurt and they're laying like on a flat surface. Maybe it's because I've seen, uh, many times driving along I've seen a dead animal, lay like that, but you can't see the complete head, or its, you see an arm or a leg sprawled out . . .

Card VI (12 seconds):

7. This I think I could just see, could picture it as a rug, an Indian rug, laying flat. (S FCh(C)+ Obj) Could be some looming, [TDI Category: Peculiar; Score: .25] you know, weaving. (E: Some what?) A rug, in the shape of a ni— [CD: 314], an interesting type of a rug with various designs in it. I'm not going to try to uh, keep thinking of animals all the time, huh, be different (S laughs). [212] No, the first thing that came to my mind was, I was thinking of Indian work, um Indian craftsmen, Indian craft. [320] (?) The uh, sort of shape, maybe, I'm thinking of uh, I have a rug similar in appearance, we have these fur rugs, you know, throw rugs, very similar in, very odd [110], you know, cut-out pieces of rug. [Tendency to fluidity; .5] (Image vacillates between fur rug and woven.) And the way the uh, the drawing went and the, the gradings of inking [Peculiar; .25; 310] could resemble the weaving or the way they work in there, uh, the Indian type of weaving, the geometric, sort of, there's sort of a design there. (?) Like right in here, see, this could be dark, and the grey, and then there's the, you know, in that way. [182] If I keep talking about ani-

mals, they'll think this is really something. **[212]** (That's a common thing people see). Yeah, why? (E starts to say something) **[211]** You mean you try to perceive something living? **[213]** You try to, read into an object? **[311]**

Card VII (17 seconds):

8. Uh, this is, uh funny. I can't think of anything, but, right now, I'm so hungry, I think of pieces of chicken or I could think of French-fried shrimp, pieces of shrimp. **[CD: 260]** Or food, either pieces of chickens, or pieces of French-fried shrimp, just, laid together. **[320]** (W F± Fd) (?) Well, like shrimp, shrimp, where you have like the claw part that's shaped there like that, so maybe at this moment I'm starving (laughs), and I'm thinking of food. When will you eat? **[212]**

9. It puzzles me, though, what this could be, in the middle here, looks like two objects are joined together by something, like a little, hinge. (D F ± Obj) Two objects are joined together like by a hinge on the bottom of the picture. It looks like to me, what those two objects are, could be, two little furry things, or like, it can't be food joined together there. **[TDI Category: Tend. Fab. Comb.; Score: .25; CD: 150]** Or it could be part of something, joined together by a hinge. Otherwise, I can't think of anything else about the picture. Then I, what comes to my mind, is chunks of food. **[250]**

Card VIII (2 seconds):

10. Well, um, to me it looks like two pink little rats, climbing around the pretty colored corals. **[CD: 330]** (D F+ A P; D CF coral, Fab.) Or it could be foliage, pretty foliage, or pieces of coral, colored coral. And I see these two, animals kind of crawling or climbing, they walk, back and forth all day, why do they do that? (S refers to patient's walking outside in hall.) **[182, 212]** (?) Pink rats, pink mice, and rats, bigger than mice, pink rats. **[320]** Sort of climbing and hovering towards **[TDI Category: Peculiar; Score: .25; CD: 310]** this pretty, greyish foliage, **[183]** and then this pretty, could be like pretty, like coral pieces, pretty colored coral chunks. (Coral?) I don't know, I'm just

thinking of coral, I've seen these colored uh, growing out of the ocean floor, could be, but then again [110], you can't have rats out of an ocean floor [311, 196], could be something that could be lying near a beach or something like that, it's coral, different colors. If that isn't imagination, honey, I don't know what is. [212]

Card IX (20 seconds):

11. Oh, again very pretty coloring. Just blobs, I don't know, on top, you could think of like two witches fighting with each other. [CD: 260] And they're standing on the, earth. (D M± (H); D CF Earth) (?) Yeah, witches with claws, going at each other. I don't know. That's all I really can see. Against coloring, pink, I can't visualize what that could be. [311] The green could be sort of the earth [181], or . . .

12. Looks like the shape of a continent that's torn apart. (W FC− Geog) (And this looks like earth, or something?) It could be like a, a country, or maybe part of a continent, that's uh, um, divided, and then again it could be—(How do you mean, it's divided?) Well, it's like a partition, like you see, like cut, it's like divided, because there's this here colored uh, line going down.

13. Or yet, it looks like three sets of, sort of animals, all, all in combat, kind of, they're sort of split down the center with this long, kind of, this long colored line. (D F+ A) But on top, it isn't so much animals, as I think of a couple of witches. [CD: 182, 250] Or they have claws and they're trying to claw each other. And the middle could be two green objects, sort of fusing together, you, I sense a feeling of a, lot of motion in the picture, the way they smear the colors. That's it. (What about the three animals?) Yeah, or I can think of it as animals fighting, you know, this is dividing in there, it's sort of like they're going at each other. This could be the heads, see, this could be the—(The what?) Their, their, whatever it is, furry, brush or, their mouths open and they're hissing at each other, there's a little eye on each one. Here's the mouth, open wide. Could be like two dragons, two dragons going at each other (S is describ-

ing center green details). (I can't see it, can you show me where the mouth is?) This, see, it's wide open, like, aah, adam's apple jutting forth [TDI Category: Peculiar; Score: .25] like steam, yeah. See and this here, the little eye, that's open, that's coming forth, they're like gushing out. (You said three sets of animals?) I don't know, what you can see down here, I think I was mistaken, I can't see anything really. [TDI Category: Fluid; Score: .75] (percept of animals unstable) Uh, then it could be like, a, two un—, it seems crazy, but like two newborn babes, these are the heads and they're laying there, two babes looking up, two babies, and they're staring up at what's going on, at all the commotion. (Additional: D M+ H) [TDI Category: Fabulized Combination; Score: .5] (So the only animals you saw were those—?) Yeah, two babies, animals, and the witches. A lot of action.

Card X (6 seconds):

14. Oh boy. Umm, I see like two spiders. (D FCarb+ A P) (?) I see these blue, big blue spiders. [TDI Category: Incongruous Combination; Score: .25] Seems to me like a lot of little series of little creatures, [TDI Category: Peculiar; Score: .25] all colored very beautifully. Bunch of little ideas in this picture.

15. I see on top there, like, two, two rats or something, digging away at something. (D FC'+ A) (?) Yeah, looked like they were gnawing at something or crawling on a thin grey object. I mean, after awhile, you get real good at this (laughs).

   Two spiders on the side. [CD: 250]

16. Could be a couple of little fishes. (D F+ A)

17. And believe it or not, in the center looks like a brassiere, a woman's brassiere, a blue brassiere, I see. (D F/C− Cg) (?) I thought of that as a brassiere, definitely, that's funny.

18. And all these animals are like, little creatures are like trying to attach themselves to this big pink, two big pink separate, I don't know what that could be, little island or something, [CD: 260, 181], I don't know. Doesn't seem to make too much sense. [191]

(D F+ A; D F/C∓ Geog; D CF Lsc) To me, looks like two little fish here? With their eyes, and they're attaching themselves to this green, green or could be part of a greenery **[TDI Category: Peculiar; Score: .25]** or something. (You said they all looked like they were trying to—) to nab— **[211]** (—attach themselves?) Yeah, attach themselves to this pink object. (What could that be?) I don't know. A long, pink thing, part of a—tree? I don't know, it's funny.

Summary of Rorschach Scores:

$$R = 24 \qquad P = 3 \qquad CD = 4.1 \qquad TD_R = \frac{5}{24} \times 100 = 20.83$$

Location:	Deter-minants:		Content:					
W	9	F	10	A	9	F%	= 21/79	Peculiar	8
D	15	M	1	Blood	2	F+%	= 60/68	Vague	1
		FC	2	Food	2	EB	= 1/6	Inc. Comb.	1
		CF	4	Geogr	2			Tend. Fab	
		F/C	3	Earth	1			Comb.	1
		FCarb	1	Obj	3			Fab. Comb.	1
		FCh	2	(H)	2			Tend. Fluid	1
		FCh (C)	1	Clg	1			Queer	1
				Coral	1			Fluid	1

Case 6:
Father of Case 2

Historical Notes

Mr. A. was a 57-year-old insurance salesman who had had postgraduate professional training but had elected not to work in his profession. He was a somewhat passive, quiet man who related himself warmly but with some anxiety to members of the hospital staff. With his wife and daughter, he appeared ineffective and often overwhelmed. He was quite reluctant to participate in the research testing procedures but finally was persuaded to come in for one session by a staff member with whom he had developed a relationship. He clearly felt threatened by the assessment procedures.

Interpretative Comments

Mr. A. has low TDI scores on both the WAIS and the Rorschach, within normal range. His communication deviance score is also low, although when combined with that of his wife, their parental-pair ranking remains quite high. His verbal IQ is superior, but he appears to have mild difficulty in staying on the track and expressing himself clearly. However, unlike his wife, who rambles off the point freely, he successfully contains his own wandering attention. His language is vague and imprecise at times, with occasional stiltedness and obsessional rumination. The lowering of the performance IQ 16 points below the verbal IQ suggests retardation due perhaps to depression. This possibility is strengthened by the absence of color responses on the Rorschach, his proneness to depreciate his own efforts, and hints that he regards himself as helpless and grotesque. These trends are masked by his use of humor, avoidance of frustration, and his denial of pain, anxiety, and dependency. Although he does engage the examiner, his interactions are usually set to forestall anxiety and to ward off frustration.

Wechsler Adult Intelligence Scale

Information Subtest:

1-4. (4 points credited)

  5. Rubber: (1)

  6. Presidents: (1)

  7. Longfellow: (1)

  8. Weeks: (1)

  9. Panama: (1)

10. Brazil: (1)

11. Height: (1)

12. Italy: Roma. (1)

13. Clothes: Let me hear that again. Because it absorbs heat. (1)

14. Washington: (1)

15. Hamlet: (1)

16. Vatican: The seat of the Catholic religion. (1)

17. Paris: (1)

18. Egypt: In south, in Africa, north Africa. (1)

19. Yeast: Oh, I guess when you heat it. (?) It causes the dough to expand and rise. (1)

20. Population: (1)

21. Senators: (1)

22. Genesis: Religion. (?) Well, it sets up a pattern of, rules of behavior, of human beings toward one another. (0)

23. Temperature: (1)

24. Iliad: That was a Greek philosopher. Let's see, I forget. You want a name. Socrates? Maybe a bad guess. (0)

25. Blood Vessels: Capillaries, ateries, and, it begins with a v, I won't say ventricle, veins. (1) **[TDI Category: Word-finding Difficulty; Score: .25]**

26. Koran: That's the Mohammedan Bible. (1)

27. Faust: I was gonna say a character, Mephistopheles. Mephistopholes, character in Faust, I don't know. (0)

28. Ethnology: I suppose the study of ethnic groups. (1)

29. Apocrypha: Is that like the apocalypse? (laughs) I don't know. (0)

Raw Score: 25

Comprehension:

1-2. (4 points credited)

3. Envelope: It wasn't post-marked? Just drop it in the mailbox. (2)

4. Bad company: Evil influence. (2)

5. Movies: Report it to the manager. (2)

6. Taxes: Support the government. (2)

7. Iron: Do it now and get it done. (1)

8. Child labor: To protect growing children. (?) Their health. (1)

9. Forest: I'd take a bead on the sun. (How would that help?)

Well, if I knew the direction, uh, where the sun was coming from, I'd know the time of day, uh, what was that? I'd know the time of day. I almost lost the question. (1) **[TDI Category: Tendency to Confusion; Score: .25]**

10. Deaf: Because they can't hear sound. (1)

11. City land: That's a very cogent question. Because it's more valuable, greater utility, greater use. (1)

12. Marriage: You know, that's a very good question! (laughs) To legalize the state of matrimony. (?) Yes, prior to 1905 in the state of Illinois, people used to live together and if they lived outwardly and openly, this was a marriage too. This was a common law marriage, and the states decided to require a license. I think to raise revenue, to a great extent. (0)

13. Brooks: I suppose it's the opposite of still water runs deep. Now you want to know what the reference is, or the meaning. I suppose it means people with not too much character make a lot of noise. (2)

14. Swallow: One success isn't 100 percent success. That's one meaning. (1)

Raw Score: 20

Similarities:

1. Orange: They're both fruit. (2)

2. Coat: Both clothing. (2)

3. Axe: Both tools. (2)

4. Dog: Both animals. (2)

5. North: Directions. (2)

6. Eye: Parts of the anatomy, or face, or head. (1)

7. Air: Part of the uh, elements, air, atmosphere, and water. I'd guess you'd call them compounds, chemically. (1)

8. Table: Furniture. (2)

9. Egg: I suppose, uh, the beginning of, a birth, of an animal and something growing. (1)

10. Poem: They're works of arts. (2)

11. Wood: Alcohol is a derivative, or it comes from wood, no, ex-

cuse me, I'm thinking of wood alcohol. They're not alike. (?) Well, both derive from growing things, I suppose. (1)

12. Praise: That pertains to the human being, as it pertains to the human being. (In what way?) Well, praise is to uplift someone, to compliment them, and punishment is to chastise somebody for misbehavior. (0)

13. Fly: They're both living things. (2)

Raw Score: 20

Picture Completion:

1. Knob: (1)
2. Tail: (1)
3. Nose: (1)
4. Handles: I can't guess this one. (0)
5. Diamond: (1)
6. Water: Somebody holding the pitcher. (0)
7. Nosepiece: I can't figure this one out. (0)
8. Peg: One of the knobs here on the violin. (1)
9. Oarlock: The oarsman. (0)
10. Base thread: The screw part on the bulb. (1)
11. Stars: (1)
12. Dog tracks: One leg missing. (0)
13. Florida: The states. (0)
14. Smokestack: The mast. (0)
15. Leg: The outline [TDI Category: Peculiar; Score: .25] of the crab. I mean, the rest of the body. (0)
16. Arm image: The chair and the legs, two legs of the table. (0)
17. Finger: I can't figure 17. (0)
18. Shadow: The sun is too big. (0)
19. Stirrup: There's no rider. (0)
20. Snow: Dk (0)
21. Eyebrow: I don't see anything wrong on 21. (0)

Raw Score: 7

Vocabulary:

1-3. (6 points credited)

 4. Winter: Oh, you mean from the other side? Oh, you want a definition? It's a season. (1)

 5. Repair: Remake, uh, fix. (2)

 6. Breakfast: Lunch, oh, that's a meal. (1) **[TDI Category: Tend. Loose; Score: .25]**

 7. Fabric: Cloth. (2)

 8. Slice: Slice is loaf, this, association? **[TDI Category: Tend. Loose; Score: .25]** No, you want a definition? A piece, not good one. Are you satisfied with a piece? (1)

 9. Assemble: Get together. (2)

10. Conceal: Hide. (2)

11. Enormous: Large. (1)

12. Hasten: Hurry. (2)

13. Sentence: Oh, words. (?) Part of a paragraph, phrase, no, paragraph. (1)

14. Regulate: Rule. (?) Or control's a better word. (2)

15. Commence: Begin. (2)

16. Ponder: Think. (2)

17. Cavern: Like a pit or a hole. A cave or a cavern, I would say, I would say, a cavern is a little cave. (1)

18. Designate: Appoint. (2)

19. Domestic: Wild. (?) Domestic would be a servant too, several meanings. A domestic animal, a wild animal, domesticated. (0)

20. Consume: Eat. (2)

21. Terminate: End. (2)

22. Obstruct: Bar. (2)

23. Remorse: Sadness. (1)

24. Sanctuary: Church. (0)

25. Matchless: Perfect. (2)

26. Reluctant: Not wanting to do something. (2)

27. Calamity: Disaster. (2)

28. Fortitude: Strength. (2)

29. Tranquil: Quiet. (2)

30. Edifice: Building. (2)

31. Compassion: Feeling. (?) Concern. (1)

32. Tangible: Real. (2)

33. Perimeter: Around. (?) The outer, the outside. (1)

34. Audacious: Aggressive. (0)

35. Ominous: Something to fear. (2)

36. Tirade: Bawling somebody else, bawling out someone. (2)

37. Encumber: To mortgage. (?) It's uh, I know fully well its meaning, well, to make something difficult maybe. (1)

38. Plagiarize: To steal. (1)

39. Impale: Be stuck on something, well, that's not the exact definition. Impale, to be caught on something, impale, or stuck, I was thinking of something sharp. (1)

40. Travesty: A wrong, travesty on justice. Some more words? (No) No more words, just when it gets fun you change the game. (0)

Raw Score: 60

Summary of WAIS Scores:

Verbal IQ: 125	Similarities: 13
Performance IQ: 109	Vocabulary: 13
Full Scale IQ: 119	Picture Completion: 6
$TD_W = 1.25$	Picture Arrangement: 10
Information: 12	Block Design: 8
Comprehension: 15	Object Assembly: 10
Arithmetic: 14	Digit Symbol: 10
Digit Span: 14	

Rorschach Test

Card I (Reaction Time 30 seconds):

1. Butterfly. (W F+ A P) (What else?) A bat! Don't tell me it's something else. It is something else? Anything you think it is.

Well, how many do I need? (Butterfly?) Some wings, the shape of the body. (Bat?) Same reasons, same reasons.

2. How about a flower? A cloud? Perfect. (W F ± Bt) (S is speaking in a brusque, humorous way) (Flower?) It looked like there were some petals and buds. (Cloud?) Uh, a cloud because it was varying shape. (Show me where the flower was?) The flower. This could look like a tulip. It can almost look like a tulip. This is the center of the tulip. (OK, that's the way it goes. I have nine more of those). Well, I don't like that game! Give me back the blocks (S laughs, playfully).

Card II (30 seconds):

Oh, how many more of these funny pictures? Oh that's terrible. Why do you do that to me! Now what do you want to know? (What it looks like). What it looks like? How many do you want? One, two, three choices? (Well, I'd like for you—) As many as I see? [CD: 211]

3. Well, two dancing bears. (D F+ A P) (?) The shape, the whole shape, two bears together, you know, like touching hands, or paws, I should say. (Any particular thing made it look like bears?) No, there are no faces. [CD: 213, 150] No, nothing else. (Where are the bears?) This would be the bodies of the bears and their hands up that way. Of course, I don't see any heads. I assume that their heads are down in between their shoulders.

4. Let's see. This could be a building up front there. And a garden in the center. (Ds F± Arch) (I didn't hear what you said). And a garden in the center. That's a building in the background. That's about all I can think of. (Building?) Well, the thing in the center which had a point. It looked like it might be a building. And these other black shapes would be forest, or maybe a garden in the center. (Garden?) Well, assuming, of course the colors weren't there, but I make out my own picture. I would assume that the landscape, or the forest, that would surround the garden leading to the building, or palace.

Card III (9 seconds):

5. Oh, two dogs. (D F± A) I can't think of any other picture. [CD: 310] That's all I can make out of this. (Don't see anything else?)

It might be something else, but I can't draw a picture in my mind. (Dogs?) Shape. (?) Uh, the way they were placed and the shape of the figures, of the drawing. That's the first thing that came to mind. **[213]**

6. Little butterfly in the center. (D F+ A P) **[CD: 260, 181]** (?) I don't know, it's part of the background (laughs). The scenery.

7. How about two birds? (D F± Aggr) How about two birds? (?) Like might be a couple of birds shot down. Look like they were falling, falling birds.

Card IV (13 seconds):

8. Ow! **[212]** It looks like the abominable snowman. (W F+ (H)) (Abominable snowman? You said—) Oh, it looked so grotesque. **[211]** This looks like a head here with two eyes, a nose, at the top of the picture.

9. It looks like a dog. That's all I see. (W F ± A) (?) A dog, looks like it had a big face, if you took a second look, with legs. If you look at it like a dog, you see two ears here and a big nose and a face here, and this is probably a tail and four legs. I hope you'll accept that. Might be the tail, in the center at the bottom of the picture.

Card V (5 seconds):

10. That has to look like a bat—and a butterfly. I can't see anything else there. Or a bee— **[CD: 260, 181]** no, no, I'll take that back. **[194]** That's about it. (W F+ A P) (Bat?) The legs and the wings. And the butterfly **[250]** was the antenna and the wings. I don't know if a butterfly has legs **[182, 183]**, but it's part of the body, I'd say the body. **[120]**

Card VI (44 seconds):

Why do all these pictures look similar? **[CD: 212]** With a slight variation. I'll tell you, I don't have any notion here. I have no imagination as to what this looks like to me. **[310]**

11. This could be some kind of an animal with whiskers. (Dd F± Ad) **[CD: 260, 181]** I can't, uh, I have no imagination **[110]** regarding it. That's all I can say for this. (?) Right up here, at the top, looked like eyes, and nose and whiskers.

Card VII (22 seconds):

12. This looks like faces. I see faces of two pigs. (D F± Ad)

13. Maybe two faces of two girls with their hair flying. (D M+ Hd P) That's all I can make out of that. OK? (?) Two girls with their pigtails flying.

Card VIII (8 seconds):

14. Oh, I see two rats. That's all I can make of it. (D F+ A P) (?) Here are the two rats. This looks like a head here and rat feet, rat legs, or legs of a rat, what else—ears, close ears [CD: 310], probably food and I don't see it (laughs). [213] I suppose that's the answer. [270]

Card IX (15 seconds):

15. This could look like a candle. (Dr F(C)+ Obj) (?) This the candle, this center. (?) Just that it has that shape. (?) Well, there might be, it looked like wax, burnt wax [CD: 310] along the sides.

16. A flower. (W F± Bt) That's all I can think of. (?) The whole thing looked like it might look like a, you know, a bulb, with petals around on the side like a tulip.

Card X (23 seconds):

17. This might look like an indescribable creature. (D F∓ (A)) I'll tell you why. You want to know now? This looks like an eye, what should I say, I can't describe it as a, [CD: 110] or give it a name. [TDI Category: Vague; Score: .25; 213] I really can't see much here. [150]

18. It looks like something out of, on which something hangs, a fixture of some kind. (D F± Obj) Some kind of fixture, something that you would hang on, or hang from a ceiling. I can't make anything else. (?) This was the piece that I said that would hang, that would—(All of that or—?) No, just this, with some *holly* (S laughs, has made pun on examiner's name), [TDI Category: Inappropriate Distance; Score: .25] how's that! (What kind of fixture did you have in mind?) Maybe a light fixture, some metal light fixture, ornamental.

19. Maybe this is an ornament? (D F ± Obj) (?) This was something over here, it seemed to have some shape, of some kind. Just the center part of that. (?) Well, just its lines, shape. (Can you tell me more about what that looked like, like what kind of ornament?) I really don't know. Could be a lavaliere, or something that a woman, or a man today, have, you know, neck, some neck ornament, around the neck. (The lines make it look like that?) Yeah, the center where you had the, uh, how do I want to say it, geometric lines.

20. This could be two men here, carrying something. That's all I can . . . (D M+ H)

Summary of Rorschach Scores:

$R = 20$ $P = 6$ $CD = 1.5$ $TD_R = \dfrac{.5}{20} \times 100 = 2.5$

Location:		Deter- minants:		Content:·				
W	6	M	2	H	1	F%	= 85/100	Vague	1
D	11	F(C)	1	Hd	1	F+%	= 85/80	Inappropriate	
Dd	1	F	17	(H)	1	EB	= 2/0	Distance	1
Dr	1			A	8·				
Ds	1			Ad	2				
				Arch	1				
				Bt	2				
				Obj	3				

References

Adler, D., and Harrow, M. "Idiosyncratic Thinking and Personally Overinvolved Thinking in Schizophrenic Patients During Partial Recovery." *Comprehensive Psychiatry,* 1974, *15* (1), 57–67.

American Psychiatric Association. *Diagnostic and Statistical Manual of Mental Disorders.* (2nd ed.) Washington, D.C.: American Psychiatric Association, 1968.

Andreasen, N. "The Clinical Assessment of Thought, Language, and Communication Disorders." *Archives of General Psychiatry,* in press.

Appelbaum, S. A., and Holzman, P. S. "Color-Shading Response and Suicide." *Journal of Projective Techniques,* 1962, *22,* 155–161.

Arieti, S. *Interpretation of Schizophrenia.* (2nd ed.) New York: Basic Books, 1974.

Astrachan, B. M., and others. "A Checklist for the Diagnosis of Schizophrenia." *British Journal of Psychiatry,* 1972, *121,* 529–539.

Atkinson, M. W., and others. "A Preliminary Report of Enquiries into the Contribution of Hereditary and Environmental Factors in the Aetiology of Schizophrenia." Paper presented at 4th World Congress of Psychiatry, Madrid, 1966.

Bannister, D. "Conceptual Structure in Thought-Disordered Schizophrenics." *Journal of Mental Science,* 1960, *106,* 1230–1249.

Bannister, D. "The Logical Requirements of Research into Schizophrenia." *Schizophrenia Bulletin,* Fall 1971, (4), 72–77.

Barison, F. "Il Manierismo Schizofrenico" ["Schizophrenic Pathology"]. *Rivista Neurol,* 1948, *18.* (Cited in Arieti, 1974.)

Barison, F. "Dissociazione e Incomprehensibilita Schizofreniche" ["Schizophrenic Dissociation and Confusion"]. *Rivista Neurol,* 1949, *19.* (Cited in Arieti, 1974.)

Beck, S. J. *Rorschach's Test.* Vols. 1 and 2. New York: Grune & Stratton, 1944.

Becker, W. C. "A Genetic Approach to the Interpretation and Evaluation of the Process-Reactive Distinction in Schizophrenia." *Journal of Abnormal and Social Psychology,* 1956, *53,* 229–236.

Behrens, M. I., Rosenthal, A. J., and Chodoff, P. "Communication in Lower-Class Families of Schizophrenics. II: Observations and Findings." *Archives of General Psychiatry,* 1968, *18,* 680–696.

Bellak, L. "Research on Ego Function Patterns." In L. Bellak and L. Lober (Eds.), *The Schizophrenic Syndrome.* New York: Grune & Stratton, 1969.

Benjamin, J. D. "A Method for Distinguishing and Evaluating Formal Thinking Disorders in Schizophrenia." In J. S. Kasanin (Ed.), *Language and Thought in Schizophrenia.* New York: Norton, 1944.

Blatt, S., and Wild, C. *Schizophrenia: A Developmental Analysis.* New York: Academic Press, 1975.

Bleuler, E. *Dementia Praecox or the Group of Schizophrenias.* New York: International Universities Press, 1950. (Originally published 1911.)

Broadbent, D. E. *Perception and Communication.* Elmsford, N.Y.: Pergamon Press, 1958.

Bromet, E., and Harrow, M. "Behavioral Overinclusion as a Prognostic Index in Schizophrenic Disorders." *Journal of Abnormal Psychology,* 1973, *82,* 345–349.

Cameron, N. "Experimental Analysis of Schizophrenic Thinking." In J. S. Kasanin (Ed.), *Language and Thought in Schizophrenia.* New York: Norton, 1944.

Cancro, R. "Clinical Prediction of Outcome in Schizophrenia." *Comprehensive Psychiatry,* 1969, *10,* 349–354.

Chapman, L. J. "Confusion of Figurative and Literal Usages of Words by Schizophrenics and Brain-Damaged Patients." *Journal of Abnormal and Social Psychology*, 1960, *60*, 412–416.

Chapman, L. J. "A Reinterpretation of Some Pathological Disturbances in Conceptual Breadth." *Journal of Abnormal and Social Psychology*, 1961, *62*, 514–519.

Chapman, L. J., and Chapman, J. P. *Disordered Thinking in Schizophrenia.* New York: Appleton-Century-Crofts, 1973.

Chapman, L. J., and Knowles, R. R. "The Effects of Phenothiazines on Disordered Thought in Schizophrenia." *Journal of Consulting Psychology*, 1964, *28*, 165–169.

Ciarlo, D. D., Lidz, T., and Ricci, J. "Word Meaning in Parents of Schizophrenics." *Archives of General Psychiatry*, 1967, *17*, 470–477.

Cohen, J. "Weighted Kappa: Nominal Scale Agreement with Provision for Scaled Disagreement or Partial Credit." *Psychological Bulletin*, 1968, *70*, 213–220.

Cooper, J. E., and others. *Psychiatric Diagnosis in New York and London.* London: Oxford University Press, 1972.

Ellman, R. *James Joyce.* New York: Oxford University Press, 1959.

Endicott, J., and Spitzer, R. L. "A Diagnostic Interview: The Schedule for Affective Disorders and Schizophrenia." *Archives of General Psychiatry*, 1978, *35*, 837–844.

Feighner, J. P., and others. "Diagnostic Criteria for Use in Psychiatric Research." *Archives of General Psychiatry*, 1972, *26*, 57–63.

Feinsilver, D. "Communication in Families of Schizophrenic Patients: Describing Common Objects as a Test of Communication Between Family Members." *Archives of General Psychiatry*, 1970, *22*, 143–148.

Fenichel, O. *The Psychoanalytic Theory of Neurosis.* New York: Norton, 1945.

Finn, J. *Multivariance: Univariate and Multivariate Analysis of Variance, Covariance, and Regression.* Ann Arbor, Mich.: National Educational Resources, 1972.

Fish, F. *Clinical Psychopathology: Signs and Symptoms in Psychiatry.* Bristol, England: John Wright and Sons, 1967.

Freud, S. *The Interpretation of Dreams.* In J. Strachey (Ed.), *The Complete Psychological Works of Sigmund Freud.* Vols. 3 and 4. London: Hogarth Press, 1953. (Originally published 1900.)

Freud, S. "Formulations on the Two Principles of Mental Functioning." In J. Strachey (Ed.), *The Complete Psychological Works of Sigmund Freud.* Vol. 12. London: Hogarth Press, 1958. (Originally published 1911.)

Friedman, H. "Perceptual Regression in Schizophrenia." *Journal of Projective Techniques,* 1953, *17,* 171–185.

Gardner, R. W. "Cognitive Styles in Categorizing Behavior." *Journal of Personality,* 1953, *22,* 214–233.

Garmezy, N. "Process and Reactive Schizophrenia: Some Conceptions and Issues." *Schizophrenia Bulletin,* 1970, *2,* 30–74.

Garmezy, N. "Competence and Adaptation in Adult Schizophrenic Patients and Children at Risk." In S. R. Dean (Ed.), *Schizophrenia: The First Ten Dean Award Lectures.* New York: MSS Publications, 1973.

Garmezy, N. "Children at Risk: The Search for the Antecedents of Schizophrenia. Part II: Ongoing Research Programs, Issues, and Intervention." *Schizophrenia Bulletin,* Summer 1974, *9,* 55–125.

Garmezy, N., and Rodnick, E. H. "Premorbid Adjustment and Performance in Schizophrenia: Implications for Interpreting Heterogeneity in Schizophrenia." *Journal of Nervous and Mental Disease,* 1959, *129,* 450–466.

Garmezy, N., with Streitman, S. "Children at Risk: The Search for the Antecedents of Schizophrenia. Part I: Conceptual Models and Research Methods." *Schizophrenia Bulletin,* Spring 1974, *8,* 14–90.

Gill, M. M. "The Primary Process." In R. R. Holt (Ed.), *Motives and Thought: Psychoanalytic Essays in Honor of David Rapaport.* Psychological Issues Monograph 18/19. New York: International Universities Press, 1967.

Goldfried, M. R., Stricker, G., and Weiner, I. B. *Rorschach Handbook of Clinical and Research Applications.* Englewood Cliffs, N.J.: Prentice-Hall, 1971.

Goldstein, K. "The Significance of Special Mental Tests for Diagnosis and Prognosis in Schizophrenia." *American Journal of Psychiatry,* 1939, *96,* 575–588.

Goldstein, K. "Methodological Approach to the Study of Schizophrenic Thought Disorder." In J. S. Kasanin (Ed.), *Language and Thought in Schizophrenia.* New York: Norton, 1944.

Goldstein, K., and Scheerer, M. "Abstract and Concrete Behavior:

An Experimental Study with Special Tests." *Psychological Monographs,* 1941, *53* (entire issue).

Goldstein, M. J., and Rodnick, E. H. "The Family's Contribution to the Etiology of Schizophrenia." *Schizophrenia Bulletin,* 1975, (14), 48–63.

Gorham, D. R. "Use of the Proverbs Test for Differentiating Schizophrenics from Normals." *Journal of Consulting Psychology,* 1956, *20,* 435–440.

Gottschalk, L. G., and Gleser, G. C. *The Measurement of Psychological States Through the Content Analysis of Verbal Behavior.* Berkeley: University of California Press, 1969.

Grinker, R. R., and Holzman, P. S. "Schizophrenic Pathology in Young Adults." *Archives of General Psychiatry,* 1973, *28,* 168–175.

Haimo, S. "Social Class, Race, and Thinking Disorder in Schizophrenia." Unpublished doctoral dissertation, University of Chicago, 1976.

Haimo, S., and Holzman, P. S. "Thought Disorder in Schizophrenics and Normal Controls: Social Class and Race Differences." *Journal of Consulting and Clinical Psychology,* 1979.

Hanfmann, E., and Kasanin, J. S. "Conceptual Thinking in Schizophrenia." *Nervous and Mental Diseases Monograph,* 1942, *67* (entire issue).

Harrow, M., Adler, D., and Hanf, E. "Abstract and Concrete Thinking in Schizophrenia During the Prechronic Phases." *Archives of General Psychiatry,* 1974, *31,* 27–33.

Harrow, M., and Quinlan, D. "Is Disordered Thinking Unique to Schizophrenia?" *Archives of General Psychiatry,* 1977, *34,* 15–24.

Harrow, M., Tucker, G. J., and Adler, D. "Concrete and Idiosyncratic Thinking in Acute Schizophrenic Patients." *Archives of General Psychiatry,* 1972, *26,* 433–439.

Harrow, M., and others. "Overinclusive Thinking in Acute Schizophrenic Patients." *Journal of Abnormal Psychology,* 1972a, *79,* 161–168.

Harrow, M., and others. "Schizophrenic 'Thought Disorders' after the Acute Phase." *American Journal of Psychiatry,* 1972b, *128,* 824–825.

Harrow, M., and others. "A Longitudinal Study of Schizophrenic Thinking." *Archives of General Psychiatry,* 1973, *28,* 179–182.

Harrow, M., and others. "Primitive Drive-Dominated Thinking: Relationship to Acute Schizophrenia and Sociopathy." *Journal of Personality Assessment,* 1976, *40,* 31–41.

Hawks, D. V., and Payne, R. W. "Overinclusive Thinking and Concept Identification in Psychiatric Patients and Normals." *British Journal of Medical Psychology,* 1972, *45,* 57–69.

Henry, G. M., Weingartner, H., and Murphy, D. L. "Idiosyncratic Patterns of Learning and Word Association During Mania." *American Journal of Psychiatry,* 1971, *128,* 564–573.

Heston, L. L. "Psychiatric Disorders in Foster Home Reared Children of Schizophrenic Mothers." *British Journal of Psychiatry,* 1966, *112,* 819–825.

Heston, L. L. "The Genetics of Schizophrenic and Schizoid Disease." *Science,* 1970, *167,* 249–255.

Hirsch, S. R., and Leff, J. P. *Abnormalities in Parents of Schizophrenics.* London: Oxford University Press, 1975.

Hollingshead, A. B. *Two Factor Index of Social Position.* Privately printed, Yale Station, New Haven, Conn., 1957.

Hollingshead, A. B., and Redlich, T. C. *Social Class and Mental Illness.* New York: Wiley, 1958.

Holt, R. R. "A Method for Assessing Primary Process Manifestations and Their Control in Rorschach Responses." In M. A. Rickers-Ovsiankina (Ed.), *Rorschach Psychology.* (Rev. ed.) New York: Krieger, 1977.

Holt, R. R. *Methods in Clinical Psychology.* Vol. I: *Projective Assessment.* New York: Plenum, 1978.

Holt, R. R., and Havel, J. "A Method for Assessing Primary and Secondary Process in the Rorschach." In M. A. Rickers-Ovsiankina (Ed.), *Rorschach Psychology.* New York: Wiley, 1960.

Holzman, P. S. "The Modesty of Nature: A Social Perspective on Schizophrenia." *Social Service Review,* 1977, *51,* 588–603.

Holzman, P. S. "Cognitive Impairment and Cognitive Stability: Towards a Theory of Thought Disorder." In G. Serban (Ed.), *Cognitive Defects in the Development of Mental Illness.* New York: Brunner/Mazel, 1978.

Holzman, P. S., Levy, D. L., and Proctor, L. R. "Smooth Pursuit Eye Movements, Attention, and Schizophrenia." *Archives of General Psychiatry,* 1976, *33,* 1415–1420.

Holzman, P. S., Proctor, L. R., and Hughes, D. W. "Eye-Tracking Patterns in Schizophrenia." *Science,* 1973, *181,* 179–181.

Holzman, P. S., and Rousey, C. "Disinhibition of Communicated Thought: Generality and Role of Cognitive Style." *Journal of Abnormal Psychology,* 1971, *77,* 263–274.

Holzman, P. S., and others. "Eye-Tracking Dysfunctions in Schizophrenic Patients and Their Relatives." *Archives of General Psychiatry,* 1974, *31,* 143–151.

Hunt, W. A., and Arnhoff, F. N. "The Repeat Reliability of Clinical Judgments of Test Responses." *Journal of Clinical Psychology,* 1965, *12,* 289–290.

Hunt, W. A., and Jones, N. F. "Clinical Judgment of Some Aspects of Schizophrenic Thinking." *Journal of Clinical Psychology,* 1958, *14,* 235–239.

Hurt, S., and others. "Schizophrenia, Thought Disorder, and Pharmacological Intervention." Paper presented at the Society for Biological Psychiatry, Atlanta, Ga., May 4, 1978.

Johnson, J. E., and Bieliauskas, L. A. "Two Measures of Overinclusive Thinking in Schizophrenia: A Comparative Analysis." *Journal of Abnormal Psychology,* 1971, *77,* 149–154.

Johnston, M. H. "Thought Disorder in Schizophrenics and Their Relatives." Unpublished doctoral dissertation, University of Chicago, 1975.

Jones, J. E., and others. "Parental Transactional Style Deviance in Families of Disturbed Adolescents." *Archives of General Psychiatry,* 1977, *34,* 71–74.

Jones, N. F. "The Validity of Clinical Judgments of Schizophrenic Pathology Based on Verbal Responses to Intelligence Test Items." *Journal of Clinical Psychology,* 1959, *15,* 396–400.

Kataguchi, Y. "Rorschach Schizophrenic Score (RSS)." *Journal of Projective Techniques,* 1959, *23,* 214–222.

Kenny, D. A. "A Quasi-Experimental Approach to Assessing Treatment Effects in the Nonequivalent Control Group Design." *Psychological Bulletin,* 1975, *82,* 345–362.

Kety, S. S., and others. "Mental Illness in the Biological and Adoptive Families of Adopted Individuals Who Have Become Schizophrenic: A Preliminary Report Based on Psychiatric Interviews." In R. R. Fieve and others (Eds.), *Genetic Research in Psychiatry*. Baltimore, Md.: Johns Hopkins University Press, 1975.

Klein, G. S. "Peremptory Ideation: Structure and Force in Motivated Ideas." In R. R. Holt (Ed.), *Motives and Thought: Psychoanalytic Essays in Honor of David Rapaport*. Psychological Issues Monograph No. 18/19. New York: International Universities Press, 1967, pp. 80–128.

Klein, G. S., and Wolitsky, D. L. "Vocal Isolation: Effects of Occluding Auditory Feedback from One's Own Voice." *Journal of Abnormal Psychology*, 1970, *75*, 50–56.

Klopfer, B., and Kelley, D. *The Rorschach Technique*. New York: World, 1942.

Kraepelin, E. *Dementia Praecox and Paraphrenia*. Chicago: Chicago Medical Book Co., 1919. (Originally published 1896.)

Kretschmer, E. *Physique and Character*. (2nd ed.) London: Routledge & Kegan Paul, 1936.

Kurland, A., and others. "The Comparative Effectiveness of Six Phenothiazine Compounds, Phenobarbitol, and Inert Placebo in the Treatment of Acutely Ill Patients: Global Measures of Severity of Illness." *Journal of Nervous and Mental Disease*, 1961, *133*, 1–18.

Kurland, A., and others. "The Comparative Effectiveness of Six Phenothiazine Compounds, Phenobarbitol, and Inert Placebo in the Treatment of Acutely Ill Patients: Personality Dimension." *Journal of Nervous Disease*, 1962, *134*, 48–61.

Lewin, K. *A Dynamic Theory of Personality*. New York: McGraw-Hill, 1935.

Lidz, T. *The Origin and Treatment of Schizophrenic Disorders*. New York: Basic Books, 1973.

Lord, F. M. "Large-Scale Covariance Analysis When the Control Variable Is Fallible." *Journal of the American Statistical Association*, 1960, *55*, 307–321.

Lorenz, M. "Problems Posed by Schizophrenic Language." *Archives of General Psychiatry*, 1961, *4*, 603–610.

Luborsky, L. "Clinician's Judgments of Mental Health." *Archives of General Psychiatry*, 1962, *7*, 407–417.

McConaghy, N., and Clancy, M. "Familial Relationships of Allusive Thinking in University Students and Their Parents." *British Journal of Psychiatry*, 1968, *114*, 1079–1087.

Maher, B. A. *Introduction to Research in Psychopathology*. New York: McGraw-Hill, 1970.

Maher, B. A. "The Language of Schizophrenia: A Review and Interpretation." *British Journal of Psychiatry*, 1972, *120*, 317.

Mahl, G. F. "Sensory Factors in the Content of Expressive Behavior: An Experimental Study of the Function of Auditory Self-Stimulation and Visual Feedback in the Dynamics of Vocal and Gestural Behavior in the Interview Situation." In *Proceedings of the 16th International Congress of Psychology*. Amsterdam: North-Holland, 1962.

Mayer-Gross, W., Slater, E., and Roth, M. *Clinical Psychiatry*. (3rd ed., E. Slater and M. Roth, Eds.) Baltimore: Williams and Wilkins, 1969.

Meehl, P. E. "Schizotaxia, Schizotypy, Schizophrenia." *American Psychologist*, 1962, *17*, 827–838.

Muntz, H. J., and Power, R. P. "Thought Disorder in the Parents of Thought Disordered Schizophrenics." *British Journal of Psychiatry*, 1970, *117*, 707–708.

Otteson, J., and Holzman, P. S. "Cognitive Controls and Psychopathology." *Journal of Abnormal Psychology*, 1976, *84*, 125–139.

Payne, R. W. "An Object Classification Test as a Measure of Overinclusive Thinking in Schizophrenic Patients." *British Journal of Social and Clinical Psychology*, 1962, *1*, 213–221.

Payne, R. W., and Hewlett, J. H. G. "Thought Disorder in Psychotic Patients." In H. J. Eysenck (Ed.), *Experiments in Personality*. Vol 2. London: Routledge & Kegan Paul, 1960.

Phillips, L. "Case History Data and Prognosis in Schizophrenia." *Journal of Nervous and Mental Disease*, 1953, *117*, 515–525.

Phillips, L., and Zigler, E. "Social Competence: The Action-Thought Parameter and Vicariousness in Normal and Pathological Behaviors." *Journal of Abnormal and Social Psychology*, 1961, *63*, 137–146.

Planansky, K. "Conceptual Boundaries of Schizoidness: Suggestions for Epidemiological and Genetic Research." *Journal of Nervous and Mental Disease*, 1966, *142*, 318–331.

Pope, B., and Jensen, S. R. "The Rorschach as an Index of Pathological Thinking." *Journal of Projective Techniques*, 1957, *21*, 54–62.

Powers, W. F., and Hamlin, R. M. "Relationship Between Diagnostic Categories and Deviant Verbalizations on the Rorschach." *Journal of Consulting Psychology*, 1955, *19*, 120–125.

Quinlan, D., and Harrow, M. "Bringing Order to Thought Disorder(s): Dimensions of Thought Disorders in Schizophrenic and Nonschizophrenic Patients." Paper presented at the 45th annual meeting of the Eastern Psychological Association, Philadelphia, April 18–20, 1974.

Quinlan, D., and others. "How Is Thinking Disordered in Thought Disorder?" Paper presented at the 41st annual meeting of the Eastern Psychological Association, Atlantic City, N.J., April 1970.

Quinlan, D., and others. "Varieties of 'Disordered' Thinking on the Rorschach: Findings in Schizophrenic and Nonschizophrenic Patients." *Journal of Abnormal Psychology*, 1972, *79*, 47–53.

Quinlan, D., and others. "Overinclusion and Transactional Thinking on the Object Sorting Test of Schizophrenic and Nonschizophrenic Patients." *Journal of Personality Assessment*, 1978, *42*, 401–408.

Quirk, D. A., and others. "The Performance of Acute Psychotic Patients on the Index of Pathological Thinking and on Selected Signs of Idiosyncracy on the Rorschach." *Journal of Projective Techniques*, 1962, *26*, 431–441.

Rapaport, D. (Ed. and Trans.). *Organization and Pathology of Thought*. New York: Columbia University Press, 1951.

Rapaport, D. "Principles Underlying Nonprojective Tests of Personality." *Annals of the New York Academy of Sciences*, 1946, *46*, 643–652. Also in M. M. Gill (Ed.), *The Collected Papers of David Rapaport*. New York: Basic Books, 1967.

Rapaport, D., Gill, M., and Schafer, R. *Diagnostic Psychological Testing*. (Rev. ed., edited by R. R. Holt.) New York: International Universities Press, 1968. (Originally published 1946.)

Reilly, F., and others. "Looseness of Associations in Acute Schizophrenia." *British Journal of Psychiatry*, 1975, *127*, 240–246.

Romney, D. "Psychometrically Assessed Thought Disorder in

Schizophrenic and Control Patients and in Their Parents and Siblings." *British Journal of Psychiatry*, 1969, *115*, 1003–1011.

Rorschach, H. *Psychodiagnostics*. Berne, Switzerland: Hans Huber, 1942. (Originally published 1922.)

Rosenthal, D. "The Heredity-Environment Issue in Schizophrenia: Summary of the Conference and Present Status of Our Knowledge." In D. Rosenthal and S. S. Kety (Eds.), *The Transmission of Schizophrenia*. Oxford, England: Pergamon, 1968.

Rosenthal, D. *Genetics of Psychopathology*. New York: McGraw-Hill, 1971.

Rosenthal, A. J., Behrens, M. I., and Chodoff, P. "Communication in Lower-Class Families of Schizophrenics. I: Methodological Problems." *Archives of General Psychiatry*, 1968, *18*, 464–470.

Rosman, B., and others. "Thought Disorder in the Parents of Schizophrenic Patients: A Further Study Utilizing the Object Sorting Test." *Journal of Psychiatric Research*, 1964, *2*, 211–221.

Rycroft, C. "Freud and the Imagination." *New York Review*, April 3, 1975, pp. 26–30.

Sapir, E. *Language*. New York: Harcourt Brace Jovanovich, 1921.

Schafer, R. *Clinical Application of Psychological Tests*. New York: International Universities Press, 1948.

Schneider, K. *Clinical Psychopathology*. (M. W. Hamilton, Trans.) New York: Grune & Stratton, 1959.

Schopler, E., and Loftin, J. "Thought Disorders in Parents of Psychotic Children: A Function of Test Anxiety." *Archives of General Psychiatry*, 1969, *20*, 174–181.

Schultz, K., and others. "The Assessment of Thinking Disorders Manifested in Families of Schizophrenics, Severely Disturbed Nonschizophrenics, and Normals." Paper presented at the 83rd meeting of the American Psychological Association, Chicago, September 1975.

Sechehaye, M. *Autobiography of a Schizophrenic Girl*. (G. Rubin-Robson, Trans.) New York: Grune & Stratton, 1951.

Shield, P., Harrow, M., and Tucker, G. "Investigation of Factors Related to Stimulus Overinclusion." *Psychiatric Quarterly*, 1974, *48*, 1–8.

Shimkunas, A. M., Gynther, M. D., and Smith, K. "Abstracting Ability of Schizophrenics Before and During Phenothiazine Therapy." *Archives of General Psychiatry*, 1966, *14*, 79–83.

Shimkunas, A. M., Gynther, M. D., and Smith, K. "Schizophrenic Responses to the Proverbs Test: Abstract, Concrete, or Autistic?" *Journal of Abnormal Psychology*, 1967, *72*, 128–133.

Singer, M. T. "Family Transactions and Schizophrenia. I: Recent Research Findings." In J. Romano (Ed.), *The Origins of Schizophrenia.* Amsterdam: Exerpta Medica International Congress Series, *151*, 1967.

Singer, M. T. "Rorschach Manual for Scoring Communication Deviances." Unpublished paper, 1972.

Singer, M. T. "The Rorschach as a Transaction." In M. A. Rickers-Ousiankina (Ed.), *Rorschach Psychology.* Huntington, N.Y.: Krieger, 1977.

Singer, M. T., and Wynne, L. C."Thought Disorder and Family Relations of Schizophrenics. III: Methodology Using Projective Techniques." *Archives of General Psychiatry,* 1965a, *12,* 187–212.

Singer, M. T., and Wynne, L. C. "Thought Disorder and Family Relations of Schizophrenics. IV: Results and Implications." *Archives of General Psychiatry,* 1965b, *12,* 201–212.

Singer, M. T., and Wynne, L. C. "Principles for Scoring Communication Defects and Deviances in Parents of Schizophrenics: Rorschach and TAT Scoring Manuals." *Psychiatry,* 1966a, *29,* 260–288.

Singer, M. T., and Wynne, L. C. "Communication Styles in Parents of Normals, Neurotics, and Schizophrenics." *Psychiatric Research Reports,* 1966b, *20,* 25–38.

Singer, M. T., Wynne, L. C., and Toohey, M. L. "Communication Disorders and the Families of Schizophrenics." In L. C. Wynne and others (Eds.), *The Nature of Schizophrenia: New Approaches to Research and Treatment.* New York: Wiley, 1978.

Spitzer, R. L., and Endicott, J. "Medical and Mental Disorder: Proposed Definition and Criteria." In R. L. Spitzer and D. F. Klein (Eds.), *Critical Issues in Psychiatric Diagnosis.* New York: Raven Press, 1978.

Spitzer, R. L., Endicott, J., and Robins, E. *Research Diagnostic Criteria (RDC) for a Selected Group of Functional Disorders.* New York: Biometrics Research, New York State Psychiatric Institute, 1975.

Spohn, H., Thethford, P., and Cancro, R. "The Effects of Phenothiazine Medication on Skin Conductance and Heart Rate in Schizophrenic Patients." *Journal of Nervous and Mental Disease,* 1971, *152,* 129–139.

Storch, A. *The Primitive Archaic Forms of Inner Experience and Thought in Schizophrenia.* New York: Nervous and Mental Disease Monographs, 1924. (Originally published in German, 1922.)

Strauss, J. S., and Carpenter, W. T., Jr. "The Prediction of Outcome in Schizophrenia. II: Relationships Between Predictor and Outcome Variables." *Archives of General Psychiatry,* 1974, *31,* 37–42.

Strauss, J. S., and Giff, T. E. "Choosing an Approach for Diagnosing Schizophrenia." *Archives of General Psychiatry,* 1977, *34,* 1248–1253.

Sullivan, H. S. "The Language of Schizophrenia." In J. S. Kasanin (Ed.), *Language and Thought in Schizophrenia.* Berkeley: University of California Press, 1944.

Tutko, T. A., and Spence, J. T. "The Performance of Process and Reactive Schizophrenics and Brain-Injured Subjects on a Conceptual Task." *Journal of Abnormal and Social Psychology,* 1962, *65,* 389–394.

Venables, P. H., and O'Connor, N. "A Short Scale for Rating Paranoid Schizophrenia." *Journal of Mental Science,* 1959, *105,* 815–818.

von Domarus, E. "The Specific Laws of Logic in Schizophrenia." In J. S. Kasanin (Ed.), *Language and Thought in Schizophrenia.* New York: Norton, 1944.

Vygotsky, L. "Thought in Schizophrenia." *Archives of Neurology & Psychiatry,* 1934, *31,* 1063–1077.

Vygotsky, L. *Thought and Language.* (E. Hanfmann, and G. Vakar, Trans.) Cambridge, Mass.: M.I.T. Press, 1962.

Watkins, J. G., and Stauffacher, J. C. "An Index of Pathological Thinking in the Rorschach." *Journal of Projective Techniques,* 1952, *16,* 276–286.

Wechsler, D. *Wechsler Adult Intelligence Scale Manual.* New York: Psychological Corporation, 1955.

Weiner, I. B. *Psychodiagnosis in Schizophrenia.* New York: Wiley, 1966.

Weiner, I. B., and Exner, J. "Rorschach Indices of Disordered Thinking in Patient and Nonpatient Adolescents and Adults." *Journal of Personality Assessment,* 1978, *42,* 339–343.

Werner, H. *Comparative Psychology of Mental Development.* (Rev. ed.) New York: Follett, 1948.

Wild, C. "Disturbed Styles of Thinking." *Archives of General Psychiatry,* 1965, *13,* 464–470.

Wild, C., and others. "Measuring Disordered Styles of Thinking." *Archives of General Psychiatry,* 1965, *13,* 471–476.

Wing, J. K., Cooper, J. G., and Sartorius, N. *Instruction Manual for the Present State Examinations and Catego.* London: Cambridge University Press, 1972.

Woodward, J. A., and Goldstein, M. J. "Communication Deviance in the Families of Schizophrenics: A Comment on the Misuse of Analysis of Covariance." *Science,* 1977, *197,* 1096–1097.

Wynne, L. C. "Family Transactions and Schizophrenia. II: Conceptual Considerations for a Research Strategy." In J. Romano (Ed.), *The Origins of Schizophrenia.* Amsterdam: Excerpta Medica International Congress Series, *151,* 1967.

Wynne, L. C. "Methodologic and Conceptual Issues in the Study of Schizophrenics and Their Families." *Journal of Psychiatric Research,* 1968, *6* (suppl. 1), 185–199.

Wynne, L. C. "Schizophrenics and Their Families: Recent Research Directions and Findings." Paper presented at the Primer Congreso de Psicopatologia del Grupo Familiar, Buenos Aires, June 1970.

Wynne, L. C., and Singer, M. T. "Thought Disorder and Family Relations of Schizophrenics." *Archives of General Psychiatry,* 1963, *9,* 191–206.

Wynne, L. C., and others. "Schizophrenics and Their Families: Recent Research on Parental Communication." In J. M. Tanner (Ed.), *Developments in Psychiatric Research.* Seven Oaks, Kent, England: Hodder & Stroughton, 1977.

Zahn, T. P. "Word Associations in Adoptive and Biological Parents of Schizophrenics." *Archives of General Psychiatry,* 1968, *19,* 501–503.

Zigler, E., and Phillips, L. "Social Competence and the Process-Reactive Distinction in Psychopathology." *Journal of Abnormal and Social Psychology,* 1962, *65,* 215–222.

Index

Absurd responses: in cases, 185, 191, 193, 194; findings on, 150, 151, 152, 153, 154, 158, 159; in reasoning, 26; as scoring category, 70, 73, 94–95

Absurd responses, tendency to, in cases, 192, 194

Active concretization, 6

Acute schizophrenics: circumstantial thinking among, 28; classification of, 108–110, 117; and cognitive focusing, 24; combinative thinking among, 27; conceptual overinclusion among, 22; and Thought Disorder Index, 173

Adler, D., 20, 24, 29, 110, 288

Adolescents, reasoning among, 27

Affect, modulation of, 28–29

Allusive thinking, 54–55

American Psychiatric Association, 108, 115, 288

Amorphous thinking, 42

Andreasen, M., 19, 288

Appelbaum, S. A., 247, 288

Arbitrary form-color response, as scoring category, 69, 85–86

Arieti, S., 6, 7–8, 10, 27, 288

Arnhoff, F. N., 32, 294

Associations: loose, as scoring category, 69, 91–92; looseness of, in cognitive focusing, 25; loosening or splitting of, 5; richness of, in concept formation, 23

Associative disorders, 72

Associative link, concept of, 8

Astrachan, B. M., 288

Asyndetic thinking, concept of, 25

Atkinson, M.W., 39, 288

Attentional dysfunction, 176–177

Autism, 20, 30

Autistic logic: in cases, 187, 210, 213, 216, 236, 237, 254, 259; in circumstantial thinking, 27; findings on, 150, 151, 152, 153, 154, 156, 158, 159; as scoring category, 70, 72, 97–98

Autistic logic, tendency to: in cases, 221, 258, 299; as scoring category, 70, 72, 98

Bannister, D., 52, 169, 288–289

Barison, F., 6, 289

Beck, S. J., 19, 289

Becker, W. C., 23, 36, 289

Behrens, M. I., 49, 130, 289, 298

Bellak, L., 30–31, 289

Benjamin, J. D., 19, 20, 289

Biases, yielding to, 24–25

Bieliauskas, L. A., 125, 294

Blatt, S., 26, 289

Bleuler, E., 5, 7, 14, 38, 42

Boundaries, fluidity of, 26–27

Broadbent, D. E., 176, 289

Bromet, E., 22, 289

Cameron, N., 7, 11–12, 14, 19–20, 21, 25, 42, 289

Cancro, R., 31, 124, 289, 299–300

Carpenter, W. T., Jr., 175, 300

Chapman, J. P., 19, 23, 24–25, 28

Chapman, L. J., 19, 22, 23, 24–25, 28, 125, 290

Chodoff, P., 49, 130, 289, 298

Chronic paranoid schizophrenia: case of, 181–202; first testing of, 182–194; history of, 181–182; second testing of, 183, 195–202

Chronic schizophrenics, 24

Ciarlo, D. D., 52, 290

Circumstantial thinking, 27–28

Clancy, M., 54–55, 296
Clangs: in cases, 187, 190, 198, 269; findings on, 150, 151, 153, 158; as scoring category, 69, 72, 83
Closure problems: in communication, 45, 46; in thought disorder, 50
Cognitive focusing: as aspect of thought disorder, 23–26; development of, 43
Cohen, J., 116, 290
Combination. *See* Incongruous combination
Combinative thinking, 26–27
Combinatory disorders, 72, 154
Communication deviance (CD): in cases, 209–214, 260, 269–277, 284–286; defects in, 45; family transmission of, 41–43; Hirsch-Leff study compared with, 162–165; measurement of, 43–45; of probands, 160; scoring of, 157–160; and Thought Disorder Index, 157–166; thought disorder related to, 49–51
Composite response, 69, 85
Concept formation, 19–23
Concreteness: of concept formation, 20–21; defined, 19; as scoring category, 69, 75
Confabulation: in cases, 191, 192, 193, 194, 213, 216, 236, 237; findings on, 151, 152, 153, 154, 156, 159; in reasoning, 26, 35; as scoring category, 70, 72, 95–97
Confabulation, tendency to: in cases, 200, 202; as scoring category, 70, 72, 97
Confusion: in cases, 190, 212, 216, 228; findings on, 150, 151, 152, 153, 154, 158, 159; as scoring category, 69, 73, 90
Confusion, tendency to, in cases, 183, 212, 215, 227, 266, 280
Constrictive thinking, 42
Contamination: findings on, 151, 152, 153, 159; in reasoning, 26, 27, 35–36; as scoring category, 70, 72, 99
Cooper, J. E., 116, 174, 290

Cooper, J. G., 169, 182, 301
Creativity, 16–17, 39

Delta Index, 33–35, 58–59, 67
Dementia praecox, concept of, 4–5
Depression, neurotic, 246–259
Details generalized, 70, 95–96
Developmental Level Scoring System, for thought disorders, 35–36
Deviant thinking, defined, 33
Deviant verbalization, Delta Index for, 33
Diagnosis, and Thought Disorder Index, 133–154
Disorganization disorders, 73, 154
Disruptive behavior: in communication, 45, 46; in thought disorder, 50–51
Distance, loss or increase of, 69, 71, 74. *See also* Inappropriate distance
Distant association, 69, 91
Drugs: in cases, 182, 202, 222; effects of, 121, 123–125; and Thought Disorder Index, 141–142

Education, of families, 52–53
Elaboration, extreme, 70, 96–97
Ellman, R., 16, 290
Endicott, J., 169, 290, 299
Ethnicity, and Thought Disorder Index, 137–140
Exner, J., 24, 27, 300
Expression: peculiar, 69, 81–82; stilted, inappropriate, 69, 78–79
External-internal response, as scoring category, 69, 86

Fabulizations, 26, 27, 35
Fabulized combination: in cases, 201, 202, 209, 210, 216, 258, 259, 276, 277; findings on, 151, 152, 153, 154, 159; as scoring category, 69, 72, 92–93
Fabulized combination, tendency to, in cases, 274, 277
Families of patients: allusive thinking among, 54–55; cases of, 259–287; characteristics of,

125–128; communication deviance transmitted by, 41–43; education, intelligence, and socioeconomic class of, 52–53; and proband scores, related, 156–157; and schizophrenia, 40–41; thought disorder in 38–55; Thought Disorder Index and communication deviance of, 160–162; thought disorder scores of, 154–157

Feighner, J. P., 175, 290

Feinsilver, D., 52, 290

Fenichel, O., 9, 290

Finn, J., 133, 290

Fish, F., 290

Fluidity: in cases, 191, 194, 215, 216, 232, 237, 276, 277; findings on, 151, 153, 154, 156, 159; as scoring category, 70, 72, 93–94

Fluidity, tendency to, in cases, 231, 237, 273, 277

Focusing, cognitive, 23–26, 43

Fragmented thinking, 42

Freud, S., 8, 9, 11, 15, 16, 29

Friedman, H., 23, 35–36, 291

Gardner, R. W., 22, 291

Garmezy, N., 39, 40, 111, 291

Giff, T. E., 300

Gill, M. M., 9, 14, 17, 19, 23, 24, 30, 32–33, 57–58, 61, 62, 71, 85, 99, 114, 142, 149, 152, 153, 175, 180, 291, 297

Gleser, G. C., 19, 292

Goldfried, M. R., 36, 291

Goldstein, K., 6, 7, 14, 19, 20

Goldstein, M. J., 40, 163, 292, 301

Gorham, D. R., 20, 292

Gottschalk, L. G., 19, 292

Grid Test, 52

Grinker, R. R., 31–32, 292

Gynther, M. D., 20, 298–299

Haimo, S., 79, 80, 137, 167

Hamlin, R. M., 35, 297

Hanf, E., 20, 292

Hanfmann, E., 20, 292

Harrow, M., 20, 22, 23, 24, 26, 27, 28, 29, 36, 110, 172, 288, 289

Havel, J., 29, 87, 293

Hawks, D. V., 21, 293

Health-Sickness Rating. See Menninger Health-Sickness Rating Scale

Henry, G. M., 174, 293

Heston, L. L., 38, 39, 293

Hewlett, J. H. G., 21, 296

Hirsch, S. R., 41, 47, 48, 160, 162–165, 293

Hollingshead, A. B., 121, 293

Hollingshead-Redlich Two-Factor Index of Social Position, 121, 123n, 128, 137

Holt, R. R., 16, 17, 29, 87, 293

Holzman, P. S., 22, 31–32, 37, 40, 79, 80, 137, 167, 176, 177, 247

Hughes, D. W., 294

Hunt, W. A., 32, 294

Hurt, S., 60, 170, 294

Idiosyncratic symbolism: findings on, 151, 154, 159; as scoring response, 69, 72, 87–88

Idiosyncratic thinking, 24

Idiosyncratic word usage, 69, 79–81

Inappropriate activity response, as scoring category, 69, 86

Inappropriate distance: in cases, 184, 185, 186, 188, 196, 198, 208, 212, 216, 224, 238, 245, 246, 250, 269, 286, 287; findings on, 150, 151, 153, 154, 158; as scoring category, 69, 70–71, 72, 74–76

Incoherence: findings on, 150, 151, 152, 153, 154, 158, 159; as scoring category, 70, 73, 99–100

Incongruous combination: in cases, 219, 220, 221, 276, 277; findings on, 151, 153, 154, 159; as scoring category, 69, 72, 85–86

Intelligence: in cases, 191, 199, 208, 218, 229, 242, 253, 260, 269, 283; and concreteness, 20–21; of families, 52–53, 128; among probands, 120–121; and Thought Disorder Index, 137–140, 142

Jensen, S. R., 35, 297

Johnson, J. E., 125, 294

Johnston, M. H., 59, 294

Jones, J. E., 48, 294
Jones, N. F., 32, 294

Kasanin, J. S., 20, 292
Kataguchi, Y., 35, 294
Kelley, D., 295
Kenny, D. A., 165, 294
Kety, S. S., 37, 294-295
Klein, G. S., 16, 176, 295
Klopfer, B., 19, 295
Knowles, R. R., 125, 290
Kraepelin, E., 4-5, 295
Kretschmer, E., 38, 295
Kurland, A., 124, 125, 295

Language: for communication or
    thought, 12-13; defined, 11;
    dichotomy or continuum of use
    of, 14-17; levels of, 13-14;
    peculiar, 45, 46, 51; primitive
    usage of, 5-6; schizophrenic, 7;
    thought related to, 11-14, 175-
    176
Leff, J. P., 41, 47, 48, 160, 162-165,
    293
Levy, D. L., 177, 293
Lewin, K., 15, 295
Lidz, T., 12, 40, 41, 52, 290, 295
Loftin, J., 53, 298
Logic, peculiar, 45, 46, 51. See also
    Autistic logic
Loose association, 69, 91-92
Looseness: in cases, 186, 214, 216,
    239, 263; findings on, 150, 151,
    153, 154, 156, 158, 159; as scor-
    ing category, 69, 72, 91-92
Looseness, tendency to: in cases,
    187, 208, 282; as scoring cate-
    gory, 69, 72, 75
Lord, F. M., 163, 295
Lorenz, M., 13-14, 295
Loss or increase of distance, as scor-
    ing category, 69, 71, 74
Luborsky, L., 110, 113, 295

McConaghy, N., 54-55, 296
Maher, B. A., 174, 176, 296
Mahl, G. F., 176, 296
Major symbolism, in cases, 210,
    215, 216, 230, 237
Manic psychosis: case of, 221-246;
first testing of, 222-237; history
    of, 221-222; second testing of,
    223, 237-246
Mayer-Gross, W., 38, 296
Meaning, private, 25
Meehl, P. E., 175, 296
Menninger Health-Sickness Rating
    Scale (HSR): in cases, 182, 202,
    222, 247; and Thought Disorder
    Index, 110-111, 112-114, 117-
    118, 119-120, 141
Metonymy, concept of, 79
Minnesota Multiphasic Personality
    Inventory, and allusive thinking,
    55
Minor symbolism, in cases, 236
Modulation of affect, as aspect of
    thought disorder, 28-29
Muntz, H. J., 52, 296
Murphy, D. L., 174, 293

Neologisms: findings on, 150, 151,
    152, 159; as scoring category, 70,
    73, 100
Neurotic depression: case of, 246-
    259; history of, 246-247; in-
    terpretation of, 247-248; testing
    of, 248-259

O'Connor, N., 110, 300
Object Sorting Test: and cognitive
    focusing, 24; and communica-
    tion deviance, 48, 51; and con-
    cept formation, 20, 23; and
    families of patients, 52, 53, 55;
    and scoring systems, 32
Otteson, J., 22, 296
Overgeneralized thinking, 26
Overinclusion, 7; behavioral, in
    concept formation, 22; in con-
    cept formation, 21-23; concep-
    tual, in concept formation, 22;
    stimulus, in cognitive focusing,
    23-24; stimulus, in concept for-
    mation, 22
Overspecific responses: in cognitive
    focusing, 25-26; as scoring
    category, 69, 75-76

Paleological thinking, 7, 27-28
Paralogical thinking, 7
Payne, R. W., 21, 293, 296

Peculiar language and logic: in communication, 45, 46; in thought disorder, 51

Peculiar verbalizations and responses: in cases, 187, 189, 192, 197, 199, 200, 201, 211, 214, 215, 217, 219, 221, 230, 234, 236, 245, 246, 250, 253, 257, 259, 261, 262, 264, 266, 267, 269, 271, 273, 274, 276, 277, 281; findings on, 150, 152, 153, 158; as scoring category, 69, 73, 77–82

Perseveration: in cases, 192, 194, 200, 201, 258, 259; findings on, 150, 151, 152, 153, 154, 156, 158, 159; as scoring category, 69, 72, 83–84

Phillips, L., 110, 111, 296, 301

Phillips Scale of Premorbid Adjustment, and Thought Disorder Index, 110, 111, 117–119, 120, 140

Planansky, K., 38, 296

Pope, B., 35, 297

Power, R. P., 52, 296

Powers, W. F., 35, 297

Present State Examination (PSE), 169, 182, 203, 221

Primary process thinking, 8–10, 16

Private meaning, 25

Probands: communication deviance of, 160; demographic characteristics of, 120–125; drug effects on, 121, 123–125; and family scores, related, 156–157; scoring by, at different levels, 149

Proctor, L. R., 177, 293–294

Proverbs Test, 20, 24, 32

Psychosis: creativity distinct from, 16–17; manic, case of, 221–246; schizoaffective, case of, 202–221, 259–287

Queer responses: in cases, 272, 277; findings on, 150, 151, 152, 153, 158, 159; as scoring category, 69, 73, 88–90

Quinlan, D., 24, 25, 26, 27–29, 51, 172, 292, 297

Quirk, D. A., 67, 297

Rapaport, D., 10–11, 17, 19, 23, 24, 28, 30, 32–33, 57–58, 59, 61, 62, 71, 85, 99, 114, 142, 149, 152, 153, 175, 180, 297

Reality testing, 29–30

Reasoning, 26–28

Redlich, T. C., 293

Reilly, F., 19, 25, 297

Relationship verbalizations: findings on, 151, 152, 159; as scoring category, 69, 72, 84–85

Relatives, first-degree, defined, 39. *See also* Families of patients

Repression, failure of, 28–29

Research Diagnostic Criteria (RDC), 169

Responses: composite, 69, 85; external-internal, 69, 86; inappropriate activity, 69, 86; overspecific, 25–26, 69, 75–76; peculiar, 69, 82; syncretistic, 69, 76. *See also* Absurd responses; Peculiar verbalizations and responses; Queer responses

Ricci, J., 52, 290

Robins, E., 169, 299

Rodnick, E. H., 40, 291, 292

Romney, D., 52, 297–298

Rorschach, H., 19, 298

Rorschach Indices of Drive-Dominated Ideation, 29

Rorschach Test: Card I, 96, 99, 191, 199, 208–209, 218, 229–230, 242, 253–254, 269–270, 283–284; Card II, 57, 96, 191, 199, 203, 209–210, 218, 230, 242–243, 254, 270, 284; Card III, 95, 96–97, 191–192, 199, 210, 218–219, 230–231, 243, 254–255, 271–272, 284–285; Card IV, 98, 192, 200, 211, 219, 231–232, 243, 255, 272, 285; Card V, 192, 200, 211–212, 219, 232–233, 244, 255–256, 272–273, 285; Card VI, 192–193, 200, 212, 219, 233, 244, 256–257, 273–274, 285; Card VII, 98, 193, 200–201, 212–213, 220, 233–234, 244, 257, 274, 286; Card VIII, 96, 97, 99, 193, 201, 213–214, 220, 234–235, 245,

Rorschach Test (continued)
257–258, 274–275, 286; Card
IX, 75, 96, 97, 193–194, 201,
214, 220, 235, 245, 258, 275–
276, 286; Card X, 84, 95, 96, 97,
98, 99, 194, 201, 214–215, 220–
221, 235–236, 245–246, 258–
259, 276–277, 286–287; in cases,
180, 182–183, 191–194, 199–
202, 203, 208–216, 218–221,
222, 223, 229–237, 242–246,
247, 253–259, 260, 269–277,
283–287; and cognitive focusing, 23, 34, 35; and communication deviance, 43, 44–45,
46, 49; and modulation of affect,
28–29; and reality testing, 30;
and reasoning, 26, 27, 28; scoring systems for, 32–36; and test
results, 130, 131, 132, 134, 142,
143, 149, 150–151, 153, 156,
158–159, 160, 162, 163, 165;
and Thought Disorder Index,
57–58, 59, 61, 62–63, 67–68,
74–100, 114, 115
Rosenthal, A. J., 49, 130, 289, 298
Rosenthal, D., 37, 39, 298
Rosman, B., 52, 298
Roth, M., 38, 296
Rousey, C., 176, 294
Rycroft, C., 9–10, 298

Sapir, E., 13, 14, 298
Sartorius, N., 169, 182, 301
Schafer, R., 17, 19, 23, 24, 30,
32–33, 57–58, 61, 62, 71, 85, 99,
114, 142, 149, 152, 153, 175,
180, 297, 298
Schedule for Affective Disorders
and Schizophrenia (SADS), 169
Scheerer, M., 292
Schizoaffective psychosis: case of,
202–221; family of, 259–277;
first testing of, 203, 204–216;
history of, 202–203; second testing of, 203, 216–221
Schizoaffective psychosis, father of:
case of, 277–287; history of, 277;
interpretation of, 278; testing of,
278–287

Schizoaffective psychosis, mother
of: case of, 259–277; history of,
259–260; interpretation of, 260;
testing of, 261–277
Schizoid, 38–39
Schizophrenia: characteristics of, x;
chronic-acute classification of,
108–110, 117, 173; chronic
paranoid, case of, 181–202; clinical and psychological test diagnoses of, compared, 115–117;
diagnostic dimensions of, 106,
108–115; disorganization in,
state of, 110–111; family's contribution to, 40–41; genetic basis
for, 39; indicators of, 114;
manic-depressive classification
of, 114, 173–174; paranoid-
nonparanoid classification of,
110, 114; patient classification
scales for, 111–114; primary
process thinking in, 10;
psychiatric syndrome diagnoses
of, 106, 108–111; psychological
test diagnoses of, 114–115; stress
related to, 53–54; and Thought
Disorder Index, 134–137
Schizophrenia State Inventory,
31–32
Schizophrenic constitution, 38
Schizophrenic language, 7
Schizophrenic thinking: analysis of
theories of, 1–17; characteristics
of, 19; example of, 1–4. See also
Thought disorder
Schizophrenics: chronic, 24; latent,
38; process, and concreteness,
20–21; reactive, and concrete-
ness, 20–21. See also Acute
schizophrenics; Probands
Schneider, K., 175, 298
Schopler, E., 53, 298
Schultz, K., 52, 298
Schwartz, F., 149, 152n
Sechehaye, M., 176, 298
Secondary process thinking, 9, 16
Sex, and Thought Disorder Index,
137–140
Shield, P., 23, 298
Shimkunas, A. M., 20, 298–299
Singer, M. T., 41–42, 43, 44, 45,

46*n*, 47, 48, 49, 157, 160, 162, 163, 180, 299, 301
Slater, E., 38, 296
Smith, K., 20, 298–299
Socioeconomic class: of families, 52–53; of probands, 121; and Thought Disorder Index, 137–140
Spence, J. T., 21, 300
Spitzer, R. L., 169, 290, 299
Spohn, 124, 299–300
Stauffacher, J. C., 33–34, 58–59, 60, 67, 300
Stilted, inappropriate expression, as scoring category, 69, 78–79
Stimulus overinclusion, 22–24
Storch, A., 5, 6, 300
Strauss, J. S., 175, 300
Streitman, S., 291
Stress, 53–54
Stricker, G., 36, 291
Sullivan, H. S., 12–13, 300
Symbolism: idiosyncratic, 69, 72, 87–88, 151, 154, 159; major, 210, 215, 216, 230, 237; minor, 236
Syncretistic response, 69, 76

Thematic Apperception Test (TAT), 32, 43, 45, 48
Thetford, P., 124, 299–300
Thinking: allusive, 54–55; amorphous, 42; asyndetic, 25; circumstantial, 27–28; class-theoretical modes of, 15; combinative, 26–27; concrete or abstract mode of, 6; constrictive, 42; deviant, 33; fragmented, 42; idiosyncratic, 24; and motivational variables, 10–11; ordered, 12; overgeneralized, 26; paleological, 7, 27–28; paralogical, 7; primary process, 8–10, 16; primitive, 9; schizophrenic, 1–17, 19; secondary process, 9, 16
Thought, language related to, 11–14, 175–176
Thought disorder: cases and interpretations of, 178–287; classical theories of, 4–8; communication deviance related to, 49–51; continuum of, 170–172; definitions and measurements of, 18–37; in families of patients, 38–55; multiple aspects of, 30–36; nature of, 175–177; psychoanalytic theories of, 8–11; rating scales for, 30–32; single aspects of, 19–30; specificity of, 172–175
Thought Disorder Index (TDI): administration of, 62–63; assessment instruments for, 60–61; categories of, 149–154; categories of, related to diagnosis, 142–154; and communication deviance, 157–166; and communication deviance, of families, 160–162; described, 59–60, 61–62; development of, 56–61; and diagnosis, 133–142; and drugs, 141–142; empirical precursors of, 57–60; findings from, 129–167; .5 level on, 69, 72–73, 88–93, 153; formulae for, 67; Good form response and, on Rorschach, 142; implications of, 168–177; and intelligence, sex, ethnicity, and socioeconomic class, 137–140; intermediate .25, .5 level on, 69, 86–88; 1.0 level of, 70, 72–73, 99–100; and patient classification scales, 117–120; and premorbid status, paranoid status, and general disorganization, 140–141; procedure for analyzing, 129–133; reliability of, 131–132; as research and clinical tool, 169–170; research population for, 103–106, 107; and schizophrenia, 134–137; scored occurrences at each level of, 143; scoring of, 63–69, 130–131; scoring categories of, 69–70; scoring manual for, 61–100; .75 level of, 70, 72–73, 93–98; statistical procedures for, 132–133; testing of, 102–128; .25 level on, 69, 70–86, 153; uses of, 129; weightings of, 61–62

Thought quality index, 27–28
Tucker, G. J., 23, 24, 29, 292, 298
Tutko, T. A., 21, 300

Unconventional verbalizations, 73

Vagueness: in cases, 204, 225, 240, 244, 246, 264, 272, 277, 286, 287; findings on, 150, 151, 153, 154, 158; as scoring category, 69, 73, 76–77
Venables, P. H., 110, 300
Venables-O'Connor Paranoid Rating Scale, and Thought Disorder Index, 110, 111–112, 117–118, 119, 141
Verbal combination/condensation, as scoring category, 69, 78
Verbalization: deviant, 33; pathological, categories of, 57–58; relationship, 69, 72, 84–85, 151, 152, 159; unconventional, 73. See also Peculiar verbalizations and responses
von Domarus, E., 7, 300
Vygotsky, L., 19, 20, 300

Watkins, J. G., 33–34, 58–59, 60, 67, 300
Wechsler, D., 60, 179, 300
Wechsler Adult Intelligence Scale (WAIS): Arthmetic, 191, 208, 229, 253, 269, 283; Block Design, 191, 208, 229, 253, 269, 283; in cases, 179–180, 182–191, 195–199, 203, 204–208, 216–218, 222, 223–229, 237–242, 247, 248–253, 260, 261–269, 278–283; and cognitive focusing, 23, 24; Comprehension, 185–187, 191, 196, 199, 205, 208, 217, 218, 225–226, 229, 238–239, 242, 249, 253, 262–265, 269, 279–280, 283; Digit Span, 191, 208, 229, 247, 253, 269, 283; Digit Symbol, 191, 208, 223, 229, 242, 253, 269, 283; Information Subtest, 183–185, 191, 195–196, 199, 204–205, 208, 216–217, 218, 223–224, 229, 237–238, 242, 248–249, 253, 261–262, 269, 278–279, 283; Object Assembly, 191, 208, 229, 247, 253, 269, 283; Picture Arrangement, 191, 229, 253, 269, 283; Picture Completion, 188–189, 191, 205–206, 208, 226–227, 229, 250–251, 253, 266–267, 269, 281, 283; and rating scales, 32; and scoring systems, 32; Similarities, 187–188, 191, 197, 199, 208, 226, 229, 240, 242, 250, 253, 265, 269, 280–281, 283; and test results, 130, 131, 132, 134, 138, 140, 143, 149, 150, 153, 156, 158; and Thought Disorder Index, 59, 60–61, 62–63, 71, 74–100, 114, 115, 120–121; Vocabulary, 189–190, 191, 197–199, 206–208, 228–229, 240–242, 251–252, 253, 267–269, 282–283
Wechsler-Bellevue, 32
Weiner, I. B., 19, 20, 23, 24, 26, 27, 30, 36, 85, 87, 153, 291, 300
Weingartner, H., 174, 293
Werner, H., 5, 6, 301
Wild, C., 26, 48, 53, 289, 301
Wing, J. K., 169, 182, 301
Wolitsky, D. L., 176, 295
Woodward, J. A., 163, 301
Word association tests, 32
Word usage, idiosyncratic, 69, 79–81
Word-finding difficulty: in cases, 194, 206, 211, 215, 226, 233, 237, 265, 266, 279; findings on, 150, 153, 156, 158; as scoring category, 69, 73, 82–83
Wynne, L. C., 39, 40, 41–42, 43, 44, 45, 47, 48, 49, 50, 157, 160, 162, 163, 165, 299, 301

Zahn, T. P., 52, 301
Zigler, E., 296, 301